THE CONSUMER MOVEMENT

The
Consumer Movement

HELEN SORENSON

ARNO PRESS
A New York Times Company
New York • 1978

Editorial Supervision: JOSEPH CELLINI

———◆———

Reprint Edition 1978 by Arno Press Inc.

Reprinted from a copy in the University of
    Illinois Library

A CENTURY OF MARKETING
ISBN for complete set: 0-405-11156-8
See last pages of this volume for titles.

Manufactured in the United States of America

———◆———

Library of Congress Cataloging in Publication Data

Sorenson, Helen Laura.
    The consumer movement.

    (A Century of marketing)
    Reprint of the 1st ed. published by Harper &
Brothers, New York.
    Includes index.
    1. Consumers' leagues--United States. 2. Consump-
tion (Economics) 3. Consumer cooperatives--United
States. I. Title. II. Series.
HD6957.U6S6 1978   381'.3   78-261
ISBN 0-405-11170-3

THE CONSUMER MOVEMENT
What It Is and What It Means

The
Consumer Movement

What It Is and What It Means

by

HELEN SORENSON

Assistant Professor of Home Economics,
University of Illinois · Urbana

publication of the

INSTITUTE FOR CONSUMER EDUCATION

Stephens College · Columbia, Missouri

HARPER & BROTHERS · PUBLISHERS

NEW YORK AND LONDON · 1941

Contents

Foreword

THE preparation of this book was undertaken as a project of the Institute for Consumer Education at Stephens College in Columbia, Mo., an organization receiving its financial support from the Alfred P. Sloan Foundation, Inc. The study was made under the joint direction of Professor J. D. Black, of Harvard University, and Dr. John M. Cassels, Director of the Institute. Helen Dallas, editor of institute publications, planned the format and played an important part in seeing the manuscript through the final stages of revision and publication. Maxine Enlow, research economist, read the whole manuscript and worked closely with me in the preparation of the final chapter. Loeta Johns, librarian, has been generous in her cooperation throughout the study and has supervised the preparation of the index. For all the help I have received in this way I am extremely grateful.

I should also like to express my appreciation to all those interested in the consumer movement who have contributed material and suggestions during the course of the two years the study was in progress. Particular thanks are due to Carol Willis Moffett, of New York City, for her continued interest and assistance from start to finish of the project. Others to whom I am especially indebted are Reign Hadsell, of the Consumers' Counsel Division of the AAA; Werner Gabler, Distribution Consultant for the American Retail Federation; Elizabeth W. Gilboy, of the Harvard Committee on Economic Research; and Dickson Reck, of the University of Pennsylvania. The interest and cooperation of my colleagues at the University of Illinois have been invaluable.

The study was undertaken with the objective of indicating what the consumer movement is, how it has developed, and what in future may be expected from it. Attention has been focused on the work of privately organized groups and data were obtained from official publications of the various organizations and through contacts with their officers. A study of the activity of government agencies in the consumer field has recently been completed by Persia Campbell and published as *Consumer Representation in the New Deal* by the Columbia University Press. Data on the rise of formal consumer education are now being collected by the Institute for Consumer Education.

Preface

BUT two witnesses in behalf of the consumer appeared before the Senate Committee on Finance while the tariff schedules of the Fordney-McCumber Act of 1921 were being reviewed. One of them represented a Housewives' League group protesting against the proposed tariff on fresh fish caught in Canadian waters. She spoke of the burden that the duty would impose on lower East Side groups in New York accustomed to getting their proteins cheaply in the form of fish. She reminded the senators of how some time earlier her league had waged a successful battle against higher prices for storage eggs in Chicago. She all but capitulated, however, when simple Senator McCumber insisted that people had to earn money before they could spend it, and that the Congress was trying to help poor people earn more money by protecting their wages.

The other spokesman for the consumers was a baker in south Chicago who asked that the duty on egg powders not be raised, saying that it would add to the cost of the Sunday cakes that his poor customers bought in his shop with their leftover pennies on Saturday night. Perhaps he was not a true consumer representative, perhaps he was thinking really of the added cost of his materials; but the manner of his speech suggested that he was in close touch with the actual final link in the chain.

It is a long way, in terms of social distance, from this simple situation to the proliferation of consumer agencies, of organizations working for the consumer, and of special interests employing the guise of the consumer, that Miss Sorenson outlines in this study of hers on the consumer movement in the United States. The change came mostly after 1930. The women's organizations *might* have fought for the consumers in the years from 1921 to 1930, as they are doing today; but they did little. The home economists of the country were already working for better standards for consumers' goods, but quietly on the whole,

There was the National Consumers League but, then as now, it was an agency working in behalf of labor rather than in the consumer interest. Once in those years this writer had an altercation with the league over its attempt to pose in a certain situation as a true consumer group—a group *of* consumers working *for* consumers. The most exasperating cases of this came in 1933 and afterward when governors of states or mayors of cities, looking around for a representative of the consumer interest to appoint on some milk control board, public welfare committee, or the like, innocently chose from the local branch of the Consumers League.

Such statements must not be interpreted as opposing the objectives of the Consumers League, which commonly are highly worthy, nor their procedure of calling upon the buyers of goods to assist them in obtaining good working conditions for the makers or handlers thereof. The point is that consumers have interests of their own which they need to defend and promote; when they are drawn off into supporting other causes or interests, they have less organization energy by so much for looking after their own interests. To this loss is added positive injury when these other interests borrow the name "consumer" and use it as a front behind which to pursue their special ends. The worst cases of all are those in which the ends thus pursued are actually adverse to the consumers.

Offsetting in part the injury done to consumers in these ways is the important assistance they have received from general women's organizations such as the Woman's Clubs and the League of Women Voters. The interests of members of these associations as consumers and as family purchasing agents are not inconsistent with the objectives of these great organizations; they do in fact provide them with important objects around which to weave their efforts. Nothing has happened to the consumer movement in the last decade so energizing as the lift it has received from women's organizations.

Miss Sorenson moves about easily among all these varied types of agencies, sorting out, classifying, and labeling them with an unerring sense. She is guided always by a conception of the place of consumption in the modern economy and of an independent consumer organization standing on its own legs and searching out and promoting a true consumer interest, which she carefully formulated early in her study.

The task which she has performed is one of great service. Perhaps its greatest service is to our democratic system of government and the capitalistic economy which evolved with it. Such a system, as is generally recognized, is peculiarly susceptible to the pressures of special interest groups. If those in charge of public affairs are to deal with these pressures without sacrificing the public welfare, they need to be fully informed as to the reason for being of each, and as to the true backing of the supporting groups. The electorate needs equally to be informed. Otherwise the public interest is no more safe than was Little Red Ridinghood from Grandma Wolf.

Not many Congresses ago, an agency parading under some such name as a legislative council was supplying to members of Congress and of state legislatures much printed matter opposing, in the name of protection of state rights, the system of federal matching of state funds for education, research, roads, and other purposes. Who will not agree that the recipients of this material needed to know that the agency in question was strongly supported, financially or otherwise, by wealthy members of the federal administration concerned with reducing federal taxes on corporate income?

Another important service is to the consumer movement itself. The charting of the past and present course of each of the organizations in this volume will enable all to lay out their own future courses more successfully. Mutual and supplementary effort will become easier. Dubious agencies operating behind false fronts will be more readily avoided. Consumers themselves can learn from this study the type of organization which they can best support, and this should have a rectifying effect on some of them. As one thinks of it, does it not seem particularly unfortunate that the two leading testing agencies now serving the public are both more or less "captive"—Consumers Union to the labor movement; Consumers' Research, speaking politely, to a highly theoretical and no longer realistic conception of "free enterprise"? Why could we not have had one bona fide organization pursuing the true undefiled ends of testing consumers' goods?

In some people's minds, the most important service which a book such as this gives is showing the way toward effective collaboration of seller and consumer groups, best exemplified by the National Consumer-Retailer Council.

It is surely high testimony to the worthiness of the consumer interest that so many other special interests have chosen it as a mask in the past ten years; but obviously this makes more difficult the task of those agencies which are honestly promoting consumer ends. Some of these difficulties should be easier to circumvent from now forward.

Are the public interest and the consumer interest identical? The answer depends largely upon definition of terms. Given the usual layman's interpretation, no doubt a public interest group such as a nation may easily have some worthy ends that are not encompassed by the ordinary conception of consumer needs. Also, although they may be the same on most issues that arise in the long run, they may differ widely in the short run. A consumer group, for instance, may be so interested in lower costs and prices as to overlook the low incomes of the producers of cotton and cotton goods.

Still it is true that, in general, the public can safely let any large consumer organization seek its own selfish ends, provided it seeks them intelligently and not in the short run, whereas it is commonly not safe to let any producer group do so. The reasons for this are: first, that, as has been recognized from Adam Smith to Keynes, "Consumption is the sole end and purpose of all production; and the interest of the producer ought to be attended to only in so far as it may be necessary for promoting that of the consumer"; second, that in the main the groups of consumers having a common interest are large and wide-embracing, whereas the producer groups acting as a homogeneous unit are small and selected. But as is carefully stated in this book, a single consumer may have a very narrow consumer interest. So also may a local consumer group, such as the families buying milk in a metropolitan market.

If consumer organizations are to wield the influence which

they should, they need to act intelligently in the public interest. This requires careful study and analysis of issues and problems. Somewhere in the total setup of groups working in the consumer interest should be women and men who know as much about cotton textiles as their makers and merchants and as much about milk and cream as their producers and distributors. On too many occasions in the past the consumer representatives at public hearings have really done little more than to say that a higher price would add to the cost of living, and "as consumers we oppose this." There are times when milk prices should rise and times when they should fall; and there are reasons in each case. The consumers must know these reasons if they are to be effective.

One can scarcely avoid the impression after reading Miss Sorenson's clinical reports on all the organizations named in her book that some of these are in considerable measure paper organizations—"letterhead" enterprises. Her book would have been somewhat more useful if she had spoken out more clearly on this phase of the subject. One has only to sit in at a single meeting of some consumer groups to know that they weigh little, and may in fact by their very weakness lessen the effectiveness of the more active agencies with which they become associated in the public mind. But this is one of the handicaps borne by nearly all movements. In the last ten years enough of the consumer movement has exhibited positive strength so that one can reasonably expect acceleration in the years just ahead.

JOHN D. BLACK

Harvard University
Cambridge, Massachusetts

THE CONSUMER MOVEMENT
What It Is and What It Means

Chapter One

THE BEGINNINGS OF THE CONSUMER MOVEMENT

No LONGER does the American housewife get eggs from her own hens or shoes from the village cobbler. The old close relation between production and consumption has disappeared. We now depend on a complex industrial system to satisfy our wants. As consumers, we are faced with special problems.

Goods and services have multiplied and become more complicated, making it difficult to choose wisely among them. Comforts, conveniences, and luxuries unheard of fifty years ago are commonplace now—washing machines and automatic heaters, electric lights and enameled stoves, radios and automobiles, frozen foods and nylon hosiery. Innumerable brands of the same product are available, making the range of choice still greater. The right kind of information needed to make intelligent selection among these myriad articles is often lacking. We sometimes are not sure what we want to start with, nor do we ordinarily get our advice from sources that are really impartial. We are constantly subject to pressure and persuasions from those whose businesses depend on the selling of their own particular products at a profit.

When times were booming this did not give most people much concern. New things were enjoyed for their own sake or felt to be necessary to keep up with the Joneses. The balance among items of the budget seemed to work out all right without thinking much about it. Workers thought much more of the size of their paycheck than of the problems of stretching it as far as it would go. Our interests as wage earners, doctors, farmers, lawyers, merchants, teachers, advertisers, government officials, manufacturers, came first. When the depression came, people were brought rather suddenly to a realization that they have problems in consumption as well as in production. To live well they began to see they needed to make their choices more independently. To get the things that would give them real satisfaction they had to manage their incomes and expenditures better than they had been doing. They needed to get as much as they could for their money. They needed information and guidance to help them decide on the relative merits of different products. As consumers they are now thinking consciously and critically of how the market serves their actual economic requirements. They recognize to a greater extent than ever before their own responsibilities for taking an active part in making it function more efficiently.

The decisions of consumers, wise or foolish, their passive acceptance or thoughtless indifference, are of great importance to the jobs and profits of those who bring us the fruits of modern invention. Certainly if the results are to turn out well, consumers should, on the whole, act rationally. But if people are to have, in adequate quantities, the things they want to consume, it is not enough that each be individually willing to work hard and that each be separately capable of spending his money wisely. In an economic society such as ours the income of each individual is a thing which depends on the coordination in production and exchange of millions of people. It is necessary that the complex social machinery of production—farms and markets, mines and railroads, factories, banks and government agencies, all taken together—should operate smoothly and continuously in such a way as to promote the welfare of the people.

When the frontier still existed, when economic units were small, and when each had a familiar place in the life of the local community, Americans had less occasion to think of their stake in the functioning of the economic system as a whole. As economic opportunities in the west diminished, as economic enterprises grew larger and more impersonal, the problems of achieving a proper balance among different groups in economic life have become greater. Inescapable decisions affecting the welfare of millions of people are made by the leaders of industry, by labor unions, by trade associations and by government bodies. As citizens of the economic community people are beginning to realize that all the decisions which shape economic policy affect them greatly. They feel they have special interests as consumers which are frequently neglected, that this neglect makes the ultimate results unworkable. As consumers they feel they have a vital concern in such questions as the tariff, antichain-store taxes, the regulation of monopoly, the cost of advertising, the fair-trade laws, the conservation of resources, the effect of war on production and prices, and many other matters.[1]

In considering these questions from the point of view of consumers, we are dealing with the final stage in the economic process of getting a living. We are concerned not simply with money income but with real wealth, with actual quantities of real goods and services as they enter into ultimate use by consumers. Nothing is more basic in the make-up of human nature, nothing more central in the concept of the consumer, than the urge to get the best standards of living that are possibly within our reach, as individuals and as a nation. While this gives the consumer movement great significance, it also gives it a diversity and diffuseness that is sometimes confusing. Different income groups, different producing groups, people of different classes see different elements in the consumer problem. They emphasize different issues in their consumer activities. No one person or group can be picked out as representing all the varied interests of consumers. The consumer interest is still an indefinite concept which can be made clear in detail only by a close examination and understanding of the nature of consumer wants and needs, of how the consumer interest at present is being articulated, by whom and on what occasions the consumer point of view is being presented.

The present study has been undertaken to give this general survey of what the consumer movement is and what it is doing.

[1] For a development of the nature of consumer problems see Corwin Edwards, "Some Consumer Problems," in *Economic Problems in a Changing World* (1939), edited by Willard Thorp; Margaret Reid, *Consumers and the Market* (1938); and Jessie Coles, *The Consumer Buyer and the Market* (1938).

The pattern which it makes has been specially influenced by a few particular events. In this chapter these threads will be picked up before examining the various parts in detail.

CONSUMER ACTIVITY BEGAN EARLY

Many of the consumer groups which are active today have been in existence for years. Some consumer cooperative societies had been established in America before the middle of the nineteenth century. Toward the end of the nineteenth century consumers, becoming conscious of their responsibilities as buyers, began to use their purchasing power to improve the working conditions of labor. The first Consumers League was organized for this purpose in 1899. New attitudes to domestic problems led to the founding of the American Home Economics Association in 1908. Home economists ever since have worked quietly and persistently for standards to help the consumer-buyer and to lay the foundations for wiser consumer choice. National women's clubs frequently worked for consumer issues. Educational work was begun by agencies such as the Bureau of Home Economics and the Cooperative Extension Service in the federal government. Some of the state governments published analyses of milk products by name of dealer, or chemical analyses of paint and similar products by brand name. The firmly rooted interest of long-established groups such as these is a major source of strength to the consumer movement as a whole.

Many sporadic efforts on behalf of the consumer appeared during the past four or five decades, which also helped to establish an interest in consumer problems. The outstanding example occurred during the passage of the first food and drug act in 1906. In the long crusade for a better law to protect the consumer from dangerous and adulterated foods and drugs, Dr. Harvey Wiley was the most prominent figure. His numerous scientific reports on food adulteration while he was chief of the Bureau of Chemistry prepared the way for general activity. The years immediately preceding the passage of the act were marked by great agitation for consumer protection. It was, in fact, dubbed an era of "muckraking" in which the press took up cudgels strongly for the consumer. The *Ladies' Home Journal* and *Collier's Weekly* were particularly vocal in campaigning against patent medicine frauds. In 1906 Upton Sinclair's book *The Jungle* became a best seller. It drew attention to conditions in the meat-packing industry which made the need for consumer protection apparent. The American Pure Food League was organized by groups such as the General Federation of Women's Clubs, the National Consumers League (which recognized the importance of this issue to the worker's living), and the State Food Commissioners, in order to coordinate their work. Even though women did not have the vote at that time, their work was of great importance. The General Federation organized a Pure Food Committee in 1904 and did everything in its power by exhibits, petitions, and speeches to arouse public interest in the bill. In spite of determined opposition, the general excitement of the public made the drive for its passage irresistible.

After the passage of the act Clean Food Clubs were organized in some places to aid in its enforcement and to push for further protection of the consumer. Mrs. John Bley's group in Chicago was an outstanding example of this type of activity. It was at first a small neighborhood group called the Fifty-First Street Club. Later the name was changed to the Clean Food Club, and finally it expanded to cover the whole of Chicago under the name of the Housewives League. The methods which it adopted proved successful: the use of official printed stationery, secrecy as to membership, and wide publicity. At first it was chiefly interested in sanitary conditions in retail stores, but later became concerned with unjustifiable price situations. In the winter of 1912 it held an egg sale on street corners to break the price of storage eggs, which were being sold as fresh. Clubwomen dropped their Christmas shopping and sold eggs at 10 cents below the prevailing price of 34 cents. A similar sale took place in Philadelphia and later the same scheme was applied to apples. Housewives Leagues became active in other parts of the country.

These leagues were sometimes revived to oppose high prices after the war, arranging informal boycotts against merchants in order to bring prices down. Unorganized, spontaneous waves of economy developed in a few places too. In the winter of 1925-1926, for example, retailers' outlets in some sections were partially closed by a decline in the demand for men's clothing. Occasionally professional workers took to wearing overalls in order to economize. There was talk of forming a Middle Class Union, but the idea soon lost its force.

The Commission on the Necessaries of Life, set up shortly after the war in Massachusetts, is an illustration of state activity on behalf of the consumer. A major objective was to prevent profiteering. One of the first things it did was to send a member of the commission to Washington, immediately after the war-time fuel and food administration ceased to function. He obtained a larger supply of army surplus stores than otherwise would have been possible, which was sold at lower than current prices. This had an immediate effect in lowering local prices. Throughout the early twenties the commission frequently threatened to go into business itself, and took credit for lowering the price of anthracite coal from $22 to $17 a ton. It relied chiefly on publicity for its effectiveness, meeting with much opposition from local merchants. Another illustration of the idea of official consumer representation was the appointment during the twenties of people's counsels to represent the public—as consumers—on some utility commissions.

The experience gathered from these early consumer activities has been of importance in the development of the present consumer movement. In more recent years, however, other developments have been responsible to a large extent for shaping the movement into the form it has taken today.

THE DEMAND FOR COMMODITY INFORMATION AND STANDARDS BECAME WIDESPREAD

During past decades science and industry have developed thousands of new kinds of products, many of which are extremely complicated. Consumers have become puzzled and confused because they have neither the time nor the technical training nor the necessary facilities to discover for themselves what goes into most of the goods that they buy. To add to their confusion, selling policies have been adopted which tend to make their powers of discrimination even less than they might otherwise be. Staple products such as motor oils are sold for their "thrilling" performance. And exactly the same oil is sold under different brand names at different prices. Dozens of brands of coffee are said to make the "best" coffee you ever tasted. Romance is assured if one only buys the right kind of face cream, toothpaste, deodorant, baking powder, laundry soap, and even shoe polish.

Without adequate means of comparison, purchasers were bound eventually to begin to wonder whether the so-called "best" that they were buying really had the best stuff in it. They began to ask whether, if they were able to make better buys, they would not obtain from their limited incomes more of the things they wanted the most. When Stuart Chase and F. J. Schlink published *Your Money's Worth* in 1927 it became an instantaneous success, a best seller, and a selection of the Book of the Month Club. The book has gone through several editions and has sold over 100,000 copies.

It crystallized a vaguely felt, but widespread, discontent. The authors set out to explore the "Wonderland" of the consumer market and the "exhilarating game" which executives play in selling their products. The Wonderland consumers admittedly enjoy. But, as Chase and Schlink said, "all of us it irks occasionally—particularly when we contemplate what it costs us; and some of us it irks continually." The book was a plea for impartial testing agencies, and for standards for staple consumers' goods. It urged consumers as individuals and through organizations to promote these objectives. Two years later Mr. Schlink, responding to popular demand aroused by the book, established the first consumer testing agency. This was followed later by two others offering similar services. The consumer testing agencies have been aptly described as the dynamos of the current consumer movement. They were staffed to a considerable extent by workers in various fields of science and members of the engineering profession who were eager to see their technical knowledge devoted to the service of the consumer.

The onset of the depression and its persistence in economic life made consumers more conscious of the importance of buying carefully. Economic necessity forced them to consider their problems of spending wisely and many carefree habits of the twenties were broken. The handicap of the absence of usable commodity standards became more and more apparent. Sizes of cans and weights of packages were altered by small degrees— but eventually these alterations were noticed. Clothes wore out faster than expected and threw budgets out of balance. Quality deterioration became such a problem that it formed the initial impetus for the organization of some consumer groups. Mrs. Dennis Jackson, chairman of the Consumer Conference of Cincinnati, for example, pointed out that the consumer movement might well be called a "child of the depression," for this very reason. "As shirts, sheets, shoes, and dresses wore out before they were normally expected to," she said, "people felt they had been cheated. Those in organized groups compared their experiences with such merchandise and began in an organized way to devise some means to remedy the situation."[2] The demand for more commodity information and standards has become a unanimously accepted plank in the consumer platform of all groups.

The introduction of rayon and the unhappy experiences many consumer-buyers had with it served to accentuate consumer discontent. Often rayon was sold as silk and when the user cleaned it as she would have cleaned silk, it would be ruined. A campaign for identification of rayon, led by Julia Jaffray of the New York City Federation of Women's Clubs, was begun in 1937. Miss Jaffray wore for many of her speeches a dress which was sold to her as "lightweight wool." While being fitted she asked the fiber content to be written on her bill. The salesclerk was gone some time and then apologetically brought back the information that it was acetate rayon. Another incident which made an effective story was concerned with a beautiful dress which went to the dry cleaners—only the buttons came back.

The members of the New York Federation of Women's Clubs decided to insist on getting the type of material identified every time they made a purchase. They had their salesclerks write the information down on the sales slips. Then they collected the slips and sent them to the Federal Trade Commission as evi-

[2] Speech before the Thirty-Second Annual Convention of the Ohio Canners' Association, December 12, 1939.

dence that women really were interested in fiber identification. This flood of sales slips did, in fact, convince the commission that the women were serious. Trade rules were finally promulgated requiring the labeling of rayon content on fabrics, and they were acknowledged to be largely due to consumer agitation.

This demand for information has been reinforced by the fact that some businessmen have felt that they have interests in common with consumers on the question of commodity information. Customers who are educated to know real values and have enough information available to take advantage of their knowledge will seek out the most efficient merchants. Distributors such as Sears, Roebuck and Co.'s mail-order house and Macy's department store, in New York, find that through informative labeling and grading they can counteract the appeal of nationally advertised brands and increase the acceptance of their private brands. The progressive retailer sees his opportunity to exercise more control over distributive processes rather than being merely the "selling agent for the manufacturer." The "returned goods problem," which has been mounting in proportions during the past two decades, and their own purchasing problems have made retailers feel the need of more information.

Actual fraud and misrepresentation have long been recognized by businessmen as introducing chaos into their markets. Through their truth-in-advertising movement and their Better Business Bureaus some steps have been taken toward keeping downright dishonesty out of the market. Accurate labeling and less gullible consumers help to make the work of these agencies easier, and they, too, have looked with some favor on the growth of consumer education about commodities. For various reasons such as these the consumer demand for commodity information and standards has been given support by the more efficient and farsighted retailers and by some other business interests.

THE STRUGGLE OVER THE FOOD, DRUG, AND COSMETIC ACT OF 1938
   BROUGHT CONSUMER GROUPS TOGETHER

After the publication of *Your Money's Worth* a series of popular books appeared more militantly debunking nationally advertised products. Especially important were *100,000,000*

Guinea Pigs, by Arthur Kallet and F. J. Schlink, and *Skin Deep*, by Mary Phillips. Their combined circulation amounted to over 250,000 and even after the passage of the act they continued to sell well. *The American Chamber of Horrors*, by Ruth DeForest Lamb of the Food and Drug Administration, and publicity given the administration's "Chamber of Horrors," an exhibit of mis-branded and adulterated products which the law could not prevent being sold, did much to help acquaint the public with the need for more protection than was afforded by the Pure Food and Drug Act of 1906. The five-year struggle which took place from the time the first bill was introduced in 1933 until its final passage in 1938 did a great deal toward consolidating elements in the consumer movement and toward giving it recognition as a force to be reckoned with in the political world.

The act of 1906 had been widely publicized by the press of the nation and was passed on a wave of strong pro-consumer public opinion. The act of 1938 never attained a like amount of attention from the general public. Except during the reporting of the tragic deaths of nearly a hundred people from the use of Elixir Sulfanilamide, it received little attention from the press and never was given a prominent place on the Congressional program. It was generally acknowledged that the defects in the existing law made some new legislation inevitable. The particular form given to the new law was to a considerable extent a test of the strength of organized consumer groups in relation to Congress, as compared with the strength of the forces lined up to oppose the reform. As a measure of definite consumer interest it brought into action the major national groups having consumer interests.

Several tendencies were noticeable in the struggle which ensued. The so-called "Tugwell" bill—really not framed by Tugwell at all—brought immediate and violent hostility on the part of industry generally. The more moderate substitute bills introduced later brought sweeping condemnation from Consumers Union and Consumers' Research—the writers connected with which had been largely responsible through their work of popularization for getting action started. The later bills were described by them as emasculated and in their publications the testing agencies urged their subscribers to vote against the substitute bills. They urged complete adoption of the consumer point of view and a centralized consumer agency in the government.

The consumer groups who supported the legislation—chiefly women's clubs—while disappointed with the changes introduced, increased rather than diminished their attempts to improve the bill as efforts were made to weaken its provisions. At the outset only two organizations, the American Home Economics Association and the National Congress of Parents and Teachers, were prepared for action. By the end of the five years sixteen national women's organizations were working for sound legislation. For these groups it was an educational and consolidating process, and has led to an attempt to obtain a permanent joint representative to follow the enforcement of the act and the regulations promulgated under it.

Through their Washington representatives the women's groups were effective in the initial stages of drafting each bill. By quiet and steady lobbying they gradually obtained wider understanding of the bill and stronger support for it in Congress. They were represented at each hearing. They helped to maintain the interest of the administration in the legislation. They did a great deal of educational work among the members of their organizations throughout the whole country. They gained experience in legislative conflicts with special interest groups opposed to them—particularly the apple-growers and proprietary medicine interests. The militant and uncompromising publicity carried on by the "guinea pig" writers and this patient and realistic lobbying by the women's clubs, though the two approaches were not formally coordinated, effectively promoted the consumer point of view.

Another tendency noticeable during the fight was the fact that industry found it worth while to try to develop its own organizations of clubwomen allies to counteract the work of the autonomous women's groups who were determined to get real consumer protection. The National Advisory Council of Consumers and Producers and the Joint Committee for Sound and Democratic Legislation, for example, testified along the same lines as industry representatives at hearings on the Tugwell and later bills. *Business Week*, in pointing this out, stated that "Business discovered that compromise on a platform of minimum reform could win for it a measure of consumer support which is helpful in withstanding the demands of the more zealous and militant consumer leaders."[3] One of the most important factors bringing consumer groups together has been their resentment at pseudo-consumer organizations of all kinds.

The bill as finally passed did represent a much greater improvement in the protection of the consumer than had been thought likely during the years just previous to its final enactment. During the struggle over the new act, consumer leaders strongly urged that control of advertising be given to the Food and Drug Administration. Although they lost on this point, the Wheeler-Lea Act gave to the Federal Trade Commission control over the regulation of trade practices and advertising with a view to their effect on consumers. The activity of consumer groups with fiber identification, particularly rayon, had already given the commission a respect for and an interest in the consumer movement and it has been active in asserting its new powers. It was the passage of the new Food, Drug, and Cosmetic Act and the Wheeler-Lea Act that did most to awaken manufacturing and advertising interests to the importance of organized consumer activity.

SPECIFIC CONSUMER REPRESENTATION WAS MADE IN GOVERNMENT AGENCIES

The depression not only developed among consumers a closer attention to their spending habits, but also brought into sharper focus problems concerned with the functioning of the economic system as a whole. Even in the best of times it has been estimated that over 40 per cent of the population existed at the subsistence or poverty level. In 1935-1936 over 60 per cent of the population had annual incomes of $1,250 or less. The spectacle of unemployed men and idle factories, of hunger in the midst of "surpluses" of pork, oranges, corn, and milk, made practical people think of themselves as consumers as well as producers. The NRA

[3] April 19, 1939.

and AAA attempted to stimulate recovery by giving aid to producing groups, through price-raising programs and by setting
up rules of market behavior. The distress of particular producing groups made this an obvious need. Nevertheless, it soon
became apparent that the interests of the consuming public also
required specific consideration. Out of the recognition of this
fact was formulated the concept of a consumer interest as a
special interest distinct from the public interest and from other
economic interests.

The history of the consumer agencies in the NRA and AAA
offers many examples of the economic problems involved in the
actual relations between consumer and other interests.[4] Only the
factors which led to the establishment of special consumer
representation and the contribution which this made to the
development of outside consumer organization can be considered
here.

In 1933 the Consumers' Advisory Board was established in
the NRA. It has been described as an "afterthought." Individuals
were to benefit from the NRA in their capacities as owners and
laborers; as consumers they were not to be injured. From the
point of view of defending policies, it was clear that there would
need to be some means of justifying the burden of higher prices
to the consumer. The establishment of a consumer board was
expected to serve as a gesture in the right direction. It became
an unexpected thorn in the flesh to the promoters of the program.
The first thing that happened was the resignation of Dr. W. F.
Ogburn as chairman of the Consumers' Advisory Board. The
newspapers gave wide publicity to his claim that the interests of
consumers were being ignored. Under the chairmanship of Mrs.
Mary Rumsey the board carried on its work and persistently
sought to obtain recognition for consumer advisers at code hearings. Only after a considerable struggle did consumer advisers
obtain even the right to make statements and ask questions.

In spite of their difficulties, it was felt that some gains had
been made by the time the NRA became defunct in 1935. One

---

[4] For a detailed discussion of the problems and work of the Consumers'
Advisory Board see Persia Campbell, *Consumer Representation in the New
Deal*, Columbia University Press, 1940.

of the most dramatic episodes in which the board was successful was with respect to consumers' cooperative societies. The oil industry incorporated an article in its code providing that no rebates could be paid to purchasers of petroleum products. This provision threatened to destroy 1,500 cooperative oil-distributing societies and to check the formation of new ones which were being organized at the rate of two a week. Mrs. Mary Rumsey attended hearings, called on Cabinet officers, deputy administrators, and other officials. On October 23, 1933, the President issued a special executive order exempting legitimate cooperative organizations from those provisions in codes which prohibited the payment of rebates, and thus prevented the destruction of cooperative consumers' societies by private enterprise through their power of control over NRA measures.

The Consumers' Advisory Board was described as the most "economically literate" group within the NRA. Part of the difficulty in its work lay in the fact that the idea of a consumer interest was itself nebulous and new, and consequently misunderstood. Among the board members and executives there was a great deal of interoffice correspondence clarifying the concept of the consumer interest. As a result the idea of a consumer interest became a part of the thinking and concern of many of the people associated with the board, who later went to other places in public and private life. Their continuing interest in consumer organization and consumer welfare has been an important part of the consumer movement.

The Consumers' Counsel of the AAA was also established in 1933. It went through periods of resignations and protests similar to those in the NRA. The office and the work, however, have been carried on continuously since its first establishment. Under the present leadership of D. E. Montgomery active presentation of the consumer point of view has been made on many public occasions and encouragement given to the formation of local consumer groups. The bimonthly publication, *Consumers' Guide*, edited by Mary Taylor, has been an invaluable aid to many families and study groups. The *Guide* has a circulation of over 150,000. Other study materials and aids to study groups are also prepared by the office of the Consumers' Counsel. Under its sponsorship a rural-urban conference of women was held in Washington in 1939 and at least seventeen similar conferences have been held in various states. At these meetings the social-economic problems of consumers were a coordinating theme. Although the Consumers' Counsel gives valuable services to consumers, the office is, of course, subordinate to the agricultural program as a whole.

One of the greatest difficulties faced by both the Consumers' Advisory Board and the Consumers' Counsel of the AAA in promoting consumer welfare was the lack of any strong organized support such as labor and industry had. In 1934 when the Consumers' Division of the National Emergency Council was set up to coordinate consumer activities of the NRA and AAA, one of its functions became the development of county consumer councils which would to some extent fulfill the need for a consumer "constituency." They were modeled on a series of "mayors' councils" which had been started by the Consumers' Counsel of the AAA. Paul Douglas, professor of economics at the University of Chicago, headed the project. He asked for $4,000,000 to set up councils in all 3,098 counties. Actually $50,000 was allotted for an objective of 200 councils on an experimental basis. They were to serve as "two-way channels" through which administration policies could be interpreted and from which consumer reaction to the new programs could be obtained. Contact was maintained with them through regular publications, such as the *Consumer, Consumer Notes, Consumers' Guide.* The councils were to be made up of appointed members approximately as follows: one member from an organization of women actively interested in consumer problems; the county agent or someone named by him; the home demonstration agent, or else a dietitian, home economist, or educator; a "dirt" farmer, a housewife of moderate or low income; a manual worker; a member of a cooperative. In this way a cross section of various consumer points of view was to be obtained. A few of the councils were extremely effective. The one in St. Louis, for example, was largely responsible for the fact that prices in the retail coal code were kept reasonable to the consumer. A few of the councils are still in existence without official support, or with the help only of WPA funds.

It is significant to note that the suggestion has been made recently that the laws against price fixing and protection against war profiteering should be backed up by the use of systematic, localized publicity. Thurman Arnold, of the antitrust division of the Department of Justice, in 1939 suggested a plan for having government stations all over the country with trained economists and lawyers who would work with existing consumer groups to prevent profiteering. Such a plan would in fact be similar in objectives to the consumer county councils—except that now consumer groups are already organized in many places and could form the basis of the plan.

Corwin D. Edwards, of the Department of Justice, speaking at the second national conference on consumer education held by the Institute for Consumer Education in 1940, further indicated the possibilities of such a scheme. "Let us envisage the relation between consumer groups and antitrust enforcement as it might conceivably prevail a decade or two hence," he said. "Consumers would be well enough organized to have an organized nucleus in most communities and to maintain loose federal ties among the various local groups. The Antitrust Division would have at least one representative resident in every state. The consumer organizations would winnow complaints by their members and supply the Antitrust Division's nearest representative with information which appeared to point to any serious consumer problems involving violation of the law. Upon receiving such complaints, the Division would be able to use a growing body of facts about consumer purchases collected by the consumer groups, as it now can use the facts collected by the complaining business groups. The department's representative on the spot could make a quick inquiry into any important complaint . . . the far flung consumer organizations . . . in helping such a staff would render one of their most important services to their members."

Although the actual part played by county councils in the NRA and AAA was limited, they helped to establish a pattern of local consumer organization. National action and national leadership were also stimulated by the New Deal program. At the invitation of Mrs. Rumsey, chairman of the Consumers' Advisory Board, and Frederick Howe, Consumers' Counsel of the AAA, a two-day conference was held in December, 1933, on "The Role of the Consumer in the Recovery Program." As a result of this meeting a Consumers' National Conference was organized with Leon Henderson as chairman, the Right Reverend John A. Ryan as vice-chairman, and Alice Edwards, of the American Home Economics Association, as secretary. The objects of the Consumers' National Conference were decided to be: to conserve and advance consumers' interests with special reference to commodity standards and to urge adequate consumer representation in the development and administration of the new policies being adopted. It was thought that the various groups represented should have an agency such as this to focus consumer interests and to exert pressure on governmental agencies. The Consumers' National Conference issued nine numbers of a *Consumers' Information Service*, January 15 to February 2, 1933. The final issue contained the following statement by Leon Henderson:

I believe the consumer's voice must be heard, and will be heard. If I did not so believe, then must I be resigned to a progressive decline in the standard of living. The consumer will find some means of mass expression . . . It may come through one of many types of associative organization . . . through government agencies such as County Councils or a Department of the Consumer.

The possibility of a department of the consumer has been a persistent idea in many organized groups. By 1939 it was an idea which even business interests looked at favorably. "Conceivably," said *Business Week* in April of that year, "one government department would be easier to deal with than ten or twenty million rugged individualists."

When the National Bituminous Coal Act of 1935 was passed specific legislative provision was made for consumer representation. The act provided for a Consumers' Counsel directly responsible to Congress and quite independent of the National

Bituminous Coal Commission. This provision was retained in the act of 1937. The Consumers' Counsel insisted on full recognition of the rights and responsibilities set forth in the act and succeeded in making effective presentation of the consumer point of view. In 1937, for example, the commission attempted to ignore the counsel's right to have evidence justifying prices set. Mr. John Carson, the counsel at that time, demanded a public hearing, and stood ready to take the case to court had not prices been revoked.

The office of the counsel undertook educational projects to make retailers and consumers better informed concerning the relative merits and uses of various types of coal. The bulletin series, Consumer Ideas, with pamphlets such as *How Much Heat, The Consumer Speaks,* are useful consumer aids. A periodical release *Coal Consumers' Digest* keeps consumers informed of current happenings. A comprehensive outline of the economics of the coal industry for use in classrooms has also been prepared. In the reorganization of 1939 the counsel lost some of his independent status, but has continued in existence in a division in the office of the solicitor in the Department of the Interior. As a part of an experiment in industrial regulation, the original setup was of great significance because of the special legislative provision for consumer representation.

The demand for commodity information and standards was closely linked with the more general interest in consumer representation in public policy. All the consumer agencies in government stressed the importance to the consumer of commodity standards as part of the consumer's stake in price fixing. In actual practice one of the most effective accomplishments of the Consumers' Advisory Board was the inclusion of grades and standards in many NRA codes. In 1933 a "Proposal to Develop Standards for Consumer Goods by Establishing a Consumer Standards Board and Funds for Basic Testing" was prepared by the board. It is generally referred to as the "Lynd Report" because of the work of Robert S. Lynd, of Columbia University. It has formed the basis for many similar proposals to establish a government agency for promoting standards for consumers' goods.

SCHOOLS ADOPTED CONSUMER EDUCATION

In 1938 the Educational Policies Commission of the National Education Association, representing the largest body of organized teachers in America, reported on the *Purposes of Education in American Democracy*. It pointed out that the one-sided emphasis on productive and vocational education is unfortunate. "Granting the importance of producer education," the commission said, "the equal and corollary importance of consumer education must not be overlooked."

The consumer movement is basically educational in all its phases, but no development has been more remarkable than the rapid rise of the interest of teachers in the possibilities of consumer education in the schools and colleges of the country. Henry Harap planted the seeds with his book *The Education of the Consumer* in 1924 and home economists have always been interested in certain phases of it. But it was during the past decade that the general idea of consumer education as an integral part of school curriculums took firm hold.

No spectacular single event can be pointed to in this field during the twenties and early thirties. Rather there was a gradual adoption in various courses and curriculums of methods and content which taken together became recognized as a "consumer approach." Teachers, gathering together, found they had a mutual bond in discussing the effectiveness of this new approach and stimulated each other's enthusiasm for it.

One convincing piece of evidence of the general extent to which consumer education had been developing was the harvest of textbooks which appeared in the middle and late thirties. Solid educational material in the consumer field is now available at every school level. Many of these books represented years of teaching experience and thinking on the subject. Another piece of evidence that consumer education had already taken hold in the schools was the unexpected attendance of more than 500 teachers at the first conference on consumer education held in 1939 in Columbia, Mo., under the auspices of the Institute for Consumer Education. The same year a Consumer Education Association was formed. This development of consumer education in the schools makes the outlook for the future growth of the consumer movement among adult members of the population seem particularly bright. A new consumer is growing up who has consciously thought of himself as a consumer and has some understanding of consumer problems.

Consumer education has itself some of the diversity and surface confusion of the consumer movement as a whole. At what age level it should be introduced, what its place in the curriculum as a whole should be, whether it should be a separate course or not—these problems have been argued back and forth at many meetings. Educators seem to be agreed that its scope is so broad that much flexibility is desirable on these questions.

Just as the demand for commodity information is the most obvious aspect of the consumer movement as a whole, the most tangible effect on school practice of the rise of consumer education is to be seen in increased instruction about buying practices and good buying habits. As such it appears wherever instruction about commodities or services is found.

More fundamental, however, is its significance as part of the changing philosophy and thinking in American education. It is characteristic of the trend toward greater realism. For many years the view has been gaining ground that education should function in action, that it should directly influence behavior, that it should be directly related to the kinds of problems which people meet in everyday life. For real life education the basic consumer decision is not whether to buy a Ford or a Chevrolet, but whether to buy a car at all. The schools recognize this and pupils now study advertising, convention, habit, customs, propaganda, and the other influences which form their opinions. They study their own wants and prejudices and try to work out their own philosophies of living and establish their own standards of value.

In line with the increased trend toward realism there has been greatly increased and vitalized instruction about the economic system. Economics courses are becoming centered around consumption instead of production; the processes of distribution gain attention as well as the techniques of factory production. The possibilities and difficulties, the advantages and disadvantages to consumer interests of private business practices, of organized cooperatives and consumer groups, and of governmental regulation of both sellers and buyers of goods, find a place for discussion in the schoolroom.

The contributions of this kind of education are basic to the development of intelligent democracy. "Consumer education is neither an ephemeral fad nor a panacea for the ills of mankind," said Professor Howard Wilson, of the Harvard School of Education, in 1939, "but it is an important phase of the realistic education for living which is the task of democracy's schools."[5]

BASIC RESEARCH AND LITERATURE ON CONSUMPTION AND CONSUMER PROBLEMS ACCUMULATED

The consumer movement has been immeasurably strengthened by a growing body of research and writing which systematically analyzes the extent and nature of consumer problems. Only by taking into account basic facts and analyzing them carefully can consumers expect to advance their position. Much more needs to be done, but in recent years a wealth of new material has been added to our fund of knowledge about consumers and their problems.

Of special importance in this country has been the completion of the colossal Consumer Purchases Study carried out jointly by three federal government agencies—the National Resources Committee, the Bureau of Labor Statistics, and the Bureau of Home Economics. It took five years to finish, and at the peak of activity more than 5,000 people were engaged in the work. It covered thousands of families in all types of circumstances and in all parts of the country. Under the careful supervision of A. D. H. Kaplan, Hildegarde Kneeland, and Faith Williams, a standard of scientific accuracy, remarkably high for the circumstances, was maintained for the research in all its aspects. It is no exaggeration to say that better data are now available on consumer incomes and consumer expenditures in this country than for any other country or for this country at any other time.

[5] "Consumer Education in the Schools," Business-Consumer Relations Conference held by the National Association of Better Business Bureaus, Inc., Buffalo, 1939, *Proceedings*, p. 49.

We know from studies such as these that one-third of the people do not have adequate incomes for the bare necessities of life; that even with adequate incomes people do not always choose adequate diets. We know more about conditions of housing and medical care. We know something of variations in patterns of expenditure from one income group to another.

We have now available more studies of commodity distribution and analyses of prices. Studies by agricultural economists and students of industrial organization are giving us a better understanding of the economic world in which we really live. From business sources we have much information about the psychology of the consumer, which is as helpful in building up sales resistance as it has been in breaking it down. Commodity information from all sources is accumulating gradually.

As more and more information of all kinds is gathered about the nature and needs of consumers the movement for advancing their interests will become more and more solidly founded. A great deal of thought is being put on the interpretation from the consumer point of view of this growing body of data. The demands of consumer leaders will be seen to be clearly founded on fact and not on personal opinion and should carry the weight of authority as well as the weight of the organized interests they represent. .

The growth of academic consumer literature in addition to popular writing has been notable in recent years. At college, secondary, and elementary levels, excellent textbooks are available on consumer problems. Increasing quantities of material are being put in a form suitable for adult study groups. Selected and comprehensive bibliographies have been prepared and are available from various sources.[6]

THE CONSUMER MOVEMENT IS CLARIFYING ITS OBJECTIVES

The broad common objectives for which consumers are working may be summed up in four key words: income, information, integrity, and independence.[7]

[6] Information as to available literature in the field may be obtained from the Institute for Consumer Education, Stephens College, Columbia, Mo.
[7] See John M. Cassels, "The Clarification of Consumer Thinking," in the

Consumers want income. They are concerned with their real income, not just their money income. So fundamental and general is this concern that it is commonly present in our minds without being consciously associated with the idea of ourselves as consumers. That, however, cannot alter the fact that it does underlie the whole consumer movement and that it undoubtedly accounts in large measure for the strong force of the current that is carrying it forward. Additional impetus is given to the force by the diffusion of information about the incomes of American families. The studies made by the Brookings Institution on *America's Capacity to Produce* and *America's Capacity to Consume*, concluded that even in the prosperous year of 1929, while many consumers were inadequately provided for, the productive plant of the country was being utilized to only 80 per cent of its capacity. Studies such as these put the depression problems in a setting which made people realize that even in the best of times there were maladjustments impairing national efficiency, maladjustments which the depression exaggerated rather than created. Then came the comprehensive studies of consumer incomes and expenditures made by the Bureau of Labor Statistics, the Bureau of Home Economics, and the National Resources Committee. These showed two-thirds of the families of the United States with incomes under $1,500; one-third with incomes less than $750 a year.

Individual experiences, supported by the evidence from such surveys and analyses, led many people to question the uncritical optimism with which we viewed our economic system prior to 1929. Much of this questioning is naturally being done from the consumer point of view. This is responsible perhaps for the feeling prevalent in certain quarters that the consumer movement is red or radical, a thing to be feared and fought against. Actually it is radical only in the true original sense of the word, meaning that consumers do want to get to the roots of their problems and they do want to find cures that will be more than temporary palliatives. That does not make it a dangerous

Proceedings (pp. 8-16) of the Business-Consumer Relations Conference, sponsored by the National Association of Better Business Bureaus, New York, 1940. The following section is a condensation of his speech.

revolutionary movement. The growing interest that people are taking as consumers in the economic affairs of the country should be considered a healthy and a hopeful thing. The consumer point of view is the point of view of the final users of goods, the ultimate beneficiaries of all economic activity, the democratic citizens of the economic community. Since all of us are consumers, this approach to our common economic problems is more likely, perhaps, than any other to lead to constructive and socially desirable results.

The second outstanding characteristic of the consumer movement is its concern with obtaining information. Part of the explanation of this is to be found in the fact that the quest for information is geared to the urge of people to better their real incomes. In order to convert money earnings into real income with a reasonable degree of efficiency, a great deal of practical information about commodities and their uses is necessary. In order to manage family income so as to get the best long-run results from the use of it, a great deal must be known about the problems of budgeting, choice making, and the whole field of personal economics. Finally, in order to play their parts effectively as citizens in the economic community consumers need to know at least a certain amount about the functioning of the economy as a whole. This desire for information accounts for the fact that consumer education is so inextricably woven in with other elements in the movement that it really has to be regarded as an integral part of the whole.

At the present time the demand for information about commodities is the most prominent feature of the consumer movement. Consumers cannot possibly become technical experts on all the types of commodities they have to buy, but they certainly could make use of more factual information than has hitherto been available to them and they could make use of simple symbols representing the facts summed up in sets of grades or standards. The proportion of consumers who are ready to make full use of the information that could be given them may still be too small to make it clearly profitable, in terms of immediate returns, for producers or distributors to provide it. On the other hand, the number of consumers asking for it is steadily increasing and the influence of consumer education in the schools is making the next generation still more fact conscious. It is a trend which promises to increase the economic efficiency of the community and enough business people are becoming convinced of its merits that developments along these lines are rapidly taking place.

Next, consumers are interested in the integrity of those with whom they deal. The highest possible standards of honesty are to be desired not only for their own sake, but also because they enable us to carry on all our economic activities more efficiently. What consumers feel most concerned about in this connection is the integrity of those from whom they buy. In this regard their interests coincide with those of reputable business concerns who suffer from the practices of competitors less scrupulous than themselves. The most dependable and the most efficient businesses have everything to gain and nothing to lose from the increased competence of consumers in the avoidance of swindles and the appreciation of real values in the things offered them in the market. Consumers are interested in joining with them to promote higher individual standards and more effective organized regulation through trade associations. They are concerned with obtaining whatever legislation is needed to protect consumers fully.

Finally, consumers want independence. They want to have independence as individuals in making up their own minds about how they will spend their incomes; they also want independence as a class in organizing and expressing their opinions. The need for the development of independent consumer education in spending money was recently pointed out by Dr. Ben Graham, superintendent of schools in Pittsburgh: "The manufacturer and his salesmen, under our system, are out to make a profit. They try to influence the public to buy those things which will yield business the greatest profits. These are not necessarily the articles which the people most need. Advertising is powerful. When you meet it, you are in the hands of professionals."[8]

It cannot be denied that the arts of advertising and selling

[8] Reported in *Advertising Age*, March 11, 1940.

have been developed to a high pitch of perfection. As an achievement in the technique of influencing other people's behavior we cannot but admire the progress that has been made. Great talent has been enlisted in this fascinating industry and hundreds of millions of dollars go annually to carrying on this work. The power over consumer spending that is exercised in this way is tremendous. Producers through their sales efforts have had a large share in making the content of American living what it is today. That content, it may be agreed, is not a bad content and yet it could be better. There are, for example, noncommercial elements in living, in support of which no promotional campaign can be financed. In the uninfluenced opinion of consumers, these might be given preference over those they have been led to exalt through the arts of aggressive sellers. It is not unnatural that consumers, now that they have started to give more thought to their problems, should want to get more of the control over their expenditures back into their own hands. This does not mean they want to abolish advertising, but that they do want to retain and develop their abilities to see other alternatives to the satisfactions suggested by advertising.

On this issue differences in point of view between consumers and business interests are often extremely difficult to overcome. The problem may be best summed up perhaps in the way it was stated by Dr. Agnew, executive secretary of the American Standards Association. Discussing a paper on advertising by Mr. John Benson, president of the American Association of Advertising Agencies, he analyzed the situation as follows:

Mr. Benson tells us that advertisers are striving to clean up their seamy tenth. I believe consumer leaders understand this effort, that they are in complete sympathy with it, and that they will be glad to cooperate in this cleaning-up effort.

But that is only a small part of the story. What the consumer leaders are after is something far more fundamental. They are asking for a major reorientation in methods, and in objectives in advertising and merchandising.

Mr. Benson is trying to make all advertisers fish only in season, throw back the small fish, and prevent anyone from dynamiting the waters and killing all the fish. He has made it clear that advertising, like fishing, is a system of techniques. The consumer leaders understand that this is so, but they dislike the idea of being treated as poor fish, whose sole function in life is to be hooked.[9]

The points of view of fish and fisherman certainly seem irreconcilable. In consumer-business relations, however, a clearer understanding of the divergence of interests in itself may contribute to a more satisfactory solution of the problems involved. The importance of consumers acting in a way consistent with their own needs and their own freely formed philosophies of life is obvious.

The other aspect of consumers' interest in independence is their freedom to act collectively on their common problems without being attacked or interfered with. They want this whether they are setting up their own cooperative enterprises, whether they are dealing directly with business leaders through representatives of their own choosing, or whether they are forwarding their interests by legislative means. In the modern economic world much more is being done by deliberate social action, and organized group activity is taking on new importance. It cannot be expected that consumer interests will be adequately looked after if consumers themselves do not make clear the ways in which they are affected by public policy. Here the issue may be summed up in the words of Stacy May, Assistant Director for the Social Sciences of the Rockefeller Foundation. In discussing the "Politics of Consumption," he said:

No one will look out for the consumers' interests unless they do it for themselves or through special agencies in government set up for that specific purpose. . . .

In my opinion consumers err when they condemn business interests as wicked when the latter merely are attempting to forward their legitimate motives of profit in a given market. But I feel equally sure that business men err when they pretend that the interests of consumers are best left in their—the sellers'—hands.

That does not make economic sense, nor does it flatter the intelligence of those whom they are addressing.[10]

[9] *Proceedings* of the National Conference held by the Institute for Consumer Education, April, 1939, pp. 169.

[10] *Ibid.*

In collective as in individual action, free formulation by consumers themselves of what they want is essential.

In the following chapters the elements of the consumer movement are described in detail. At this stage it seems to be roughly true that groups in the consumer movement have collected around their professional or occupational interests, but gradually are coordinating the contributions to the consumer interest evident from their special points of view. Scientists are turning their services to the direct use of the consumer through testing agencies. Educators are integrating consumer education with education as a whole and giving leadership to adult groups. Women are thinking of what can help them with their jobs and responsibilities as homemakers and how their interests can be protected. Other groups, such as religious, labor, farm, and welfare organizations, are becoming more interested in the protection and recognition of their interests as consumers. The consumer cooperative movement is growing and is recognized as an integral part of the movement as a whole. All these efforts are being coordinated, chiefly at community levels, but to some extent on a national scale. Business and government are giving recognition to organized consumer groups in shaping their policies.

The common goals of a better real income, more information, integrity, and independence run throughout the programs of all consumer groups, with varying special emphases. Only by examining the separate groups, with their particular emphasis, can a satisfactory understanding of the whole be reached.

Chapter Two

SCIENTISTS BECOME CONSUMER CONSCIOUS

SCIENCE naturally found its first application in the field of production. It is true that because of all the improvements that have been made in production techniques higher standards of living are possible today than ever before. Yet as a result of technological progress many of our consumer-buying problems have been tremendously increased. There is an increased complexity of goods; synthetic fibers and complicated mechanical devices have come to the market. Consumers have found themselves confronted with deliberate aggressive campaigns by producers to influence their choices. Advertising on radio and billboard, in newspapers and magazines, has attempted to tell consumers what to buy. But in the midst of all these appeals the consumer is beginning to wonder how well some of the products fit his actual needs or desires. When he learns that there are 10,000 brands of wheat flour, 4,500 brands of canned corn, 500 brands of mustard, he begins to wonder about the particular advantages of the brand he happens to be using and how it differs from all the others, or even whether it is really different at all in any essential respects.

Industrial purchasers often buy by specification, or analyze competing brands to determine which will best suit their needs. Government and institutional buyers in many places have made outstanding economies through purchasing on this basis. The Hospital Bureau of Standards and Supplies has for thirty years been developing a purchasing service to aid member organizations in this way. This bureau, which is only an example of thousands of similar types of organizations, has over 200 members and purchased in 1939 nearly two and one-half million dollars' worth of goods for them. According to it, "Competent and economical purchasing can be achieved only through specifications sufficiently detailed to enable buyers to know what they are getting and suppliers to submit their bids on the basis of the intrinsic merits of the materials offered, rather than on brand names."[1] The bureau issues confidential reports to its members comparing branded products. Buying surveys indicate a saving to its members at the present time of over a third of a million dollars annually.

In recent years the household purchaser has shown an interest in the possibilities of receiving similar aid. The movement for standards and specifications has attained momentum. Scientific advisers are available to help the consumer in choosing economically what he or she wants, whether it be vitamins, glamour, or pride of possession. Testing agencies have been set up "to make science serve more effectively the interest of the consumer—to give the consumer counsel and information comparable to that supplied industry by its technical staff."[2] From lipstick and automobiles to furnaces and floor wax, these agencies try to guide the ultimate buyer through the complexities of the modern market, filling as best they can the gaps in the individual consumer's information and technical skill. The task is not an easy or a simple one. It is of interest to ultimate consumers to know something about the setup and nature of these agencies which tackle with their scientific tools, not the problems of producing and selling goods, but those of buying and using them.

CONSUMER COMMODITY TESTING AGENCIES

Three national organizations are engaged in rating branded products for the consumer on the basis of scientific tests: Consumers' Research, Intermountain Consumers' Service and Consumers Union. Table 1 indicates some general information about them.

[1] Thirtieth Annual Report, 1939, p. 3.
[2] Intermountain Consumers' Service, *Buying Guide*, vol. 5, Feb.-Mar., 1937.

TABLE I. COMMODITY TESTING AGENCIES IN THE UNITED STATES

Organization	Date Established	Approximate Membership	Director	Head-quarters
Consumers' Research	1929	60,000	F. J. Schlink	Washington, N. J.
Intermountain Consumers' Service	1932	3,500	S. A. Mahood	Denver, Colo.
Consumers Union	1936	85,000	Arthur Kallet	New York, N. Y.

It will be observed that their total membership amounts to almost 150,000. This represents family or larger groups. It includes, however, an unknown number who may subscribe to more than one of the services. Consumers Union publishes a monthly news release, *Your Dollar,* which is carried by trade-union and labor newspapers whose circulation is estimated at 3,000,000. Consumers' Research data are used in a monthly journal, *Consumers' Digest,* published by a legally independent corporation. It sells on newsstands at 15 cents a copy.

The primary purpose of rating and testing commodities is carried on in essentially the same way by all three agencies. Commodities for testing are bought for the most part at random on the open market. Attempts are made to choose products which subscribers appear to be most interested in, for which the need for testing appears to be most urgent, or for which tests are most readily available.

Based on test results, products are generally classified into three groups, dividing them into first and second best, and those not recommended for use at all. Consumers' Research rates products as recommended, intermediate, and not recommended, according to quality. Price ratings also are made—1, 2, 3—in increasing order of price. All quality ratings are independent of price and all price ratings independent of quality. Consumers Union ratings are based on both price and quality. Its top rating (Best Buy) may not indicate a product of as high a quality as one given the rating "also acceptable," because of an unfavorable price difference. As a result of an analysis of membership preference, Consumers Union adopted the policy of giving the order of quality in addition to Best Buy for most products. It was found that out of 2,600 replies to questionnaires, 68 per cent favored the inclusion of strict quality ratings; 11 per cent favored ratings in order of quality only; and 16 per cent were satisfied with the method of rating on quality in relation to price. The idea of a "Best Buy," however, represents a specially important contribution to consumer thinking, since it stresses economy as well as quality. Among the middle-class groups where the circulation of testing agency material is widest, this is sometimes neglected. Intermountain Consumers' Service rates commodities on quality and correlates price with it. Products are rated on a basis of A, B, C, followed by numerical figures 1, 2, 3 indicating fair, high, or excessive prices. Occasionally products are given an exceptional rating of AA. A further rating *ad* is given to indicate "advertising not warranted by the facts, not informative." Intermountain Consumers' Service computes an "index of dependability" to gauge the maintenance of quality over two or more years.

In addition to testing products and devising ways of relating their intrinsic merits to the prices at which they are sold, the agencies give general information about the care and construction of the goods. After each rating, information about the test and reasons for the rating, whether favorable or unfavorable, is given. It is expected that this general information will be read by the subscriber and taken into consideration in purchasing for his particular needs. It is perhaps the most useful part of the service.

It is quite wrong to think of the material of testing agencies as mainly critical. Dexter Masters, publications director of Consumers Union, pointed this out at meetings of the American Marketing Association in 1940. "Only 15 per cent of the products tested," he said, "are rated 'not acceptable.'" Much of what is said about products that are found worthy by tests is highly commendatory, and this is often true of widely advertised as well as of less known products.

Each of the agencies issues periodic bulletins summarizing the results of their tests. Consumers' Research and Consumers Union, in addition, prepare annual cumulative buying guides summarizing their ratings for handy reference for shoppers. Consumers' Research *Bulletins* and Consumers Union *Reports* are printed and illustrated. Intermountain Consumers' Service's *Buying Guide* is mimeographed. Subscription rates to Intermountain Consumers' Service and to Consumers' Research are $3 a year, to Consumers Union $3.50. Reduced rates for study groups or students are also available from all of them. Special bulletins or reports on topics of limited interest or requiring more extensive treatment are issued by Consumers Union and Consumers' Research. Consumers Union prepares an abridged edition omitting some luxury items for $1.50, group rates $1; four nonconfidential bulletins issued each year by Consumers' Research may be subscribed to for $1.

Subscribers to all the services are required to sign a pledge to keep certain designated material confidential. Membership is open to anyone on this basis. The only confidential issue from Consumers Union is its annual *Buying Guide*. Consumers' Research issues four confidential bulletins annually. Intermountain Consumers' Service material is almost entirely confidential. According to Consumers' Research the purpose of the confidential status is to lessen the possibility of legal difficulties with manufacturers who think their products may have been unfairly treated. Intermountain Consumers' Service states also that it helps to maintain circulation.

Consumers' Research and Intermountain Consumers' Service confine themselves chiefly to the commodity field. Consumers Union offers an insurance advisory service and has a medical section in its *Reports*. Intermountain Consumers' Service and Consumers' Research will test products for individual subscribers on a fee basis.

ORGANIZATION, FINANCES AND PROMOTION

All three agencies are incorporated under nonprofit laws. Of the three, Consumers' Research is most strictly controlled by its director. Intermountain Consumers' Service draws on the advice and experience of representatives of various types of community interests. It has a board of five directors and its sponsors include leaders from welfare, education, labor, and professional fields, who are willing to give some time and thought to the work which IMCS is doing. Consumers Union has a board of directors of seventeen, including seven staff members, elected by ballots mailed to members. An annual questionnaire is sent to members which the board may use in shaping its policies. Annual meetings are held in which all members are invited to participate. In June, 1940, about 200 out of its 85,000 members attended a two-day conference at Massachusetts State College, where the theme "Science in the Service of the Consumers" was discussed jointly with the Boston and Cambridge branch of the American Association of Scientific Workers. All the agencies welcome the experience and help of their members in contributing to the fund of information about commodities.

Altogether Consumers Union and Consumers' Research each report on about 2,000 products annually. Intermountain Consumers' Service covers a smaller range in its mimeographed bulletins. All the agencies are supported mainly by subscriptions. Sometimes small gifts are received from subscribers or others, provided they have no commercial interests. Consumers Union income in 1939 amounted to a little over $200,000. Consumers' Research is somewhat less, and Intermountain Consumers' Service's income is around $10,000.

Annual breakdowns of expenditure are available to subscribers to Consumers Union. For the year ending May 31, 1939, according to figures in the November *Report*, about 23 per cent of CU's expenditures went into the preparation of material for the *Reports* and *Buying Guide*; about 25 per cent into the publishing and mailing of the *Reports* and *Guide*; promotion and renewal costs absorbed 23 per cent; cost of keeping membership records and preparing wrappers for mailings came to 7 per cent; work with membership groups, speakers' bureaus, preparation of material for classroom use, work on consumer legislation, etc., took 5 per cent; administrative and general expenses amounted to 17 per cent.

A criticism sometimes made of the testing agencies is that the actual work of testing absorbs too low a fraction of total income, and that in any case their resources are too small to allow for an adequate job of testing, especially in comparison with the huge sums spent for research by manufacturing concerns. The figures, however, should be interpreted in the light of three other facts.

In the first place, some of the cost of testing is unusually low. Many of the workers in the testing agencies are willing to contribute their services at lower salaries than they would get for similar work in industry. A great deal of voluntary help is received from outside consultants, who like the originators of the agencies, feel the desire to turn their talents and training immediately toward the helping of the consumer. There is no way of knowing what the commercial value of this low-cost or free service from technical sources is, but if valued in monetary terms it would materially alter the apparent relations between cost of technical work and cost of administration.

A second point which should be remembered is that the problems of industrial and consumer testing are different. The object in consumer testing is not the development of new products, but the comparison of two or more similar products. Sometimes only simple tests are necessary to determine, for example, the presence of lead in cosmetics. This is a much less difficult and expensive task than devising formulas for the making of products. More funds would certainly be desirable and are needed, but the actual smallness of the budget in comparison with the millions spent for industrial research need not be considered evidence of futility in the efforts that are being made.

In the third place, the ordinary channels of sales promotion—the press and radio—are closed for the most part to agencies which are critical of many business practices and hostile to exaggerated claims of advertisers. Sixty-two publications have turned back Consumers Union advertising. The New York *Times* accepted some advertising from them in 1936 but soon dropped it. Most of the publications, according to CU, "didn't say yes . . . and most of them didn't say no. They hemmed and hawed, most of them. They said that they weren't sure about the copy, that they didn't know enough about CU, that they never accept 'controversial' advertisements, that they have policies against CU's 'type' of advertising." Many of these same publications, however, have carried "scientific" advertising for such products as Fleischmann's Yeast and Vicks VapoRub, and testimonial advertisements of doubtful authoritativeness. The "censorship" of their advertising is not only a bitter issue with the testing agencies, but it also forces them to rely on expensive direct-contact methods of promotion for increasing their membership and finances. Consumers Union has undertaken active promotional campaigns, relying chiefly on mailing pieces and personal contacts, and has had the most rapid increase in members. Twelve hundred new members were obtained by a prize contest in 1938 and more than 6,000 members were obtained through their booth at the New York World's Fair in 1939.

TESTING METHODS

Perhaps the most important single requisite for a satisfactory testing agency is that of independence of control from any commercial interest having a stake in the ratings made. Offers of assistance from commercial interests have frequently been made. They have necessarily been rejected by the testing agencies. Sometimes attempts are made to use their ratings promotionally, or to suppress information. Many examples of such attempts and resistance to them are available in their files. Each of the agencies buys its samples almost exclusively on the open market, as would an ordinary purchaser, and often the ratings of different lines of goods from the same manufacturer will be widely different or will vary greatly from time to time.

Any authoritative appraisal of the soundness of the technical work of the three agencies (within their financial limits) would require a detailed investigation of their results and methods by competent authorities in many fields. No such study is available. Isolated examples of inconsistency in their work have been pointed out and the general limitations have been frequently discussed. The agencies themselves clearly recognize the difficulties which confront them but they still feel that their technical advice puts the consumer in a better position than he would be without it. Consumers' Research, the oldest of the three, states the typical position:

CR does not seek to force its findings or opinions on its subscribers. The technical staff, to the extent of its ability, aims to act as consulting expert for all those who support the work, giving to CR's subscribers the kind of advice available to a few large industrial corporations in their own purchases through their technical staffs and consulting experts. It is out of the question that we should be able to provide answers to all possible queries of consumers, which are infinite, almost, in number and diversity.

CR's recommendations make no pretense to completeness or unfailing exactness. Certainly not one subscriber in a thousand would have access to information in any field as extensive as is CR's in many. Only a few specialists in certain kinds of consumers' goods could possibly have as complete and comprehensive data available, and more than likely theirs would not be in quickly and conveniently usable form as they are in CR's *Bulletins* especially its *Annual Cumulative Bulletin*. . . .

CR does not claim infallibility in the material which it presents. In any work operating on limited funds and involving the cooperation of so many individuals and the recording of so many thousands of observations and references, errors of fact and of judgment unavoidably creep in. All scientific work is in a state of continual change, and it is only such vendors of certainty as tooth paste and patent medicine advertisers who quickly and assertively achieve finality in their statements. It should be noted, however, that CR promptly issues corrections when errors are made; the small number of corrections needed in the course of a year gives a very good indication of the general reliability of CR's work.[3]

The technical work of Consumers' Research is under the direction of F. J. Schlink, co-author with Stuart Chase of *Your Money's Worth*. Mr. Schlink is an engineer-physicist. He was formerly assistant secretary of the American Standards Association and formerly technical assistant to the director of the National Bureau of Standards of the federal government. Consumers' Research has a staff of experts and its own laboratory in Washington, N. J. It has recently finished building new laboratories. As stated in the *Introduction to Consumers' Research*, a fifteen-page pamphlet explaining its scope and nature to new members, the major part of CR's work rests on the large number of tests and studies of consumers' goods which are planned

[3] Quoted from the *Introduction to Consumers' Research*, pp. 7-8, November, 1939, by special permission of Consumers' Research, Inc., Washington, N. J. Italics in original statement.

and carried out in its own laboratory or for it by investigators in colleges, universities, some commercial laboratories which it regards as properly equipped, and other institutions. Much of the information issued is derived from tests, investigations, or researches made by its consultants, of whom there are more than a thousand. These are experts who have signified their readiness to help along the lines of their specialties and include agronomists, physicians, dentists, engineers of all sorts, physicists, chemists, photographic technologists, entomologists, biochemists, home economists, nutritionists, and many other classes of scientists and technicians. At their own request none of these is named because they hold official positions elsewhere in which their work with consumer testing agencies might involve controversy or censure. Use is made of the data published by the National Bureau of Standards, by the American Medical Association, and other research or investigating bureaus, associations or individual experts.

IMCS similarly draws together pertinent information from all possible sources which may help the consumer in deciding among brands. Dr. S. A. Mahood, the president and research director, is a chemist with degrees from the University of Nebraska and Cornell and has done special investigations at Yale. He formerly taught at Lawrence College in Nebraska, at Cornell and Tulane universities and was also formerly senior research chemist in the U. S. Forest Products Laboratory affiliated with the University of Wisconsin. He has taught courses dealing with consumer education in several Colorado colleges and universities. All material used is edited and checked for reliability by his own staff before publication.

According to official statements, all of Consumers Union's technical work is handled under the general supervision of a Technical Control Committee. The chairman of this committee is Dr. William M. Malisoff, professor of biochemistry at Brooklyn Polytechnic Institute. It includes also Arthur Kallet, director of Consumers Union, a graduate of Massachusetts Institute of Technology; Dr. Harold Aaron, head of Consumers Union's medical department; Dexter Masters, publications director; and

Mrs. Florence Gluesing, librarian, who was for several years librarian of the American Standards Association.

Projects are initiated by the Technical Control Committee on the basis of studies of questionnaires and communications from members. The first step in every project is a search for all applicable standards, specifications, and methods of test, under Mrs. Gluesing's direction. At the same time the Boston and Cambridge branch of the American Association of Scientific Workers, which officially cooperates with Consumers Union in its technical work, is notified of the initiation of the project. A special committee of the branch calls upon those members who have special knowledge in the field of the project for advice with respect to methods of test and the general conduct of the project. Another member of the staff is assigned to making market surveys of the product concerned, with the aid of shoppers employed by Consumers Union in leading centers throughout the country.

Each project is assigned to a member of the technical staff who on the basis of standards and tests and the market surveys submits a preliminary report to the Technical Control Committee. On the basis of the preliminary report and, where necessary, of correspondence and discussion with authorities in the field concerned, the Technical Control Committee decides whether the project is feasible, what methods of test are to be used, what brands are to be covered, how many samples of each brand are to be tested, and whether the test is to be conducted in Consumers Union's own laboratories or by outside consultants, and finally assigns the project to a particular issue of the *Reports.*

If the necessary technical equipment is available in the Consumers Union laboratories, and a member of the technical staff is competent to do the work, the test is done in Consumers Union's laboratory. If specialized equipment and specialized experience or knowledge are required, the work is assigned to one of the many outside laboratories with which Consumers Union maintains contact. A new laboratory has recently been completed. All textile work is done in an outside textile laboratory. Most heavy electrical equipment, such as refrigerators or washing machines, is tested in a university laboratory which has the special equipment needed for such work. The grading of canned foods is done for Consumers Union by the grading service of the U.S. Bureau of Agricultural Economics. Between January and May, 1940, Consumers Union submitted nearly 4,000 cans to the grading service to be rated.

In addition to direct supervision of the work as it progresses, the Technical Control Committee keeps in touch with the progress of tests through weekly reports and through conferences with the technicians. In this way any special problems, requiring new tests or new samples, are handled as they arise. Projects in the medical field are handled with the assistance of a Medical Advisory Committee of physicians. Assistance is also obtained regularly from leading authorities in various medical fields.

When tests are completed the technician in charge submits a technical report to the Technical Control Committee, and on the basis of this technical report prepares an article and the ratings for Consumers Union *Reports*. In every case the technical data and the ratings are checked by a member of the technical staff other than the one in charge of the project, and in most cases the reports are sent to outside consultants for further checking before publication.

ARE THE TESTING AGENCIES WORTH SUBSCRIBING TO?

This is the question consumers ask most frequently. The answer to it depends largely on the consumer himself. The testing agencies offer only an advisory service with no claim to infallibility. Consumers who are looking for perfection, or who consider themselves pretty good buyers already, are likely to be disappointed. Those who simply hope to make fewer mistakes are generally able to save both time and money. For products which can be tested by chemical analysis—such as soap, tooth paste, paint, floor wax, gasoline, cosmetics, drugs, and so on, the analyses seem least open to question. For other products, such as textiles and canned food, specifications or grades established by government or recognized standardizing bodies are available and used. For shoes, shirts, stockings, refrigerators, radios, and other products where personal preferences or complex mechanisms are involved, the difficulties are greater. Performance tests may be inadequate or almost impossible to obtain because of the lack of suitable tests or because of the varying conditions of use. The tests may not take account of personal tastes or characteristics of the user. Once the limitations are recognized, however, the consumer may still find the ratings and even more the accompanying technical information an aid to selection. They at least give him defense ammunition against some of the general and often exaggerated claims that may be made for the highly advertised product or for the retailer's specialty. With some knowledge about the relative merits of products, customers may discover the salesclerk's own ignorance. This may be the initial impetus to obtaining more satisfactory information from manufacturer and merchant.

Generally speaking, the information which the testing agencies give has offered to the buyer a degree of protection to pocketbook and health which far outweighs incidental cases of error; and consumers have found that these economic comparisons are as interesting to them as is the competitive game to businessmen. The appeal made by testing agencies to consumers is well illustrated by one of CU's promotion pieces—"The Case of Mr. and Mrs. X." It tells the story of how a "make-believe consumer family" saved nearly $170 in a year. They began with a little figuring on milk and soap and then, "Fascinated, Mr. and Mrs. X rolled up their sleeves. At two in the morning, bleary-eyed but happy, they sat back and surveyed their handiwork." Their results are shown in the table on page 44.

The continual changes made in products and the fact that ratings go out of date are sometimes considered a further serious limitation to the services of the testing agencies. As in the case of performance testing, however, the consumer may still obtain some aid from his buying guide, provided he uses it wisely. If he indicates to the seller that his choice is based on a consumer rating he can more readily find out what changes have been made. If improvements have been made, it is usually easy to extract the information.

The fact that the testing agencies cover only a small fraction of the total number of commodities and of the brands of the

THE RESULTS OF THE X's NIGHT OF FIGURING:

What we can save a year by changing from "Not Acceptable" or "Acceptable" brands listed in Consumers Union Reports to the "Best Buys."

From	To	Estimated Yearly Savings
Grade A milk	Grade B milk	$ 16.38
Cashmere Bouquet soap	Colgate Big Bath	2.45
Ivory flakes	Kirkman's	3.75
No-Nox Gulf*	Gulf Traffic	28.00
Mobiloil	Penn-Rad	17.50
Dunlop tires	Goodrich	22.00
Walk-Over shoes, men's	A. S. Beck	5.54
Apex Washing Machine	ABC	19.05
Kolynos toothpaste	Craig-Martin toothpowder	3.48
Holeproof socks	Woolworth's "Worthtwist"	6.00
Stove coal	Pea coal	30.00
(with proper adjustment of boiler and careful firing)		
Beechnut tomato juice	Royal Scarlet	6.08
Gillette Model G Electric Shaver	Sunbeam Shavemaster Model M	7.50
Total Savings for a Year		$167.73

* This change was based on the fact that Mr. X was driving an old car for which premium gasolines were considered less effective than for newer models.

commodities from which consumers must choose is a greater limitation to their usefulness. Many who subscribe to them feel that they are helping to support a long-run development which is still at a preliminary stage and which must attain a bigger scale to give the amount of help needed. Their rapid growth since their first establishment, in spite of the handicaps in promotion already referred to, indicates that consumers have found their services of value.

It is not possible to say which agency is best. Opinions vary as to which agency fulfills individual needs the best. Their ratings correspond reasonably well although they do not always agree precisely. This is partly due to inadequacies or differences in testing methods, partly to lack of standardization of products themselves.

Ideally much of the work performed by the testing agencies would be carried out, on the one hand, by a government agency adequately financed and equipped to do the work necessary for developing standards and grades (including arrangements for cooperating with affected interests) and, on the other hand, by fully informative selling policies on the part of advertisers, retailers, and manufacturers, with social and legal institutions that would check and control tendencies to misrepresentation and fraud. The need for private testing agencies would probably still be present, but their functions would be more largely concerned with helping in the enforcement of laws against fraud and misrepresentation, with explaining the use of standards and specifications, and with giving supplementary information.

Such a goal is recognized by the agencies themselves. Consumers' Research has helped in the drafting of a bill which would coordinate existing machinery in the federal government for consumer protection and provide additional protection and technical aid. Intermountain Consumers' Service strongly advocates grade labeling and adequate legal protection for the consumer. Consumers Union takes a similar position and one of its representatives takes part in the work of the Advisory Committee on Ultimate Consumer Goods of the American Standards Association.

Dexter Masters, publications editor of Consumers Union, indicated his general point of view at hearings before the Temporary National Economic Committee. In answer to a question as to how far he thought CU meets the problem of showing consumers the way to spend their money more wisely, he said: "Well, it doesn't go far enough, and doesn't go nearly as far as the problems go; it is a stopgap to control or provide a balance to the upset in distribution. . . . I might compare Consumers Union or any organization operating on that basis to insulin in the control of diabetes; i.e., the insulin does control it by providing a counterbalance, but the important thing would be to prevent the diabetes. Whether the upset in distribution is as incurable as diabetes, I don't know."

The question as to why three agencies exist is best explained by looking into their historical development and their differing views on the place of the consumer and consumer agencies in the economic order.

HISTORICAL DEVELOPMENT AND POINTS OF VIEW OF THE THREE
AGENCIES

Consumers' Research, Inc.

After devoting half a year of weekends, holidays, and other
spare time to answering questions from readers of *Your Money's
Worth*, F. J. Schlink decided that a local consumers' club which
he had organized should be expanded. The result was the establishment in 1929 of Consumers' Research, designed to do on a
larger scale the work formerly undertaken by the club. This
pioneering organization states its aims as twofold: "to provide a
clearing house where information of importance to consumers
may be assembled, edited, and promulgated; and to develop an
art and science of consumption by use of which ultimate consumers may defend themselves against the invasions and aggres-
sions of misleading advertising and high pressure salesmanship.
Consumers' Research is founded on the belief that consumers
have as much right to increase the purchasing power of their
dollars as have business enterprises, and that many consumers,
given an income above the subsistence level, will as a practical
matter achieve better results by learning how to get more for
their money than by continually striving to get more income as
the sole means of realization of their economic rights."[4]

No words have ever been minced in opposing many current
business practices and advertising copy. Many of the evils of
modern society are attributed by Mr. Schlink to mass production
and industrialization of the food supply. In his book *Eat, Drink
and Be Wary* he advises the consumer to "follow your grand-
mother's instincts—back to the ante-bran, pre-crisco days."
The pasteurization of milk he regards as a stopgap device designed to cover up an essentially bad situation. The excesses of
not only advertising and manufacturers, but of women's magazines, scientific nutritionists, professional dietitians, home economists, vitamin zealots, and food faddists generally are warned
against. Recommendations for home production of common
articles such as ink and dentrifices are also features of CR's
service which have attracted special notice.

The management of Consumers' Research is antagonistic to

[4] *Introduction to Consumers' Research*, p. 3.

labor organization, and to any alliance of consumer groups with other groups. No employees of CR are allowed to belong to any other organization without written permission. In the *Introduction to Consumers' Research* subscribers are told that such social questions as the wages, hours, contractual relations, and factory surroundings of employees engaged in producing and distributing goods are outside the scope of its work. This, of course, is true, but it is further stated that "unbiased reports on such subject matter are not available from any quarter"—a rather sweeping statement about a subject that has received extensive research by many social scientists and is subject to investigation by government agencies.

Enthusiasts in the consumer movement often see rational consumer choice as the element needed to make a competitive system effective and to eliminate the need for other kinds of control. This perhaps explains some of the general views which characterize CR's approach to economic questions. Editorially in the *Bulletin* for February, 1940, Mr. Schlink indicates his point of view with respect to some important economic issues. "All forms of price fixing by manufacturers or dealers in concert," he says, "or by contract or under governmental auspices is *against the interest of consumers*. It is an essential characteristic of the American system of doing business (the system known as capitalism) that prices should be allowed to reach the level which results from open competition in manufacturing and distribution among a multiplicity of makers and sellers of differing skills, talents, faculties, and points of view."[5] No reference is made to any interest of the consumer in such economic problems as cutthroat competition, labor exploitation, and the concentration of economic power. Many groups consider these and similar problems of great importance to the consumer.

Within the consumer movement CR is in a somewhat curious position. It has been the most vigorous of the testing agencies in attacking many advertising practices. It has therefore been grouped with all such agencies as "subversive" by the reactionary interests using these tactics to attempt to discredit the con-

[5] Quoted from *Consumers' Research Bulletin*, February, 1940, by special permission of Consumers' Research, Inc., Washington, N. J.

sumer movement.[6] At the same time it has been aggressive in attempting to discredit groups which it believes to be "communistic." J. B. Matthews resigned his position with Consumers' Research to become research director for the Dies Committee (his wife is still on the CR staff) and in a report to the committee in 1939 gave special attention to Consumers Union.[7] Because of such personal affiliations his report has been regarded by other organizations as part of the private feud between CU and CR, arising from the way in which CU was established as explained in the following section.

Consumers Union of the United States

In September, 1935, a strike occurred at Consumers' Research. Members of the staff, organized in the Technical, Editorial and Office Assistants Union affiliated with the American Federation of Labor, charged that three union members, including the president, were dismissed after making a request for formal recognition. They asked reinstatement and a minimum weekly wage of $15 instead of $13.13. The director of Consumers' Research refused arbitration or mediation and after four months of bitter struggle the strike was called off. The National Labor Relations Board ordered Consumers' Research to cease and desist from refusing to bargain collectively and to offer reinstatement to the dismissed workers. Consumers' Research refused to comply. The directors believed that the strike was originated by the Communist party and certain hostile commercial interests in order to obtain control of their laboratories.

An association of Consumers' Research subscribers had been formed to help in settlement of the strike, and they formed the nucleus for a new organization. Its object was to perform the same kind of testing and rating service for its members that Consumers' Research did for its subscribers and it adopted on the whole the same methods. The first issue of Consumers Union *Reports* appeared in May, 1936. Its physical appearance and setup is strikingly different from Consumers' Research *Bulletins*. The style is lighter and numerous photographs and cartoons are

[6] See Chapter Seven.
[7] See Chapter Five, pp. 131-136.

included. In interest and readability it compares with many popular magazines. Its scope, however, is not limited to the purely technical interests of consumers. It reports on labor news and labor conditions, especially as related to conditions of organization, for the products it rates. A section on legislation, news, and articles of general interest to consumers is also included. Since September, 1939, a monthly feature "War and Prices, a Guide for Consumers" has been run. All these features are kept separate from technical ratings.

The fundamental aim of Consumers Union, as stated in its charter, is also in marked contrast to that of Consumers' Research: "To give information and assistance on all matters relating to the expenditure of earnings and the family income; to initiate, to cooperate with, and to aid individual and group efforts of whatever nature and description seeking to create and maintain decent living standards for ultimate consumers." Commenting on this, it is stated editorially that "the directors of Consumers Union do not feel that they have done their job when they have provided information which permits the saving of a few pennies, or even a few dollars, by buying one brand instead of another . . . All the technical information in the world will not give enough food or enough clothes to the textile workers' families living on $11 a week. They, like the college professor or the skilled mechanic, are ultimate consumers; but the only way in which any organization can aid them materially as consumers is by helping them, in their struggle as workers, to get an honest wage."[8]

At the second annual meeting (1938) three resolutions were introduced proposing that Consumers Union be restricted to rating and analyzing consumer goods and not give its attention to the problem of labor, the threat of fascism or "other ideologies." (Consumers Union had run several articles on fascism and boycotts of Nazi goods shortly before.) After some debate the members present voted to adopt a resolution continuing to report on these. In 1939 this position was reaffirmed. At the same time the resignation was accepted of Dr. Charles A. Marlies, who was one of the founders, a member of the Board of Direc-

[8] Consumers Union *Reports*, Vol. 1, No. 1, May, 1936, p. 2.

tors and Executive Committee, and former head of the Chemical Section. In accepting his resignation it was stated that "In the rapid growth of Consumers Union to a position of leadership in the consumer field, we have encountered disagreements with Dr. Marlies as to the authority of the Director of Consumers Union, and the proportion of the resources of the organization to be devoted to strictly technical work." At the annual meeting in June, 1940, a resolution was passed offering support and cooperation to Miss Harriet Elliott, consumer representative on the President's Advisory Commission on National Defense "in such actions as she may initiate to the end that the fulfillment of the defense program shall not result in a decline of the standard of living of consumers."

Consumers Union has been active in support and promotion of organizations such as the Consumers National Federation, the Milk Consumers Protective Committee of New York, High Cost of Living Conferences, etc. It is also interested in the development of consumer cooperatives and at the 1938 annual meeting a resolution was adopted to the effect that Consumers Union should assist cooperatives in promoting higher quality standards by giving them technical advice and informing members through the *Reports* of important developments in the field of consumer cooperation.

The approach to consumer problems made by Consumers Union represents the alliance of consumer-labor interests in a struggle for a higher standard of living. It has worked militantly to extend consumer organization and arouse consumer consciousness on general issues as well as on the issue of commodity testing.

Returns from a questionnaire sent out to a sample of 2,600 CU members in 1939 indicated that almost half were professional workers, with teachers and school administrators first and engineers second. About one-third of CU's members were employed in manufacturing and merchandising industries and about 8 per cent were government employees. The median income was about $2,600; about 5 per cent had less than $1,000 and about 13 per cent more than $5,000.[9]

[9] Consumers Union *Reports*, October, 1939.

Intermountain Consumers' Service

This agency was organized in 1932. Its research director, Dr. S. A. Mahood, states that as a university professor he had noted the way in which his students were drawn into the exploiting treadmill of science as practiced in industry. He saw these youngsters, as producers and potential creators of valuable products and processes, required to contract with the employing corporation to assign the results of all their investigations to it, so that they were in a more unenviable position than the share-cropper who has at least the possibility of possessing a share of what he produces. These and other observations led him to consider a means for making science serve more effectively the needs rather than the greed of humanity. His investigations made him feel that Better Business Bureaus were concerned mainly with policing "blue-sky laws" on stocks and bonds and settling "false advertising" disputes among competing firms, and gave scant consideration to commodities and the interests of ultimate consumers. This resulted in the germination of his idea of a Scientific Better Business Bureau from which evolved his present research and information service.

IMCS is a service which "hopes to contribute in an enlarging degree to the health, economic well-being, and happiness of ultimate consumers, whose scientific and technical counselor it is privileged to be." Its function is regarded as chiefly limited to that of testing commodities and of education in the field of consumption. Dr. Mahood states that it has "no axe to grind and is motivated simply by a desire to see honesty and fair play prevail against fraud, misrepresentation, deception and greed . . . it desires the good will of business." He sees a need for commodity testing regardless of the form of the economic system. Professional testing groups should not be regarded as part of a radical movement designed to create unjustified suspicion of business and its methods, but rather the inevitable outgrowth of scientific and technological development in industry. "To such groups it is plain," he says, "that any economy which is scientific on its production side and pre-scientific on its consumption side is unworkable and that attempts to make it workable through the medium of advertising and salesmanship only create greater unbalance."[10]

Besides the work of testing, IMCS provides speakers and lecture courses on consumer education. It reports editorially on news of consumer interest. In a survey by the Consumers National Federation its director ranked the following organized consumer activities in order of importance: commodity testing services, consumer cooperatives, education (including the American Home Economics Association), welfare organizations and civic groups, religious and women's organizations.

The members of Intermountain Consumers' Service are advised, if they are interested in cooperatives or labor organizations, to pursue these interests independently. The position with regard to cooperatives is indicated by the following statement:

Cooperation among humans for high social ends is always commendable and so we have expressed ourselves as sympathetic toward all such endeavors. The cooperative idea, however, is not new and not all of the experiments in that direction have been successful. Without going into a detailed discussion of the reason for success or failure, let us say with H. G. Wells that "the human being, when fully adult, is still fundamentally a highly individualized and ego-centered animal, and his social life is based on subjugation and education. Economic and social cooperation . . . is cooperation against the grain." In the past there has been too much subjugation and not enough education.

Our enterprise is therefore centered around education which we feel is a necessary prerequisite to any thorough going cooperation which will not only supply honest goods at honest prices, but will also develop enthusiasm for the cooperative idea, and produce goods with greater novelty and increasingly better quality at a socially equitable cost. We are cooperators not only upon the basis of economics, but also on the basis of life enrichment in all its phases. Our objective is that social and economic order in which ethical and intelligently informed individuals can function on the basis of true mutuality.[11]

[10] "The Problems of a Consumers' Testing and Rating Agency," National Conference of the Institute for Consumer Education, April, 1939, *Proceedings*, p. 80.

[11] *Consumers' Buying Guide*, Vol. 3, Pt. 5, October, 1935, p. 1.

FOREIGN CONSUMER TESTING AGENCIES

The idea of testing and rating consumers' goods by brand names is essentially American. Observing experience in this country, other countries have considered the possibility of establishing similar organizations. A group of scientific and technical workers in England began making plans in 1938 for starting an organization modeled on Consumers Union. They proposed to begin in a small way, with a few advertised products. These were to be examined in the light of their advertising statements and the results circulated confidentially among members. In 1939 an organization in Canada was started called Consumers of Canada, Inc. Its aims were to report on commodities of interest to Canadian readers and to issue a publication *Consumer Standards*. It drew its inspiration chiefly from Consumers' Research. Shortly after its formation it became affiliated with the Canadian Association for Adult Education. Since the war these British attempts have been discontinued because of pressure of other tasks on their promoters. It is expected, however, that they will eventually be revived.

THE AMERICAN ASSOCIATION OF SCIENTIFIC WORKERS

This association, modeled on the twenty-year-old British Association of Scientific Workers, was organized in the summer of 1938 by a group of biologists at Woods Hole, Mass. In 1940 there were branches in Philadelphia, Boston and Cambridge, New York City, Chicago, Berkeley, New Haven, and Amherst. Membership is open to all who have a genuine interest in science and a college degree. The president is Dr. Anton J. Carlson, professor of physiology at the University of Chicago, and there are now about 800 members. The aims of the organization are to promote and extend the application of science to all problems of human welfare; to develop in the minds of the general public a better understanding of pure and applied science; to educate scientists to a better understanding of the social implications of their work.

The Boston and Cambridge branch has a Consumer Committee, which acts as a technical advisory board to Consumers Union and has begun dealing with scientific matters raised by

CU. In Boston and Cambridge a Committee on Group Medicine has been set up. In Chicago a nutritional survey is planned. In New York the possibility of cooperation with consumer organizations is being considered. Philadelphia has a consumer committee which will cooperate with similar committees in other branches.

At the joint meeting of the Boston and Cambridge branch with Consumers Union, June 17-18, 1940, the program included the following events and speakers:

What the Consumer Expects from Science
    Dr. William M. Malisoff, Special Technical Consultant for CU
Government Research in the Interest of the Consumer
    Dr. Louise Stanley, Chief, Bureau of Home Economics, United States Department of Agriculture
What the Consumer Should Know about Vitamins
    Dr. Helen Mitchell, Massachusetts State College
Diet, Oral Hygiene and Teeth
    Dr. Theodor Rosbury, College of Physicians and Surgeons, and School of Dental and Oral Surgery, Columbia University
The Automobile from the Consumer's Viewpoint
    Dr. C. Fayette Taylor, Professor of Automotive Engineering, Massachusetts Institute of Technology
The Need for Standards and Specifications in Consumer Goods
    Dr. Paul G. Agnew, Secretary, American Standards Association
What Recent Textile Developments Mean to Consumers
    Dr. Warren E. Emley, Chief of the Textiles Division, United States Bureau of Standards
What the Consumer Should Know about Cosmetics
    Dr. Marion B. Sulzberger, Editor of the Journal of Investigative Dermatology
The Reorganization of Medical Care
    Dr. Henry E. Sigerest, Professor of the History of Medicine, John Hopkins University
What the Science of the Future Holds for the Consumer
    Dr. Raymond E. Kirk, Head of the Department of Chemistry, Brooklyn Polytechnic Institute

Speakers at the dinner meeting were Professor Anton J. Carlson, of the Department of Physiology of the University of Chicago, and Dr. John M. Cassels, director of the Institute for Consumer Education, Stephens College, Columbia, Mo.

CERTIFICATION OF CONSUMERS' GOODS

There are many professional and business groups which issue seals of approval of various kinds—the American Medical Association, the American Dental Association, the Underwriters Laboratory, the Electrical Testing Laboratories, and so on. Many of them are extremely useful. They offer a protective minimum standard to the consumer without, however, making any comparison of relative values. Some certifications are mainly promotional selling devices. One well-known agency—the Good Housekeeping Institute—was in 1940 under examination by the Federal Trade Commission on the ground that it deceives the consumer. Amid the welter of seals of approval and certification agencies of all kinds which recent years have brought, many consumers are losing faith in all of them. They are asking for an "appraisal of the appraisers" of goods and the wider use of official grades and standards.

Chapter Three

EDUCATORS LOOK TOWARD THE CONSUMER

CONSUMER education in the schools of America is the property of no single department or age level. Chemistry teachers are beginning to analyze brands of tooth paste; arithmetic teachers compare relative prices in their work; history teachers draw attention to changing standards of living; commercial teachers are concerned with the newer methods of informative selling; and so on. Developments such as these may all be regarded as part of the increasing tendency for educators in general to adapt their methods and orient curriculums in terms of the immediate needs of their pupils. Furthermore, the failure of social institutions to adapt themselves in a rapidly changing economy is putting a severe strain on democratic societies. This has given still greater force to the idea of "education for living" in terms of immediate needs as individuals in present-day economic life and responsibilities as interdependent members of a great and complex economic community.

The consumer approach to these individual problems and to broader social and economic problems is a natural one. A National Committee on Economic Education appointed by the United States commissioner of education in 1933 reported in 1938 that there was great need for a vigorous expansion of economic education. It recommended a personalized approach through the consumption interest as a means of vitalizing economic education at all levels of maturity.

All branches of formal education of the younger generation

—elementary and secondary schools, colleges, graduate schools, and teachers colleges—now show the influence of these new ideas. Many varied concepts of consumer education are present. Sometimes it is the use of goods that is emphasized—how to wash rayon or how to bake a cake. It may be basic human needs that are considered—how to choose a diet with the proper balance of nutritive elements. Most often it is the buying problems of the consumer that receive attention—how to get best values in sheets or insurance. With increasing frequency problems of personal and family finance are taught—how to apportion expenditures among food, clothing, housing, recreation, and so on. Economic issues are being discussed more and more from the consumer point of view—the advantages and disadvantages of chain stores, the economics of advertising, what makes the price of meat or milk what it is, the use of our natural resources as a whole, and problems connected with public consumption goods.

The consumer point of view is a thread tying together all these various types of content. Only gradually are the aims and appropriate methods for different age levels and different types of schools being clarified. Special consumer courses have been added to many curriculums and consumer units to many regular courses in commercial, mathematics, science, civics, and other courses. Sometimes "core" curriculums are developed around the idea of consumption and the activities of the individual as a consumer.

It is almost impossible to make an accurate estimate of the extent of consumer education now being given in American schools. Approximately two-thirds of the high schools of the nation have home economics departments. Education in consumer cooperation is compulsory in some states and taught in many others. All signs indicate that there have been tremendous increases in all forms of consumer education in recent years. A survey by James Mendenhall and Maurice Wieting showed that, while only about 35 per cent of the texts published from 1930 to 1937 had sections on consumer problems, about 50 per cent of the 1938-1939 texts had sections on such varied problems as testing, labeling, buying wisely, and prices.[1] In 1938 B. J. Rivett submitted a questionnaire to 1,000 public and private secondary schools, all members of the North Central Association.[2] Out of 486 schools which replied about 8 per cent had separate courses in consumer education. Nearly all the schools reported that they taught the subject as units in home economics, economics, commerce, agriculture, chemistry, and health, with a frequency in the order named. One of the most convincing signs of the rapid growth in consumer education comes from studies made by Henry Harap.[3] In making a survey of courses in consumption in 1935 he was able to obtain only 28 course outlines. Three years later he repeated the survey and was able to collect 71 courses of study in consumer education, an increase of over 250 per cent. The survey did not include all the courses being taught. In 1940 the Institute for Consumer Education wrote to 200 colleges and universities for information about plans for including consumer education in their summer sessions. During the summer 125 different courses were offered in 63 of the 200 institutions. Such courses are designed primarily for teachers both in service and in training. Several of the institutions also sponsored summer conferences and workshops on consumer education.[4]

The most significant contribution of consumer educators is their influence on the thinking of the younger generation. As new consumers grow up, the practical results of this influence can be more clearly observed. The general direction of the work of educators and their immediate influence in national policy can best be seen, however, by an examination of the extent and nature of their organized activity. The American Home Economics Association is the oldest educational organization with major consumer interests and will be considered first. In the

[1] Maurice Wieting and James Mendenhall, "A New Consumer Grows Up," *Retailing*, Executive Edition, April 17, 1939.

[2] "Consumer Education in the North Central Schools," *North Central Association Quarterly*, April, 1939.

[3] "Seventy-one Courses in Consumption," *School Review*, October, 1938.

[4] See Joseph de Brum and James Mendenhall, "Consumer Education—Its Implications for Business Educators," *National Business Education Quarterly*, Summer, 1940.

past few years other types of organization of consumer educators have become important and will be considered later in this chapter.

I. THE AMERICAN HOME ECONOMICS ASSOCIATION

The American Home Economics Association was organized in 1908 and is concerned with the development of education, legislation, and research that will contribute to standards of home living satisfying to the individual and profitable to society.

The founding of the organization was largely due to the work of Mrs. Ellen H. Richards, an instructor in sanitary chemistry at the Massachusetts Institute of Technology from 1884 to 1911. She saw the need of intelligent direction from within the home if it was to keep in step with the rapid industrial advances. "The home economics movement," she said, "took rise in a realization of the 'inconvenience of ignorance.'" The changing nature of domestic life was only part of the stimulus to organization. New responsibilities of the home to society also were recognized. "What forces in the community can be roused to action to secure for the coming race the benefits of material progress?" asked Mrs. Richards.[5]

At a series of informal conferences held at Lake Placid during the years 1899 to 1908 these problems were discussed by a group of women interested in the new problems of the home. A minor accomplishment which indicated the line of their thinking was the insistence that their subject should be removed from its library classification as one of the useful arts under "production" and be put under the "economics of consumption." By this they felt that something could be done to suggest to students that home economics involves matters connected with social economy as well as with the arts of cooking and sewing. The Lake Placid Conferences finally culminated in the establishment of a formal and permanent association in 1908.

By 1940 the American Home Economics Association had, in affiliated state associations, more than 15,000 members including deans, directors, supervisors, teachers, research workers and executives in federal and state governments, rural extension

[5] Cf. Caroline Hunt, *Life of Ellen H. Richards* (1912).

workers, home economists in institutions, in commercial and business enterprises, in magazine and newspaper work, in relief and public health agencies, and in the practical business of home-making. There are in addition about 2,300 home economics clubs in colleges and high schools with around 80,000 members, and 6 homemaking groups. It has 18 standing committees, 13 special committees, and is affiliated with 16 other organizations. It is organized into five subject matter divisions: the family and its relationships; family economics; housing; food and nutrition; textiles and clothing. These include the aesthetic, economic, sociological, psychological, and applied science aspects of the home.

The association publishes a monthly *Journal* which follows developments of professional interest along all these lines; and two mimeographed services which cover in more detail news and activities in special fields: *The Consumer Education Service*, begun in 1936, and the *Family Life Education Service*, begun a year later. In 1940 the *Journal* had a paid circulation of 6,823, the *Consumer Education Service* had 900 subscribers, and the *Family Life Education Service* had 310. A quarterly *Bulletin* goes to every paid-up member of the association. A *National Magazine of Home Economics Student Clubs* is issued four times a year and has a circulation of 2,300.

Total budget for the year 1938-1939 amounted to $65,345. Of this approximately 30 per cent came from membership dues and registrations at the annual meeting, 23 per cent from *Journal* subscriptions, 24 per cent from *Journal* advertising and commercial exhibits at the annual meeting, and the remainder from registrations, sales of pins and publications, and miscellaneous sources.

HOME ECONOMICS AND NATIONAL POLICY

From the point of view of national policy making as well as of the education of the individual, the contribution of home economists to scientific knowledge about consumption is especially important. Some of the most remarkable achievements of recent years have been the discoveries associated with newer knowledge of nutrition. The work of United States Bureau of

Home Economics is internationally recognized for its outstanding work in economic aspects of this field. The study by Hazel Stiebeling and Medora M. Ward, *Diets at Four Levels of Nutritive Content and Cost* (USDA Circ. No. 296) and its popular version *Diets to Fit the Family Income* (USDA Farmers Bull. 1757) have received wide attention both by homemakers eager to improve their food choices and by economists interested in the long-run use of national resources. In the study made by the Brookings Institution in 1934 of *America's Capacity to Consume*, for example, these dietary standards formed the basis for speculating as to land-use possibilities. Since then other similar studies have drawn upon this type of data.

The effectiveness of the work of the Bureau of Home Economics on diets is indicated by the fact that in 1935 the following proviso was attached to the Agricultural Appropriations Bill as reported to the House of Representatives, March 14, 1935: "No part of the funds appropriated by this Act shall be used for the payment of the salary of any officer or employee of the Department of Agriculture . . . who issues or causes to be issued or to be made public any statement, oral or written, which advocates reduced consumption of, or which asserts that it is undesirable to use, any wholesome agricultural food commodity or any manufacture thereof." This sweeping amendment was inserted as the result of pressure from flour millers. They objected to the fact that for higher incomes a diet was recommended calling for more use of meat and milk and less of cereal products. Although the bill did not pass Congress with this rider, the bureau had to spend much valuable time in counteracting the propaganda of the millers. A typical example of what they were up against is indicated by the caption in *Northwest Miller and American Baker* in February, 1935; "Five Thousand More Copies of Four Diet Plan are Ordered, Bureau of Home Economics Proceeds Defiantly with its Anti-Wheat Propaganda." In actual fact the bulletin about which the millers complained is one of the most significant contributions to better living standards that has been made and the defense by the bureau of the right to give consumers honest educational material in this as on other occasions has added strength to the consumer movement as a whole.

From Hazel Stiebeling and Esther Phiphard's more recent study of the *Diets of Employed Wage Earners and Clerical Workers in Cities* (Circ. 507, USDA, 1939) based on data from the federal Consumer Purchases Study for 1935-1936 we know that 40-60 per cent of the diets of white families, in the four regions from which most extensive data were obtained, were judged to be in need of improvement. Over 60 per cent of the diets of Negro families in the South were in this class. No white families succeeded in obtaining diets which could be classified above the poor grade when they spent, a person a week, less than $1.60 in North Atlantic cities; $1.55 in East North Central; $1 in East South Central; or $1.60 in Pacific cities; and no Negro families in the South, when they spent less than 95 cents. It was found that many families spending more than these sums obtained poor diets, but that the chances for better diets increased with rising per capita expenditures for foods.

Information like this accumulating from many sources has served as a stimulus to new kinds of research in economics and related fields. Besides the federal Consumer Purchases Study for 1935-1936 which was undertaken with the cooperation of home economists all over the country, much research is in progress in state institutions. Land-grant colleges in 1939-1940, for example, had completed or under way 289 projects on foods and nutrition. During the same year 193 projects were in progress or completed on various phases of textiles and clothing, housing, and family economics.[6]

Home economists have shown a growing interest in public housing programs, and in other fields some progress in consumption standards has been made. In the development of such standards, in the comparison of these standards with actual consumption, home economists make a basic contribution to the development of consumer welfare. Any program of long-run planning for higher living standards will require a foundation of the kind

[6] See *Notes on Graduate Studies and Research in Home Economics and Home Economics Education*, issued by the Bureau of Home Economics, June 1940.

of scientific and practical research that is part of their special field. In immediate and emergency planning such as was begun for national defense in the fall of 1940, one of the first recommendations made to the consumer adviser of the National Defense Council was that everything possible be done to improve the nutritional status of the population through community action. The American Home Economics Association registered all its members in order to make them available for local participation in plans for increasing consumption and improving dietary practices. At the annual convention in Cleveland in June, 1940, the following resolutions were adopted:

WHEREAS, The home is the first line for national defense and the center of influence in the development of the democratic way of life, and whereas home economics is concerned with the best use of time, material, and human resources within the family; therefore,

Resolved, That the American Home Economics Association, assembled in annual convention in Cleveland, pledge its support to national defense and urge the President of the United States to utilize the services of its members.

Resolved, That the Amercian Home Economics Association offer its assistance to Harriet Elliott, the consumer representative of the Advisory Commission to the Council of National Defense, and stand ready to organize its members for such technical service as they can suitably render in connection with her work.

A further resolution was adopted requesting the executive committee to get in touch with agencies both regular and emergency which promote these aims, in order to find out the ways in which the services of the association and its members could be made most useful.

HOME ECONOMICS AND ADULT EDUCATION

One feature of the work of home economists which is of great importance is their connection with the extension service of the Department of Agriculture. For more than twenty years the Cooperative Agriculture Extension Service of the Department of Agriculture has, through its land-grant colleges, provided educational services for women, chiefly in rural areas.

This is the most systematic long-time adult education program for women in existence in this country.

It is jointly directed by the United States Department of Agriculture and the various land-grant colleges of the states. Participants in local programs help to shape policies and share in the responsibility for financing the work. Twenty-five hundred home economists are engaged in directing the "home demonstration" program for women. Each county home demonstration agent may direct an educational program in from twelve to thirty-five communities in her county. Once a month or more the women come together, usually in one of their own homes, to discuss their problems and add to their education.

Interest in family finance and consumer buying problems is long standing. In 1920 extension groups in Illinois, for example, were discussing such subjects as "Shopping Habits As They Affect the Budget." Testing circles in which women passed around pieces of equipment and kept performance records helped the homemaker decide what she wanted. Food values as related to health were discussed. Since the early twenties interest in programs such as these has steadily increased. In 1939 topics taken from random on the extension programs in Illinois included:

Financial planning for the family in relation to business cycles and in relation to cash income for family living and outgo.
Purchasing commodities for the women in relation to quantities and price change.
Buying electrical equipment for the farm home.
Textile identification.
Durability problems caused by weave and finish.
The selection of canned food.
The homemaker reads food advertising.
The cost of instalment buying.

Since 1923 most land-grant colleges have been holding outlook conferences to discuss the general economic situation, especially as it relates to agriculture. At these meetings the men and women consider the outlook for the farm business and for the farm home. They realize that they cannot decide what to produce, what to sell, when to buy, or when to borrow on the basis of their experience in one small community. They know these questions are related to national and world affairs.[7] In the spring of 1939 a conference of rural and urban women was called in Washington, D.C. Since then numerous regional conferences bringing town and country homemakers together have been held under extension sponsorship.

It is estimated that more than two million women and girls are reached annually through the extension program. Home economists in the Farm Security Administration are also reaching an increasing number of low-income rural consumers and helping them with their problems of management and buying.

HOME ECONOMICS AND CONSUMER BUYING PROBLEMS

Since consumer buying problems play such an important part in the consumer movement at the present time, the activities of the home economists through their association merit special attention. Specifically included as part of the interests and activities of the American Home Economics Association is cooperation with the commercial and business world by continued fostering and stimulating of interest in quality and performance specifications for consumers' goods and in the increased use of grade labels on the retail market.

At the first annual meeting of the association in 1908 a member from Tennessee said, "We pay money for goods and we know not what we get . . . I have found a great necessity for textile standards."[8] Since that time the association has been continuously concerned with the development of standards, grades, specifications, and simplified practice rules for consumers' goods. Unlike the testing agencies, however, the method adopted and followed consistently has been that of attempting to work cooperatively with business or government without trying to evaluate the relative merits of particular branded products.

[7] See K. VanAken Burns, *Adult Consumer Education*, Buffalo Conference of the National Association of Better Business Bureaus on Business-Consumer Relations, 1939, *Proceedings*, pp. 43-45.

[8] Cf. Harriet Howe, "Solving the Buying Problems of the Conusmer." Address before the Mid-Year Convention of the National Retail Dry Goods Association, June 22, 1937.

Work in the field of textile standards has been a major concentration. In 1918, when all fabrics were high in price and uncertain in quality, the textile division of the association launched a definite program to bring on the market staple fabrics labeled with quality specifications. The association invited the cooperation of associations of manufacturers, jobbers, and retailers to determine such standards and put on the market a limited number of standardized fabrics of various grades which would carry some identifying symbol. A committee was set up by the textile section to secure the cooperation of the industry, to educate consumers to ensure intelligent use of standards, and to provide the necessary research for testing fabrics.

An example of a successful cooperative project between clubwomen and merchants was that carried out by Rosamond Cook, an association member, in Cincinnati in 1934. The local merchants agreed to give the specifications recommended by Miss Cook's committee on all sheets offered in their stores during the white-goods sales. Through study groups and meetings the members of the committee taught consumers the meaning and significance of the items included in the specifications and urged them to purchase sheets sold under specifications.

When the commercial standards set up by the American Standards Association governing labeling of fiber content on wool and part-wool blankets became effective, the association brought their significance to the attention of consumers. It continued to point out the need for further information such as the facts about heat transmission, weight per square yard, and tensile strength. This publicity attracted commercial attention and the Chatham company introduced a "specification" blanket. In Virginia, the state committee on standardization listed all the manufacturers in the state and let each one know that consumers are interested in seeing informative labels on Virginia products. Similar projects have been carried on in Texas, Mississippi, Michigan, and Minnesota.

Among the textile projects in which the American Home Economics Association has co-operated are: the development, in cooperation with the National Bureau of Standards, of a standard abrasion machine for measuring durability; a study of the wear of textiles through the Textile Committee of the National Research Council; studies of women's purchasing habits to determine what fabrics are bought in largest quantities; a survey of women's opinions on what fabrics could and should be sold under standard specifications. It has also helped to develop practical performance tests for such commodities as sheets, hosiery, and slips. Textile research fellowships have been given by the association.

Cooperative efforts in the general field of standardization have been made with the two major bodies for the promotion of industrial standards—the National Bureau of Standards of the federal government and the American Standards Association. In 1927 a standing committee was appointed by the American Home Economics Association on the Standardization of Consumer Goods. In 1928 the association became a member of the American Standards Association, the only consumer body officially affiliated with it. It is also one of the most active consumer members of the National Consumer-Retailer Council.

At the present time work with the American Standards Association includes projects for the development of standards for bedding and upholstery, boys' clothing fabrics, shoe shanks, hosiery, dry cleaning, silver-plated tableware, safety rules for radio installations, household refrigerators, gas-burning appliances, waterproof materials, definitions of terms used in retailing, and children's garment and pattern sizes.

The project on sizes for children's garments and patterns was introduced under the sponsorship of the American Home Economics Association. The sectional committee set up by the American Standards Association to formulate the standards includes representatives from various trade associations and manufacturers and from government agencies. The committee has voted to recommend the establishment of a standard system of children's body measurements based upon height and hip measure which could be used as a basis for garment and pattern sizes. The recommendations are based on a study of body measurements initiated and carried out under the direction of the Bureau of Home Economics. The use of standards in this field should go a long way toward removing one common cause of consumer irritation.

For various reasons, the accomplishments of home economists over this period of more than thirty years are somewhat less than might have been expected from such continuous efforts directed toward the improvement of consumer buying. It should be remembered, however, that the movement for standardization is young, even in the industrial field. Home economists, with their close acquaintance with commodities, have been particularly conscious of the difficulties involved in the standardization of consumers' goods. They are particularly aware of the difficult human relations involved in developing and promoting standards. In the actual working out of practical programs they play a role of major importance. They have the needed information about commodities but do not themselves take responsibility for exerting great pressure.

A factor which has had a hampering effect in the work of promoting grades and standards has been a somewhat inconsistent attitude with respect to theory and practice. During the very period when the association was most active in attempting to promote standards, home economics classrooms were an outlet for great quantities of commercially sponsored educational material promoting particular branded products. The uninformative selling policies of much of this material tended to defeat the very objectives which the association was trying to advance. For example, in an analysis of approximately 300 advertising booklets used by teachers of home economics in their classrooms, the information given in them was rated by specialists trained in various phases of home economics. When scored on the basis of a maximum of ten points, the average score of the booklets was 6.7 for quantity and 7.0 for the quality of the information. It was also found that 75 per cent contained questionable statements, 43 per cent unsubstantiated statements, and 60 per cent contained misleading statements.[9]

Another indication of the type of commercial material some-

[9] Elizabeth Winkelhake, "Advertising from the Consumers' Standpoint," *Journal of Home Economics, February,* 1937, pp. 88-92.

times used by home economics teachers is the *Home Makers Bulletin*, published as part of the Home Makers Educational Service especially for home economics instructors. This service has been in existence for twenty-four years and is received by 18,000 teachers of home economics in schools and colleges and 2,000 home demonstration agents, WPA adult educators, and other groups. Editorially business and advertising are glorified. The main purpose, however, is the introduction of samples of various nationally advertised products into the schools by subscribers. The service is free. Fourteen products were listed in April, 1940, as having the "Home Makers Educational Service Symbol of Reliability." Lesson helps are provided to ensure the proper use of the products. The only tests actually made in awarding the "Symbol of Reliability" are the manufacturers' own and personal use by the staff of the service. The work is entirely financed by the manufacturers of the products being promoted, but this is not specifically stated. By material such as this the classroom becomes an extension of the salesroom rather than a true educational institution.

Attempts are now being made by the American Home Economics Association to get at the problem and work it out on a factual basis. One of the major steps in this direction was the appointment of a committee in 1934 on the Educational Use of Commercial Materials. This committee has prepared a check list to help teachers, students, and club leaders to evaluate commercial materials. The check list is planned for commercial materials produced for educational use as differentiated from advertising for direct selling. It offers a guide for checking such points as accuracy of subject matter, its timeliness, method of presentation, and lack of bias. At the Cleveland meetings in 1940 the committee reported that its work so far had brought from business the question "Do educators want information which business can give; and if so, how do they want it presented?" It was suggested that this was a question on which the committee might profitably spend its efforts in securing an answer from educators and interpreting it to business.

With the publication in 1936 of the *Consumer Education*

Service, edited by Mrs. Harriet Howe, the association began
to follow developments in the broad field of consumer education more closely than is possible in the *Journal*. This mimeographed publication is issued periodically as a newsletter and
miscellany series and covers activities in legislation, government
agencies, standards and standardization, grading and labeling,
cooperatives, distribution, advertising, trade promotion, the consumer movement, business-consumer relations, new books and
other publications in the consumer field. It is an important publication conveniently keeping workers abreast of developments
over a wide range of topics. Subscribers include libraries, business organizations, advertising agencies, publishing houses, and
department stores, although it is predominantly bought by home
economists. The income from subscriptions covers about 80 per
cent of the overhead costs, the remainder, including the salary
of a part-time worker, being contributed by a grant from the
home economics fraternity, Phi Upsilon Omicron. The second
year of its establishment showed an increase in subscribers of
16 per cent.

LEGISLATIVE PROGRAM OF THE ASSOCIATION

Through its legislative committee the American Home Economics Association plans programs for legislative support in
Congress. The association does not claim in any way to represent consumers themselves, but only the consumer interest as
seen by its members. Its programs are submitted for approval
to its executive council at the annual meeting. Two council meetings are required before final approval can be given. Representatives are sent to give testimony at hearings on bills which are
concerned with items for support. It is often represented at Federal Trade Commission hearings and trade practice conferences.
The chairman of the legislative committee maintains close contacts with the state legislative chairmen of affiliated associations
and the general membership by articles in the *Bulletin* and *Journal*. The legislative program for 1938-1939 included action on
the following measures of consumer interest: protection of the
ultimate consumer under the Food, Drugs, and Cosmetics Act;

block booking and blind selling of motion pictures; punitive taxation against chain stores; federal aid for housing.

The legislative program for 1939-1940 included the following items of interest to consumers: support of satisfactory measures for the protection of the consumer, such as adequate representation in the federal government; legislation for improved regulation of foods, drugs, and cosmetics and adequate enforcement of existing laws; legislation for the development and establishment of standards of quality and performance for consumers' goods, with the authority for fixing and establishing standards vested not in one government agency such as the National Bureau of Standards, but contributed to by the many governmental agencies working in this field, with final approval vested in large part in those bureaus long known to represent the consumer point of view, such as the Bureau of Home Economics; adequate regulation of weights and measures; fiber identification. It also went on record as opposing legislation for resale price maintenance and other forms of price fixing and legislation which discriminates against specific forms of distribution. Continued approval was given to the support of housing measures and continued opposition to blind selling and block booking of motion pictures. Approval was given to the support of measures which will improve the cultural and educational values of motion pictures and radio broadcasting.

WORK WITH OTHER CONSUMER GROUPS

No active interest in the problems of labor and the consumer has been taken by the association, although the responsibilities of the consumer with respect to conditions of labor has at times been pointed out in the *Journal*. It supports protective legislation for labor, particularly women and children. Until recently it has shown little interest in the consumer cooperative movement. No articles on this subject appeared in the pages of the *Journal* until September, 1936, except for minor notices about cooperative dormitories. The leading editorial in that issue reports that "In the coming months the *Journal* hopes to help its readers follow and appraise the development of consumer cooperatives." The *Consumer Education Service* gives careful coverage to this phase of the consumer movement.

The American Home Economics Association works closely with women's organizations. It helps them to prepare and develop educational materials and programs in consumer education. It cooperated, for example, in the preparation of the pamphlet *Scientific Consumer Purchasing* published by the American Association of University Women. This was written by Alice Edwards, formerly executive secretary of the association, and author of *Standardization of Consumer Goods* published by the Columbia University Press in 1940. In 1937 the association worked with the National Congress of Parents and Teachers to promote active cooperation between state leaders of the two organizations. Joint meetings with other organizations are sometimes held. It has worked closely with consumer groups through its work on the National Consumer-Retailer Council and on the Advisory Committee on Ultimate Consumer Goods of the American Standards Association. The Home Economics Association cooperates with other education associations and has been represented at the numerous education conferences that have been held during the past few years. Many home economists attended the two conferences held by the Institute for Consumer Education in 1939 and 1940. More than a dozen home economists took active parts in the programs.

II. ORGANIZATION OF OTHER CONSUMER EDUCATORS

So far there has been little formal organization of consumer educators as such. Most of the big long-established national organizations, such as the National Education Association, the Progressive Education Association, the American Federation of Teachers, and the National Commercial Teachers Federation, are giving increasing attention to consumer education as part of their regular programs. The National Education Association recently published a report by its Educational Policies Commission entitled the *Purposes of Education in American Democracy* in which a whole section was devoted to consumer education. In 1938 at its annual meeting in New York a special session was held on consumer education, with exhibits of educational material; and again in 1939 at San Francisco. The Progressive Education Association held a panel discussion on consumer education at its meeting in Chicago in February, 1939. It held a workship in consumer education in the summer of 1940. The National Council for the Social Studies devoted one of the sessions at its annual meeting at Kansas City in 1939 to "The Consumer Approach to Economics." At the American Marketing Association meetings at Detroit in December, 1938, a breakfast session was held on consumer problems and a special session at meetings of the American Economics Association in 1939 at Philadelphia. The Mid-West Economics Association meetings in April, 1940, also devoted a session to considering the problems of the consumer.

At the annual Commercial Education Conference in June, 1939, a meeting was held to discuss consumer education and again at its meetings at Pittsburgh in December, 1939. The increased attention given to understanding the consumer movement among commercial and business school teachers is an important development in the educational field. Many of these teachers are as eager to promote the consumer point of view in their work as teachers concerned entirely with nonvocational education. At a meeting of the Business-Consumer Relations Conference held by the National Association of Better Business Bureaus in 1939, Professor F. G. Nichols, president of the National Council of Business Education, expressed his surprise at a clubwoman who referred to "misguided crusaders" in the consumer field. Any crusade against questionable business practices, blatant advertising, and fake testimonials, Professor Nichols regarded as a healthy thing.[10] Business educators like this believe that consumer education will bring about stability to business enterprise, and stimulate its most efficient development. One recent event in the educational field of special importance to consumers was the passage in 1937 of the George-Deen Act providing educational funds for distributive education, an occupation which has been comparatively neglected. Merchandise information is particularly stressed in the new program.

[10] Discussion on "What Consumers Want," *Proceedings* of the Buffalo Conference, 1939, pp. 35-36.

Numerous regional, state, and local conferences on consumer education are being held in increasing numbers. In May, 1940, 250 educators from all the Southern states met in Nashville, Tenn., under the leadership of Henry Harap, of Peabody College. Pennsylvania held a conference in Williamsport in June on the theme "Where Shall Consumer Education be Taught?" Plans are being developed to include a course in consumer education in the state curriculum in Pennsylvania. A Consumer Education Institute was held at Kalamazoo, Mich., under the direction of Howard F. Bigelow in July, and a Consumer Education Conference was held in Colorado at about the same time. No complete record of all such conferences is available but their number is constantly growing, contributing much to the solidarity and growth of the consumer movement as a whole.

The Institute for Propaganda Analysis established in 1937 issues a monthly bulletin, prepares study material, and issues special reports which are valuable aids in many phases of the work of consumer education.

At the present time only two national groups are concerned specifically with the development of formal consumer education in schools and colleges: the Consumer Education Association and the Institute for Consumer Education, both organized in 1938.

CONSUMER EDUCATION ASSOCIATION

The Consumer Education Association was started by Edward Reich and Carlton J. Siegler, educators in the field of merchandising, who had long had an interest in the development of consumer education. In 1937 they published a book *Consumer Goods*. Because of their increased mail after this, the idea came to them of forming an Association of Secondary School Teachers of Consumer Education. A committee was formed to lay plans for the proposed association. At the National Education Association Convention in June, 1938, an organizing committee was formed. A small amount of initial help was received indirectly from the Alfred P. Sloan Foundation through the cooperation of the Institute for Consumer Education in building up a mailing list. The further development of the organization was largely due to the interest of Reich and Siegler and the contributions of their own time and money to the venture.

The association as finally organized includes teachers at all levels—colleges as well as secondary schools. It will be financed eventually through membership fees which at present are $2. It is now dependent to some extent on private contributions from members, none of which have exceeded $50. The objectives of the association as drawn up in 1939 were to:

1. Provide a common source for discussion of problems of consumer education.
2. Develop a central bureau for collection of information, source material, research material, etc.
3. Conduct original research on a national scale.
4. List factories and schools open for study by members.
5. Interchange problems of methodology.
6. Initiate and develop a *Consumer Education Journal.*
7. Become a force for the greater welfare of our young and adult consumers in American life.

Membership is open to teachers who are interested in some phase of consumer education. The officers and directors of the association for 1940 are: Harold F. Clark, Columbia University, president, and Carlton J. Siegler, executive secretary; Jessie V. Coles, New York University; Loda Mae Davis, San Mateo Junior College; Elizabeth Hoyt, Iowa State College; Colston Warne, Amherst College; Donald Montgomery, Consumers' Counsel of the AAA; Helen Hall, Consumers National Federation; Ada Kennedy, Pasadena Junior College; James E. Mendenhall, Stephens College; G. E. Damon, Greeley, Colo.; Sidney Galper, Salem Vocational School; Edward Reich, New York City.

The Consumer Education Association published the first issue of its *Journal* in October, 1939, and had at that time about 400 paid-up members. Later issues have carried articles, reports, news, and other material of special interest to consumer teachers interested in all aspects of the content and methods of consumer education. The board of editors of the *Journal* includes many distinguished leaders in the field of consumer education.

A drive for new members is under way, and plans are on foot

for the organization of state associations which would be affiliated with the national organization, thus building up the work on a firm foundation of local groups. The first national convention was held in St. Louis in 1940 at the same time as the meetings of the National Education Association. Other conventions are to be held annually.

The board has had some preliminary discussions on matters of policy. Advertising in the *Journal* is to be limited by putting the ultimate decisions in the hands of a small committee which is to meet and discuss all applications for advertising space. They are experimenting with the policy of accepting no commercial advertising except that of book publishers, manufacturers of scientific equipment valuable in consumer courses, and genuine consumer research organizations. Policy with respect to legislative action and cooperation with other consumer groups has not yet been definitely worked out.

INSTITUTE FOR CONSUMER EDUCATION

This institute was established in 1937 at Stephens College, a junior college for women in Columbia, Mo. Financial support is derived from the Alfred P. Sloan Foundation, an educational foundation devoted to the increase and diffusion of economic knowledge.

Although the institute does not represent any organized group of consumers or educators, the first National Conference on Consumer Education which was held under its auspices in the spring of 1939 brought together over 500 consumer educators, club leaders, government workers, labor representatives, scientific workers, and others interested in consumer problems and consumer education. This informal educational gathering served to give an impetus and coordination to the movement as a whole. A similar conference was held in 1940 with an attendance of over 600.

The speakers and other participants at the conferences represented a wide range of points of view and made possible personal contacts among people interested in the same general problems but approaching them from different angles. After the first conference *Time* magazine referred to the institute as the "unofficial capital" of consumer education. The first conference was so impressive from the business point of view that after it Werner K. Gabler, distribution consultant, wrote for the American Retail Federation a pamphlet *Labelling the Consumer Movement*, indicating its strength and permanence in economic life and the need for taking it into consideration in making business policy. High light of the second conference was a speech by Harold Rugg, of Teachers College, Columbia, whose textbook *Problems of American Culture* has been under fire from advertising groups. The enthusiasm with which his address was greeted was a tribute to the solidarity of consumer educators in opposing the particular kind of attacks which have been made on his work.[11]

Proceedings of the conferences have been published under the titles of their respective themes: *Next Steps Forward in Consumer Education* and *Making Consumer Education Effective*. The institute's monthly newsletter *Consumer Education* with a circulation of nearly 5,000, helps to further its coordinating activities.

Actually there was some misunderstanding at first as to the independent position of the institute. The fact that it receives its financial support, indirectly at least, from big business through a comparatively recently established foundation induced many on both left and right wings of the consumer movement to believe that it was intended primarily as a gesture towards promoting better consumer-business relations. Some business interests reacted hostilely to the first conference because of the limited representation given to business and advertising and the absence of manufacturing representation. Editors of women's magazines were particularly incensed because they felt insufficient attention was given to their contributions to helping the consumers. Hostility was less openly in evidence at the second conference. The strictly educational nature of the institute's activities seems now to be generally recognized.

The budget of the institute for 1939-1940 amounted to $49,-900. The budget is granted yearly by the Sloan Foundation and it is expected that eventually the institute will become par-

[11] See Chapter Seven.

tially self-supporting through the sale of its publications and material. Its program has been conceived not as one of quick or striking response to the particular consumer complaints of the moment, but rather one of patient, gradual work on problems that are of a fundamental and persistent character. Consumer education is broadly interpreted to relate to those matters of economy concerning consumers as individuals and consumers as members of society. It has a three-point program of fact finding, fact organizing, and fact using, designed eventually to reach consumers at all levels of education—elementary, high school, college, and adult.

A definite statement of policy was issued by the institute in March, 1940:

We accept the following definition of consumer education:
Consumer education is development in attaining the maximum individual and group satisfaction for time, effort, and money expended.
We hold that consumer education, thus defined, will increase the efficiency of the system of free enterprise and will have a beneficial effect on public economic policy.
We consider that individual development for the ends in view can take place only through
    (a) A realistic comprehension of one's own personality and position in life.
    (b) An intelligent understanding of the workings of the economic order.
    (c) A consciously trained ability to analyze and appraise accurately the competitive claims for goods and services offered as necessities, comforts, or luxuries of life.

An insignia consisting of a family group, a food basket, a house and clothing, has been adopted for its publications, "because it emphasizes the importance of food, clothing, and shelter as the three basic wants of the typical American family of four. It is from this combination that the consumer movement stems."

Its director, John M. Cassels, is an economist, formerly of Harvard University now on leave from the institute as executive assistant to Miss Harriet Elliott, the consumer adviser on the National Defense Advisory Commission; the associate director of the institute, James Mendenhall, is an educator, formerly of Lincoln School, Teachers College, Columbia University. Altogether the institute had in 1939 a full-time staff of seventeen. A consumer library has been accumulated with 2,500 books, as well as magazines, pamphlets, government documents, and exhibit material. Besides the newsletter, *Consumer Education*, a publications program has been launched for the preparation of a series of pamphlets. Two of these, *Chain Stores—Pro and Con* and *Read the Label*, have been issued as Public Affairs Pamphlets and others will be included in this series later. A lithoprinted pamphlet, *Buyer Guidance Please*, and a series of study outlines to go with this and other pamphlets have been prepared.

The institute gives a course in consumer problems to students of Stephens College, with an enrollment of 140. The purpose of the course is to translate economics into understandable language and then to apply these principles to common problems that Mary and Jane face every day. Students have no textbook but use material from a great variety of sources. They begin by thinking of their own buying motives and what influences them. They study budgeting, standards, grades and labels, what determines the price of goods, the place of consumer cooperatives and government regulation. They go on to a study of life insurance, health service, housing, instalment buying and other forms of credit. They make field trips to study housing conditions in different parts of the town, and go to see cooperatives actually working in practice. They made an investigation of prices in different stores in Columbia and tried to find reasons for the differences in prices.

A consumer clinic gives students advice and help in keeping personal budgets. A personal finance book especially designed to meet the needs of Stephens College girls has recently been prepared and put into use by Rufie Lee Williams of the home economics staff of Stephens College, and Dr. Mendenhall. Many of the girls who take advantage of the help in personal finance and budgeting find they have "extra" money to spend. After keeping a budget for some time one girl saved up enough money so that she didn't need her next month's allowance; she sent the check for that month back home. One of the things stressed in the clinic is that the girls in learning to spend their allowances more wisely now are not only reaping the present benefits of the extra money saved, but are preparing themselves for the future as homemakers.

An important part of the institute's program is the undertaking of educational and economic research. A high school survey is being made for the purpose of finding out how extensively consumer education is being taught, at what level and by what department. This covers all consumer education courses in elementary schools, high schools, and colleges. Other educational projects include cooperation with selected schools in the use of materials and developing methods; working with adult groups; cooperation in an experiment to determine the effect of education on diet; preparation and study of the value of radio transcriptions in the classroom teaching. A transcription on the subject "To Rent or Own" was prepared during 1939-1940 and used in high schools and colleges to determine the value and effectiveness of this kind of material. Basic economic research under way includes a study of the consumer's milk problem.

At the conference in 1940 a special committee under the leadership of Professor Margaret Reid, of Iowa State College, gave careful thought to the problem of making research in the field of consumer economics as effective and purposeful as possible. The wastes involved in spasmodic unplanned efforts by separate individuals or institutions was stressed. Acting on the results of these discussions and cooperating closely with members of the committee, the institute is working on preliminary plans with the expectation that the task of continuing coordination will find appropriate permanent sponsorship when the time comes.

The institute provides each year a number of visiting fellowships for students or workers in the field who wish to make use of its facilities for research in consumer education. Nine such visiting fellows were received during the year 1939-1940. Some came to get additional material for books they were writing, others to get new ideas to use in teaching. One came to get background material to use in making a survey of the living costs in her city. This policy of giving fellowships facilitates the exchange of ideas and makes it possible for the institute on its side to gain a better understanding of the work being done in various parts of the country.

Chapter Four

GENERAL ORGANIZATIONS ADOPT CONSUMER OBJECTIVES

THE consumer movement has a "rank and file" but for the most part it is not organized under a single banner. Most people in America already belong to some kind of organization. Since everyone has consumer interests, it might well be expected that a large part of consumer activity would develop through the addition of consumer sections to the programs of existing organizations. And this had proved to be so. Women in America, already highly organized for social and charitable purposes and for protecting their rights as women, have given increasing attention to consumer education and activity in recent years. Welfare, religious, farm, and labor groups have become more and more aware of their interests in consumer welfare.

At present nationally organized women's groups are particularly outstanding for their promotion of consumer interests. Although we are all consumers, men as well as women, agelong division of labor gives special importance to the work of women as managers and spenders of the family income. They are concerned most directly with the gains to be made through wise consumption. More than 25,000,000 women are full-time homemakers. The unspecialized small households under their care are the typical consuming units. It is their budgets which get upset when they get poor buys; when they yield to high-pressure salesmanship and purchase some gadget which turns out to be useless; or when they buy some more expensive piece of equipment than is justified by their income. As consumers housewives are beginning to consider more carefully what they really want most and are trying to get information that will tell them what products can do for them in comparison with other products. They are conscious, too, of changes in the prices of the things they buy. When the price of milk goes up it is a matter of genuine concern to them. They know that their real income depends on the cost of living as well as on how much money comes into the family purse. More and more women want to understand the economic processes which affect them so vitally. They want to know if their interests are being adequately considered in all those complex processes which determine what is produced and how it gets to them.

The fact that women have worked together on broad issues, such as suffrage, and on more specific issues, such as establishing a women's bureau in the Department of Labor, has given them valuable experience for promoting their common interests as consumers. With diverse methods they often work toward common goals. It has been remarked by many of those closely associated with the consumer movement that the women seem to be taking it up with something of the same spirit in which they took up getting the vote. They are campaigning for effective enfranchisement in a democratic economic society. In this connection it is interesting to point out a comment made by Mrs. Harvey Wiley, widow of the famous promoter of the first food and drug law. In testifying for the adoption of the so-called Tugwell bill she said: "The First Lady of the Land has written a book entitled, *It's Up to the Women.* That idea certainly applies here. Who manufactures poisonous cosmetics which maim and kill? Who manufactures patent medicines with their false and misleading claims . . . ? Who uses false and misleading advertisements to break down our buying resistance and make us the victims of fraud? Isn't it generally speaking men? The great body of women are homemakers and consumers. So it's up to the women, to us, to start housecleaning."

Burr Blackburn, whose work as director of research for the Household Finance Corporation has brought him in close touch with consumers, has pointed out the determined way in which women are tackling consumer problems. Writing to the editor of an advertising journal in February, 1939, he said:

I am afraid business executives do not appreciate what they are up against when they face the fast growing consumer movement. Industry has taken most of the work of the home out into the factory, freeing the upper middle class women to participate in political and economic activities. They are taking hold of this consumer movement in the same spirit that women leaders fought for Woman Suffrage and Prohibition. If business refuses to cooperate with them they will enjoy a fight.[1]

Middle-income groups have in recent years found more leisure and have engaged in more organized activity. Women are taking their responsibilities seriously as voters and buyers and as members of society. Many in business and political life are contributing their experience toward the problems of the consumer. This special interest of women is a matter of great importance in the consumer movement. The nationally organized groups which have been most active will be considered first.

THE AMERICAN ASSOCIATION OF UNIVERSITY WOMEN

Next to the professionally interested American Home Economics Association, the organization that has given greatest attention to consumer problems is the American Association of University Women. Its present Committee on Social Studies was originally begun as a Consumers' Interests Committee. The purposes of the association's program imply the belief that actual consumer needs should ultimately determine the planning of production and that consumers must understand economic processes in order to perform their rightful function in the economy.

Its active interest in consumer education was stimulated by the New Deal consumer agencies. "Though the demand for material on consumer purchasing grew out of the interest of members in education in general," wrote Esther Cole Franklin, associate in social studies, "it was the need for informed consumer representation precipitated by the AAA and NRA programs that offered greatest stimulus for study of consumer

[1] From carbon copy sent to author.

problems. Members became interested to investigate local enforcement of codes and a number of them were appointed to County Consumer Councils. In November, 1934, the General Director was asked to serve as a member of the advisory board sponsoring a milk survey which was conducted by the AAA; in May, 1935, she was asked to become a member of the NRA Consumers' Advisory Board."[2]

The association was among the pioneering groups in preparing study outlines indicating available data on testing, standardization, and the informative labeling of foods, drugs, household equipment, and clothing. The syllabus, *Scientific Consumer Purchasing*, by Alice Edwards was first prepared in 1932 in cooperation with the American Home Economics Association, and was revised in 1933, 1934, 1935, and 1938. Altogether nearly 3,000 copies have been sold. Study groups in approximately 300 branches have studied consumer purchasing.

Reports indicate an ever-increasing interest in consumer education in all sections of the country. Local activities include, besides the study of individual buying problems: (1) community education in consumer buying through forums and demonstration exhibits, through establishment of consumer library facilities, through support of consumer education courses in the schools; (2) activity on consumer protective measures—municipal, state, and federal; (3) consumer-retailer cooperation toward making available more commodity information and toward obtaining standards and grades; (4) participation in the national program of the association by furnishing representatives for committees and conferences and sending in original materials prepared in the study groups which may be circulated to other branches.

The *Journal* of the association in January, 1937, gave particular notice to the consumer exhibit which the Bethlehem, Pa., branch held in November, 1936. Information on the quality and value of many commodities was in this way made available to the whole community. In the branch in Decatur, Ill., a consumer study group during 1937-1938 summarized their findings for the year in a playlet, *Shoppers' Heyday*, presented

[2] In survey by Consumers National Federation 1939 (mimeo).

at an open meeting in the community. Out of this program such an interest developed that a new Consumer Center was established at Millikin University. It now has a library and exhibit room open to all persons interested in consumer information.

Consumer institutes, held by branches or state divisions, sometimes in cooperation with other organizations, give opportunity for a one- to three-day discussion of consumer problems under the leadership of specialists. In the fall of 1937, the New Jersey branches were represented in a consumer institute at Rutgers University, jointly sponsored by the Home Economics Extension service and the principal women's organizations in the state. A test project on informative labeling under the auspices of the Committee on Local Consumer Groups of the National Consumer-Retailer Council has been carried out in 1939-1940 in Newark, N. J. Representatives of the AAUW took part in this work. Meetings were held with retailers on the labeling of silk hosiery and an informative label satisfactory to both consumers and retailers was developed. It was introduced into all participating stores in May, 1940. A one-day institute is held each year in Philadelphia. The branch at Knoxville, Tenn., has developed a consumer program during the past three years and offers a good illustration of the close relation between study and community work, for it has sponsored radio programs and community forums. In Charleston, W. Va., the local AAUW branch has made a careful survey of local consumer problems and is planning action based on the results of the facts discovered. At the second national conference held by the Institute for Consumer Education, Dr. Franklin led a round-table discussion on "What and How to Teach Adults of Average Income Levels." In this way the experience of the AAUW became available to a larger group.

An exhibit sponsored by the AAUW of Washington, D. C., in February, 1940, included a consumer section which received nation-wide attention. It started off with a sign "Today's Consumers Live in Blunderland." A big cardboard hand clutching a fistful of paper money bore the slogan "More Power to Your Dollar." The exhibit itself included samples of can sizes, graded products, and similar articles of consumer interest. Large-size illustrations from Trilling, Eberhart, and Nicholas's textbook *When You Buy* showed the consumer's plight and possible ways out. The whole exhibit was extremely effective in arousing consumer interest.

The association is becoming more and more interested in working next for consumer standards of quality. Expansion of their use through informative labeling is being promoted both locally and nationally by the members. Through the subcommittee on consumer interests of its National Committee on Social Studies, the association is represented on the Advisory Committee on Ultimate Consumers' Goods of the American Standards Association, a national clearinghouse for establishment of standards. Commodity committees are now working on standard specifications for bedding and upholstery, sheets and sheeting, children's garments and patterns, household refrigerators, silver-plated tableware, and hosiery. The association is a "charter member" of the National Consumer-Retailer Council. Dr. Faith Williams of the AAUW is a member of the council's board of trustees and chairman of its Labeling Committee.

The AAUW is interested also in governmental recognition of consumer interests. For five years prior to the passage of the federal Food, Drugs, and Cosmetics Act of 1938, it was on record for amending the old Food and Drugs Act to secure adequate food, drug, and cosmetic control; and at present several state divisions are working for state food and drug laws to supplement national regulation. Support of the Bureau of Home Economics has been a specific tenet in AAUW's legislative program since 1935. AAUW consumer groups have studied the bureau's bulletins on foods and diets, textiles, and household equipment, and on family income and expenditures, and have frequently urged enlargement of the bureau's activities. At its convention in June, 1939, the AAUW adopted the following policies for protection of the consumer:

1. Coordination of consumer activities in the federal government under a joint committee representing all the federal agencies working in the field.

2. Development of standards of quality and performance for consumer goods.
3. Opposition to the so-called "fair trade" laws authorizing price-fixing contracts between manufacturer and retailer.
4. Protection of the consumer against unfair trade practices.

Emphasis has been placed on legislation for a consumer agency in the federal government. On November 1, 1939, Dr. Kathryn McHale, general director, sent a letter to President Roosevelt urging the establishment of a central agency "as a separate entity or as a bureau in some department where it could be thoroughly representative of the consumer interest." She praised the Consumers' Counsel Division of the Department of Agriculture for its service to consumers but pointed out that it was "necessarily subject to certain limitations . . . since the interests of the farmers must come first in the formulation of the Department's policies." The proposals included concrete suggestions showing the kind of consumer agency that might be appropriate.

The legislative program is based on careful study by the branches. It is democratically adopted and close touch kept with branches as current developments take place. In discussing the need for greater attention to studying political issues, it was pointed out at the Savannah convention in 1938 that

Economic and social forces are at work over which the individual has no control. . . . The trend toward government participation in economic and social affairs seems to be inevitable; therefore the question of the nature and extent of such participation is one which must be faced by all citizens.

The association was founded in 1882 for practical educational work, for the collection and publication of statistical and other information concerning education, and in general for the maintenance of high standards of education, with particular emphasis on the educational opportunities for women. It has attempted to promote these purposes through establishing and maintaining standards of education, through research and study programs, and through legislation. Each branch is expected to study local needs and build a program that embodies the objectives of the national association as adapted to local needs. In all fields it is the aim to develop study programs that will produce informed leadership for participation in current activity, in the realm of both opinion and action. All the AAUW branches are expected to function on a level which makes full use of their college training. This ideal of leadership in public opinion makes the organization much more influential than the size of its membership (62,000) would suggest.

Membership in the AAUW is limited to the women graduates of certain approved colleges. It has 880 branches in 48 states and in Alaska, Hawaii, and the Far East. It is not a federation of local clubs but a national organization whose program is largely realized through these branches. The administration and operation of the association are carried on by a general director, assisted by staff members. The national association is divided into nine geographical regions, each under the leadership of a sectional director. There are 43 state divisions. The organization is set up on democratic principles with ultimate authority lodged in the biennial convention at which all national members are entitled to representation. Between conventions the governing body is a board of directors, consisting of the national officers, the nine sectional directors, and chairmen of standing and special committees. The national officers and sectional directors are elected by the national convention; they in turn appoint the committee chairmen. The AAUW issues a quarterly *Journal*, and has an extensive and impressive catalogue of publications in the fields of education, international relations, social studies and the arts.

GENERAL FEDERATION OF WOMEN'S CLUBS

The General Federation of Women's Clubs was founded in 1890 at a meeting of 91 women's clubs in New York. It is now a large, loosely integrated federation of over 15,000 clubs with a membership of well over two million. Its original constitution provided that the chief object of the clubs belonging to it should be literary, artistic, or scientific culture, but by 1896 this rule was dropped and the motto "education not for self, but for service" adopted.

During the twenties the federation had a committee on standardization which took a special interest in such products as hosiery, woven dress fabrics, wool and part-wool fabrics, dress measurements, washable cotton gloves, women's leather shoes, and enamel kitchenware. A pamphlet *Buy Intelligently* was prepared in cooperation with home economists. In 1931 the federation conducted a study in cooperation with the Department of Commerce which resulted in a bulletin *The Consumer Viewpoint on Returned Goods*. This bulletin gave official sanction to the following Shoppers' Creed:

I believe that the American Woman, through control of a large share of the family budget, exerts a vital influence upon today's economic order.

Therefore, I hold it my duty to help make this influence constructive; to govern my buying so that waste will be reduced and the greatest good to all realized from my expenditures.

I believe that, as a measure of true economy, I should:

Make known my merchandise needs and preferences in advance whenever the opportunity is presented;

Remember that cheapness in itself is not always a bargain, and consider suitability and durability as well as price;

Avoid merchandise known to be produced under unfair competitive conditions, such as sweat shop or prison made goods;

Be reasonable in my demands for service, such as credit, alterations, and deliveries;

Refrain from returning merchandise unless the goods or the store is at fault.

This is my creed. I believe in it; I shall support it.

The District of Columbia federation, in addition, formulated a resolution and a petition for a uniform returned-goods policy by merchants. These achievements were one-sided in their emphasis on consumer responsibilities; the federation is now promoting the interests of the consumer more directly.

At present the federation has nine departments. Consumer interests and programs are advanced through the Division of Family Finance and the Division of Consumer Information of the Department of the American Home. In cooperation with the Institute for Consumer Education the federation has drawn up study outlines on such topics as the consumer and the chain stores; buyer guidance; consumers and the agricultural programs of the federal government; food and drug laws; consumer financing; grades, labels, and brand names; consumer testing; consumer cooperation. It takes part in a weekly broadcast in cooperation with the Consumers' Counsel of the AAA.

Commercial interests and self-seeking leaders have not been slow to see the value of getting endorsements of their special interests by this influential group of women. Perhaps the most striking example goes back to the effort of the utilities in the middle twenties to use the influence of the general federation in their gigantic campaign to mold public opinion in their favor. More recently systematic attempts have been made by anti-tax groups to capture the local and state branches. Under the present national president, Mrs. Sadie Orr Dunbar, a healthy skepticism is developing. There is no way of knowing how far her work has penetrated to local groups but attempts are being made to help clubs maintain strict independence in dealing with all special interests. This is done by placing before local officers all information available at national headquarters.

Speaking before the National Conference on Consumer Education at Stephens College in 1939, Mrs. Dunbar said, "During this first year of my presidency I have learned—to my dismay— of the tremendous pressure that is put on this organization by various private interests, who in the name of the consumer are attempting to use the General Federation in their self-interest. Most of the past year I have spent trying to investigate and to weed out the spurious consumer organizations that have attempted to use the General Federation for one reason or for another."

From the point of view of business groups, the General Federation of Women's Clubs is undoubtedly one of the most important forces in the consumer movement, both because of its numbers and because it represents consumers who are economically powerful and can be called upon to indicate the reactions of the middle- and upper-class housewife. As a politically conservative and socially prominent group, it is to businessmen a sort of barometer for the consumer movement at large. Strategically important, therefore, is the fact that the president of the general federation has attained prominence as spokesman for consumer groups. Along with the American Association of University Women and the American Home Economics Association, a platform of consumer-business relationships has been drawn up and Mrs. Dunbar has on several occasions put this before business groups. In August, 1940, Mrs. Dunbar acted as chairman of a group discussing the general question "How can the problem of the consumer-buyer be so handled as to contribute positively to their own welfare and to the total defense program?" at a conference of national civic leaders called by Miss Harriet Elliott, consumer adviser on the Advisory Commission to the National Defense Council.[3]

The governing power of the General Federation of Women's Clubs is vested in a board of directors, comprised of the executive committee, state directors, department chairmen, extension secretary for international clubs, and the board of trustees. Conventions are held triennially, and councils in each of the two intervening years. It has an annual budget of $100,000 for the national program and impressive headquarters on a tree-bordered street in Washington, D. C. Local clubs are free to build their own programs in any way they like, but the central organization prepares educational material, suggests programs, and proffers advice. Members are kept in touch with each other through the monthly publication, *The Clubwoman GFWC*. Clubs federate by county, city, and state, as well as in the national federation. At the annual council meetings a legislative program is adopted and the program is forwarded by sending representatives to hearings on appropriate bills. It took an active part in the promotion of food and drug legislation.

NATIONAL CONGRESS OF PARENTS AND TEACHERS

The National Congress of Parents and Teachers was organized in 1897 as the National Congress of Mothers. Its present membership of nearly two and one-third millions includes both men and women interested in promoting the welfare of children and

[3] The findings of this group are discussed in Chapter Nine.

raising the standards of home life by bringing together teachers and parents in intelligent cooperation. The scope of its work is consequently broad and consumer interests are only one part of its general program. It represents one of the most important consuming elements—parents with school-age children—and it also reaches down into lower income groups than women's clubs. The membership is not selective like that of the General Federation of Women's Clubs and the American Association of the University Women. Its work is of special importance on a community basis.

Growing interest of local groups in consumer problems was reported at the meetings of the National Congress of Parents and Teachers in 1939. Local and state chairmen expressed a need for more low-cost reference material for classes in consumer buying. Attention was called to the *Consumers' Guide* of the Consumers' Division of the AAA and to the publications of the Bureau of Home Economics. The group was reminded that much valuable material for consumer education is right at hand within any group when an opportunity is given for the members to bring and discuss some of their own particularly good or poor buys of the last year. Miss Florence Fallgatter, of the Department of Home Economics at Iowa State College, is chairman of the Committee on Home Making, through which consumer education is carried on. At the National Conference on Consumer Education in Columbia, Mo., in 1940 she acted as chairman for a meeting on "What is Consumer Education?"

In a small book, *Our Homes*, the National Congress has brought together authoritative discussions of many aspects of home life. A section on Home Planning and Management includes statements by Lita Bane, Head of the Department of Home Economics of the University of Illinois, on "Planning the Home Budget," and by Rosamond Cook, of the Home Economics Department of the University of Cincinnati, on the "Education of the Consumer." Also included are such topics as The Child and Money Management, Radio as a Source of Home Education, Health Education and the Home, The Safe Home, and others related to consumer welfare.

Some states such as Illinois, California, and Ohio have been especially active in consumer work. In Illinois, for example, a study course outline for consumer education includes bibliography and study questions on advertising, meat, milk, textiles, and clothing. A "Consumer Alphabet" opens up the subject and its ABC's include such items as the following:

Are you Aware of what consumer problems are? Ask for information about what you buy.

Beware of "Bunkum" in advertising. Bargains are not always a Best Buy. Begin your consumer education by reading consumer literature.

Consumer Cooperation and Credit unions are Consumers' Creations which Concern you. Other Countries are already using them.

Tell your friends about the consumer work. Talk about it at your club meetings and sewing meetings, even at your missionary meetings, for it is real missionary work. Thrift will make you Thankful when you have to pay your Taxes.

Utilities of all kinds are Under attack. Should these be managed for the Use of the consumer or for the profit of a few? Or is there a middle ground?

Vegetables Vary. Vigorous insistence on Value is Vital, if you would provide the family with Vitamins.

Welcome all the consumer information you can get. It Will Work Wonders. Wills should be made by everyone—Women as Well as men.

XYZ. You may Yet expect to balance that budget if you cut out the extras. Yearn not for what you cannot afford, and be Zealous in saving the pennies, the leftovers, and Yourself.

In Ohio a course of study planned by the Home Service Department "To encourage homemakers to study their problems as consumers" was drawn up around the following topics:

The Homemaker's responsibility as a buyer
Information available to the consumer
Grades, Standards and specifications as an aid to consumer buying
Legislation and organization
Study of canned goods
Study of hosiery
Study of sheets and sheeting

Study of cosmetics
Study of a piece of electrical household equipment

Of particular interest in connection with the consumer work of the national congress is the "noncommercial policy" adopted as one of its six "Guiding Principles." Noncommercial guideposts for PTA associations warn against giving out membership lists, endorsing or sponsoring commercial products or enterprises, making advertising announcements at meetings, accepting gifts or materials with any commercial implications or identification, distributing materials of commercial organizations. The formulation of the guideposts is based on experience of many local groups. In one group a department store made a generous offer to the local PTA groups and it was accepted. A full-page advertisement in the paper drew attention to the fact that a percentage of every sale made the next day would be given to the local PTA for its child welfare activities. PTA local officials acted as department managers and customers were urged to buy from their favorite manager. The scheme worked but brought rebukes from other parent-teacher people for the violation of the noncommercial policy—and still more from another department store which had had a similar scheme refused a few years earlier.

A magazine, the *National Parent-Teacher*, is issued ten times a year by the national organization. This is controlled by a separate board of directors. It carries no advertising and each issue is devoted entirely to articles, features, and book reviews of both lasting and current interest to parents and teachers. Among organizations of its type the present form of the magazine is unique. It has been evolved from experience during many years of publishing. Originally it was called *Child Welfare* and carried a great deal of advertising. In April, 1938, all advertising was dropped and the present setup adopted. The occasion for the change arose in connection with a desire on the part of the national congress to maintain complete control with respect to reading and editorial content of the magazine. Although the new policy has involved a temporary decline in circulation, subscriptions are rapidly being built up again on a basis that is felt to be sounder and more in harmony with the long-run objectives of the organization.

The national congress with its big membership is an important group in legislative matters. It took an active part in developing new food and drug legislation and through the Women's Joint Congressional Committee works with women's groups on legislative questions. In 1939 the chief measures of consumer interest which it supported were the Neely bill to abolish block booking and blind selling of motion pictures and the Johnson bill to prohibit the advertising of alcoholic beverages by radio. Legislative programs are adopted after study by individual associations at annual conventions. Individual associations are free to determine their own programs.

THE NATIONAL LEAGUE OF WOMEN VOTERS

The National League of Women Voters is unique among the women's organizations because its primary purpose is the development of a program of legislative action, based on a study of the issues involved. The league was founded in 1920 after the suffrage victory. It was organized by the leaders of the National Woman's Suffrage party to carry out the political education of women needed for their new role in public life. The militant suffrage group, smaller in number but more spectacular in action, has carried on in the Woman's Party which works primarily for complete equality of rights under a "blanket" amendment that would make unconstitutional any differentiation in legislation between the sexes.

In April, 1938, there were 533 local leagues in 30 affiliated state leagues and 26 college leagues, having a total individual membership of 50,000. There is a national headquarters in Washington, D. C., which employs a staff of nineteen. The national league is in constant communication with the state leagues by form letters, a *Newsletter*, and by field visits from headquarters. National expenditures for 1937-1938 amounted to $57,720; state and local leagues spent about $200,000. Finances are raised by dues, contributions, and special events. Its membership is open to all women and it is a group in which organization for purely social reasons plays a smaller part than in any of the other groups.

The primary interest of the league is in development of good government on democratic principles. According to the league, the economic basis of the need for the protection of consumers lies in the cardinal principle "private business must be either subject to effective competition or else government regulation or control if the evils of monopoly are to be avoided. . . . Basic to all problems connected with the consumer is the question of consumer representation in all agencies—federal, state, or local —that deal with problems affecting the consumer. . . . [These] administrative boards make decisions of vital concern to the consumer regarding price, quality, and quantity of goods. The consumer should be represented on them." Specific measures of support have been food and drug legislation, quality standards and labeling, government operation of Muscle Shoals as a yardstick; downward revision of the tariff. The present program includes housing as a main interest. Cooperatives are recognized as an important means of obtaining effective consumer protection, and some state leagues have put the cooperative movement on their programs for study.

The league is nonpartisan in political affiliations, and it expects its members to work through regular party channels as individuals. Its officers generally refrain from political party activity, however, so as to maintain a strictly nonpartisan position. It enters into joint action with other groups only at the point where action begins. The program includes lobbying activity as well as immediate action at the polls. Belle Zeller, in discussing the work of the New York State league, points out the following typical methods:

1. Seeing and informing the local legislator.
2. Seeking the active cooperation of other organizations.
3. Interrogating candidates for public office and informing the electorate accordingly.
4. Seeking the assistance of public opinion by publicity.[4]

According to Professor E. P. Herring, "The lobby of the

[4] *Pressure Politics in New York* (1936), p. 214.

League at the capital possesses particular influence in so far as it presents the deliberated sentiment and disinterested opinion of a large and highly organized body of women voters. As a matter of fact, a high percentage of the measures advocated by the League have been passed by Congress. Whether this is due to the intrinsic merit of the measures or their support by the League, working along with other organizations, is a question that can not be answered."[5] Although the work of the league is directed toward an action program, it operates slowly. It takes two years for a problem to move from the study to the action stage. Once a measure is adopted, however, it is followed up persistently.

Some of the most effective work on consumer interests by the league is carried out in local groups. The New York City league, for example, has been particularly active. Under the chairmanship of Ruth Ayres the consumer section of the department of government and economic welfare has included work on housing, costs of living, coal distribution, cosmetics, public utilities, price fixing, and other topics of consumer importance. At the first annual conference held by the Institute of Consumer Education, Dr. Ayres was chairman of a discussion on "Choosing, Using and Improving Materials in the Field."

Another example of effective local action is the School of Citizenship held yearly by the Des Moines league. In 1939 this took the form of a two-day conference on consumer problems, with the general theme "Education for Economic Efficiency." At this meeting educators, religious leaders, economists, sociologists, and representatives from other women's groups, retail merchants' associations, Rotarians, the local Retail Credit Association, Housing League, Labor Federation, Welfare Society, government, consumer cooperatives, the Advertising Vigilance Committee, Chamber of Commerce, and the Freedom of Opportunity Foundation, met and discussed various aspects of consumer problems. Besides a total registration of 590 clubwomen and businessmen, it was estimated that between 100 and 200 businessmen attended the sessions without registering.

[5] *Group Representation Before Congress* (1929), p. 203.

The National Federation of Business and Professional Women's Clubs represents the woman whose interests are organized around her earning rather than around her spending activities. In 1939 it had over 71,000 members in 1,600 clubs. The federation's activities center around the specific problems of women, "recognizing their inevitable relation to legislation, government, business, international affairs, and to all social and economic progress." Those activities were given focus in 1931 by the adoption of an objective to the effect that the federation "should fit itself to assume real leadership in thinking on economic problems and their social implications, with a view toward helping in the establishment, through scientific methods, of conditions which assure to women, and to men as well, the fullest possible opportunity and reward for the development of whatever capacities they may possess." In 1934 a general theme "Economic Security," was adopted for the year's study, and each year since then a new study theme for club work has been chosen. Outlines, study materials, and practical suggestions have been prepared to help local clubs with their problems.

At the biennial convention in 1936 the following statement was officially called to members' attention:

As business and professional women we have a double stake in consumer problems; we are consumers and distributors of goods and services for the ultimate consumer.

Although the federation has not been prominent in consumer activity, consumer problems have been included in all its study programs in recent years. In 1937-1938 the theme chosen for study was "Our Town's Business." This included a study of consumer problems. For 1938-1939 the theme chosen was "My Business and Yours" and the program outline covered problems connected with budgeting, informative labeling, grading, and prices. The program for 1939-1940 was entitled "Business Women in a Democracy." It brought out the correlation between government and business. Consumer interests in this program were centered around problems connected with raising standards of living.

The federation has been giving increasing attention to its legislative program. In 1938 a part-time paid legislative secretary was appointed to be resident in Washington. The federation does not support particular parties but is realistic in its attitude toward working through the party system. Consumer legislative interests have been chiefly food and drug legislation, antiprice-fixing legislation, and housing. In 1940 a full-time worker was added to the staff to do basic economic research.

ORGANIZATIONS COORDINATING WOMEN'S ACTIVITIES

The five groups just discussed are the major national women's organizations which have shown an important interest in consumer problems. It is not possible to estimate accurately their combined membership, since there is a considerable amount of duplication of membership among the clubs. Their recorded membership, too, must be regarded as a minimum estimate, for there are countless unaffiliated local, state, and regional clubs which reinforce the programs of affiliated clubs or promote consumer programs of their own. Five million might be suggested as a rough minimum estimate for the clubs discussed.

Through their consumer interests these groups have often worked closely together. The General Federation of Women's Clubs, the American Association of University Women, and the American Home Economics Association have been brought particularly close through their cooperation on the National Consumer-Retailer Council and in the preparation of a platform for Consumer-Business Relations; and with the League of Women Voters and the National Congress of Parents and Teachers through their work on the Advisory Committee on Ultimate Consumer Goods of the American Standards Association. All this has added greatly to the strength of the consumer movement. Efforts are being made to coordinate consumer work further by setting up some kind of joint committee.

Women have already formed the habit of pooling their strength in legislative matters through the Women's Joint Congressional Committee. Located in Washington, this organization serves as a clearinghouse for groups engaged in promoting Congressional legislation of special interest to its members. It does not itself endorse, promote, or propose any measures; it merely provides the machinery by which member organizations can pool their efforts. It operates on a budget that is no larger than is required to cover the cost of mimeographing and mailing the minutes of monthly meetings and incidental expense. It keeps its members advised on the status of legislation through a Look-Out Committee and a Follow-Up Committee and members interested in particular measures work through special legislative committees. Its members work individually when action is actually taken on a particular measure. At the present time, the committee has eighteen members, and it was through this committee that work for the Food, Drugs, and Cosmetics Act of 1938 was marshaled.

Similar organization has been effective on a state-wide scale. In 1932, for example, the New York State Women's Joint Legislative Forum was organized on the initiative of the New York State Federation of Women's Clubs. In 1935, fourteen state and twenty local women's organizations were members of the forum. Weekly meetings are held in Albany during the legislative session to study current state legislation. This has served to strengthen their work considerably.

The lobbying methods of women's groups are highly respected. E. P. Herring and Belle Zeller, political scientists who have made special studies of pressure group activity both point out the increasing strength and importance of the "women's lobby."[6] Women's groups, they say, are the best examples of the "front-door lobby" and have more influence than is usually credited to them. This growing importance of women's groups in the legislative field will undoubtedly be a factor tending to make much more effective the demands of consumers.

A Woman's Centennial Conference, under the chairmanship of Carrie Chapman Catt, the former suffrage leader, was held in November, 1940. The program included special sections on Eco-

[6] E. P. Herring, *Group Representation Before Congress* (1929) and *Public Administration and the Public Interest* (1936); Belle Zeller, *Pressure Politics in New York* (1936).

nomic and Social Welfare and on Government and Politics. Delegates were invited from the American Association of University Women, the General Federation of Women's Clubs, the National Board of the YWCA, the National Council of Church Women, National Council of Jewish Women, National Federation of Business and Professional Women, National League of Women Voters, National Women's Christian Temperance Union, and the National Women's Trade Union League.

WELFARE ORGANIZATIONS

Welfare organizations, almost by definition, are greatly concerned with consumption problems. Most welfare workers help the families under their care with budgeting and buying problems. They are highly conscious of the difficulties of low-income groups in doing the best possible with what they have, even though they recognize that raising income and obtaining work are the basic problems. They are especially conscious of changes in the cost of living as they affect families living close to the subsistence level. It is to be expected, therefore, that these organizations will cooperate actively with other groups which can demonstrate the effectiveness of consumer action in improving the position of low income families. In New York City, for example, welfare groups have helped to establish cheap milk depots where milk can be bought by needy families at lower prices than through regular outlets. The Henry Street Settlement House decided to cooperate with the Milk Consumers Protective Committee in 1939 in order to draw attention to the milk problem. A "baby-carriage parade" by mothers wound up at Foley Square and presented their view of the milk situation to the governor and the State Department of Agriculture. The Dairy Farmers' Union cooperated by meeting them at Foley Square with a cow. It turned out to be a day of sleet and rain so that the mothers did not actually bring the babies, but several hundred women came and the cow was milked in Foley Square. A large sign on her side said, "I am a union cow. I give milk for babies, not for the milk trusts." The result claimed for the demonstration was the granting of a license for a Consumer-Farmer Milk Cooperative which has been operating since 1937.

In less spectacular ways welfare groups have worked to advance consumer welfare, through conferences on human needs, support of consumer departments in government, and so on. They often show special interest in the development of consumer cooperatives.

The National Federation of Settlements, organized in 1911 and having in 1939 a membership of 156 agencies all over the country, accepted the following statement at their 1939 annual conference:

From our close knowledge of household and neighborhood life, we hail the spread of the consumer movement. Our neighbors are now taking a hand in their own self-protection, especially in the securing of the necessities of life. The cooperative movement brings into play that self-help which characterized our pioneers and which we now so greatly need in facing our new social challenges.

A committee on Consumer Education provides material for member settlements for use in adult groups. It collects the experience of settlements in this field for use by others. The methods used include conference programs, regional and national; bulletins; consumer bibliographies; consultation service in consumer education. Housing, health, credit unions, consumer cooperatives, and milk are main fields of interests.

The federation is an organization member of the Consumers' National Federation, and uses its services. It has participated in several consumer conferences such as the "People vs. the High Cost of Living" in New York City in December, 1937. A delegate went to Washington, D. C., in February, 1938, to press for a department of the consumer along with other consumer representatives. As an associate group of the National Conference of Social Work, it provided a consumer program for the Buffalo, 1939, conference of that body. Besides approval of working for a federal consumer agency and for consumer representation on regulatory bodies, it has approved strengthening food and drug control in the consumer interest and took an active part in the passage of the 1938 law. The fact that the Social Work Yearbook for 1940 added a twenty-page section on Consumer Interests indicates the growing interest of social workers in this field.

RELIGIOUS GROUPS

Another instance of the way consumer programs have come to have a place in programs of existing organizations is given by religious groups. Two women's groups which have often worked with the women's groups already discussed are the National Council of Jewish Women and the National Council of Catholic Women.

The National Council of Jewish Women at their Triennial Convention at Pittsburgh in 1938 adopted the following resolution:

WHEREAS: every person in the United States is a consumer and is affected by the way in which consumer goods and services are supplied, and

WHEREAS: consumers generally are not organized to combat the waste and exploitation in the production and distribution of the necessities of life

WHEREFORE: be it resolved, that the National Council of Jewish Women in Triennial Convention assembled recommends the study of the trends and problems of Consumers Welfare.

Their study programs are planned to lead toward constructive legislative action. No legislative action can be taken until 1941, however, after the two-year study program has been undertaken. The council has a membership of over 40,000.

The National Council of Catholic Women, a part of the National Catholic Welfare Conference, has no definite plan for developing consumer programs, but consumer activities can be appropriately included under the general program. It occasionally acts as sponsor to consumer conventions and cooperates locally with other groups on consumer programs. It is interested in raising the moral standards of moving pictures and radio broadcasting. Included in its study program for social action are consumer cooperatives, prices, economic power, and other problems of consumer significance.

The National Board of the Young Women's Christian Association included the following under their Public Affairs Program for 1938-1940: "Encouraging the participation of our members in the cooperative movement and other organized

efforts to deal with the interests and problems of consumers."
Their official interest in consumer problems dates back to 1933
and since then the subject has been carried along in a general
way.

The National Council of the Young Men's Christian Association reported in 1939 that, although consumer education is
carried on throughout the country, there is as yet no collection
of facts about it. A number of their organizations have been
active in forming consumer cooperatives or in spreading information about them.

The Federal Council of Churches of Christ in America is
the most important religious group with an interest in consumer
problems. This federation of twenty-four national denominations, representing a total membership of over 20,000,000, reports that "by 1937 the interest in many church circles was so
great, and at the same time such large sections of the Church
were so clearly unreached, that it was decided to set up a special
committee on the Church and Cooperatives under the Industrial
Division."

Eight special conferences on the Church and Cooperatives
were conducted in 1938. Forty-five hundred copies of the report
of the conferences held at Washington, Boston, and Columbus
were sold or distributed through church channels. The council
has taken part in study tours to Nova Scotia to observe the
Antigonish cooperative movement. These have had a stimulating
effect on the cooperative movement in America. Through cooperation with other established church agencies further stimulus to the study of cooperatives has been possible.

James Meyers, who is chairman of the Committee on the
Relations of Organized Labor and Consumer Cooperatives of
the Cooperative League, as well as secretary of the Committee
on the Church and Cooperatives of the Federal Council, has
helped to plan meetings and conferences of organized labor and
consumer cooperatives. The committee has felt it a peculiarly
appropriate function for a church group to bring together economic groups which have too little sympathy with understanding of each other, such as farm and city and farm and labor
groups, and many conferences have been arranged. The com-

mittee is promoting a fund-raising campaign for furthering the work in this field.

PRODUCER GROUPS WITH CONSUMER INTERESTS
Labor

Before the worker's wife can go shopping, there has to be a wage envelope with something in it. But this does not mean that the worker considers his role as a consumer unimportant, and there are many signs that labor groups are beginning to pay more and more attention to consumer education and consumer protection as a means of improving their current living standards.

Workers in industry can make an important contribution to other consumers through their knowledge of the quality of the materials with which they work and the conditions under which the goods are made. Through joint action in consumer cooperatives and with cooperative farm groups some leaders see the possibility of a means to a long-run solution of some of the problems of modern industrial society.

Mark Starr, educational director of the International Ladies' Garment Workers Union, at an address made before the Second National Conference of the Institute for Consumer Education in 1940 outlined what labor groups are doing. This includes distribution of Consumers Union Quiz Tests and *Consumers' Guide* to educational directors of trade union classes, and women's auxiliaries. The number of lectures and courses on consumers' problems in workers' educational activities has increased greatly during the past few years. The feature column "Your Dollar" issued by Consumers Union is distributed regularly to 110 labor newspapers. Among younger women in the International Ladies' Garment Workers Union classes in charm include talks on price and quality in cosmetics and clothes. In a printers' trade school in New York City, five English classes with about twenty students each discuss consumer problems. The American Federation of Hosiery Workers at Reading, Pa., reported regular consumer courses, and until pressure from local advertisers ended them, radio talks. The ILGWU has issued a pamphlet *The Worker as a Consumer* by Mark Starr and Helen Norton for use in study groups. One of the most popular songs from the ILGWU's hit revue *Pins and Needles* was "Nobody Makes a Pass at Me," a satire on advertising appeals.

Just as labor can make gains through collective bargaining in its trade-unions, consumer cooperatives are a means for improving the position of the consumer by collective action. Many consumer cooperatives insist that their societies observe trade-union conditions and so the efforts to raise standards of living become integrated. Reports of the American Federation of Labor, the CIO, and independent unions show that the credit union is most effective in starting cooperative societies among labor groups. The AFL reported in 1939 that more than 350 credit unions were serving its affiliated unions. There are six credit unions in the ILGWU. The cooperative mail-order house, Cooperative Distributors, has four unions affiliated as members and 18 unions as customers. Trade-unions have been a leading influence in establishing successful cooperatives in such centers as Racine, Wis.; Kenosha, Wis.; Dillonvale, Ohio; Minneapolis, Minn.; Waukesha, Wis.; Marvin County, California. In some of these, farm groups as well as labor and consumer are included.

Labor's Non-Partisan League and the American Labor party have also been active in helping to promote consumer interests. In Boston Labor's Non-Partisan League helped to organize a Consumer Committee on Milk and a Consumer-Farmer Cooperative in the metropolitan area. The American Labor party in New York was one of the chief groups behind the campaign for a Department of the Consumer there in 1938. Louis Waldman, representing it at Albany, said, "It is a moral obligation, an inescapable obligation, for the state to assume a responsibility for those citizens who cannot gamble with the products they buy. . . . We have a duty toward those who are nevertheless forced to gamble, because they are not informed on what is fair value for the money they spend. Our people have a right to guidance, when as consumers they make purchases. They have a right to greater protection than they now enjoy."[7]

[7] Reported in *Retailing*, Executive Edition, June 27, 1938.

Farmer

For the most part rural consumer interests have found expression through Home Demonstration Clubs, mothered by home demonstration agents of the Cooperative Extension Service of the Department of Agriculture and through the consumer cooperative movement. The Associated Women of the American Farm Bureau Federation, which was an outgrowth of the activities of the extension service, in 1937 recommended increased support to federal and state agencies supplying factual information regarding consumer education, repeal of the Miller-Tydings Act, and support of pure food and drug legislation.

The importance of organized activity such as the women's clubs discussed earlier is probably less for rural women because of the fact that systematic education has long been available to them through the Cooperative Extension Service. Representatives of this service at the two annual conferences on consumer education held by the Institute for Consumer Education have indicated the growing interest in rural areas in education in problems of budgeting, buying, housing, health, and similar problems which they have in common with urban homemakers.

One of the most significant and interesting experiments which is of interest to the consumer movement was the conference held in Washington, D. C., in the spring of 1939 under the sponsorship of the Consumers' Counsel of the AAA. Twenty-five rural women and twenty-five city women met together for two days and discussed their mutual problems in obtaining better living standards for themselves, their neighbors, and the nation. Representatives included delegates from farm organizations, home demonstration clubs, church, school, labor, cooperative groups, and similar organizations from all over the country. No resolutions were made. The women were interested in finding out facts about economic and social problems and in contributing their own experiences. Out of it has developed further interest among the various groups represented in broad problems of consumer welfare, and the underlying causes of economic maladjustment. About seventeen state-wide conferences and several county conferences of a similar nature have been held.

Other Buying Interests

The problems of the small-scale household buyer are, in some respects at least, similar to those of commercial and institutional buyers. Purchasing agents have for years recognized the handicaps which buyers of ultimate consumers' goods are up against: lack of standards, lack of informative labels, lack of testing facilities. Some states and cities have tried to overcome this handicap by setting up testing laboratories to be used by these agents in the purchase of goods for institutional and public use. Like the household consumer, they are interested in getting best value for the money spent. Many purchases of the institutional buyer and other agents are used for purposes much the same as those of the household buyer—floor wax, towels, sheets, ink, and so on. In the purchasing agents' fund of knowledge about commodities there is a great deal of technical information which could be turned to the service of the household consumer. In many colleges, teachers have a great buying advantage in being able to draw on the knowledge and sources of supply of the purchasing agent for the college in buying their household goods. One of the most frequent demands of consumer groups is that information from the National Bureau of Standards should be made available to the ultimate consumer in forms which he can use, a service which the bureau renders for the government as a buyer.

Purchasing agents have organized in associations for the exchange of information and experience. Groups such as the National Association of Purchasing Agents, the Educational Buyers' Association, and the Simplification and Standardization Committee of the American Hospital Association have done extensive work in connection with the establishment of minimum prices through federal agencies such as the National Bituminous Coal Commission and in setting up quality standards. The National Association of Purchasing Agents was one of the groups in the Consumers' Advisory Board of the NRA which was most effective in promoting consumer interests. J. W. Nicholson, of Milwaukee, and Russell Forbes, of New York City, have done outstanding jobs in their cities of buying by carefully drawn specifications rather than by brand. The Hospital Bureau of

Standards tests and supplies products for purchase by its members, and gives the information in a confidential bulletin. Information of all kinds from sources such as these could be of great significance to the ultimate consumer, and workers in these fields might eventually be drawn into much closer relation with the consumer movement.

Chapter Five

CONSUMER GROUPS ORGANIZE

THE consumers of Little Rock, Ark., have become articulate. They have a "Society for the Booing of Commercial Advertisements in Motion Pictures." Many other more elaborate organizations have developed in recent years specifically for purposes of protecting and promoting the consumer interest. The sample organizations included here should not be regarded as a comprehensive survey. They simply represent a few types which have grown up around the concept of a special consumer interest. Both national and local groups have been included. No attempt has been made to classify them strictly according to income groups, methods, aims, origins, and so on. A valid classification of this sort would require a systematic and inclusive survey of the thousands of consumer groups all over the country. The arrangement of organizations in the present chapter is based chiefly on convenience in presenting different types.

CONSUMERS NATIONAL FEDERATION

Outside of the consumer cooperative movement there is little organization on a national scale which represents exclusively the interests of consumers. At numerous national conferences consumer problems have been discussed but no permanent national headquarters exists for organized consumers as a whole. An organization which might form a nucleus for the coordination of national consumer activity is the Consumers National Federation.

This federation is an outgrowth of a local New York group,

the Consumers' Emergency Council, and was established in the spring of 1937. Although membership includes some national organizations such as Consumers Union and the National Federation of Settlements, most of the 20 to 30 organizations which belong to it are of a local character. The chairman of the federation is Helen Hall, director of Henry Street Settlement House, and Robert S. Lynd, professor of sociology at Columbia University, is vice-chairman. Other members of the executive committee include officers of the Bureau of Cooperative Medicine, the New York branch of the American Association of University Women, the New York City League of Women Voters, the Farm Bureau Cooperative Association of Pennsylvania, the National Consumers League, the Consumer Distribution Corporation, the Federal Council of Churches, the Milk Consumers Protective Committee of New York, Russell Sage Foundation, and Greenwich Settlement House.

The federation seeks to give coherence and focus to the consumer movement by providing centralized services of information and education. It believes that such services should provide help for its members, both as organizations and as individuals, in making more intelligent decisions for action and in facilitating their cooperation with each other. Objectives center around general economic problems from the consumer point of view rather than around specific problems of factual information or particular price situations. The scope of its activities is indicated by the following statement from the first issue of its publication, the *Consumer*:

The experience of the Consumers' Advisory Board under the NRA showed that the "problem" of the consumer is not confined to the confusion of the housewife at the retail counter. One of the main weaknesses of the consumer movement in the past has been the want of leaders able to explain the processes of industry and finance to consumers and at the same time effectively to represent the consumer point of view in public councils.

Accordingly, the federation has set up a series of expert committees to follow and interpret developments in different fields of interest to the consumer—cost of living, price and production policies, standards, housing, cooperatives. The federation is pro-motional in that it encourages the formation of legitimate consumer groups. Its purposes as stated in its by-laws are as follows:

1. To exchange and disseminate information among its members relating to their respective consumer programs and plan of action.
2. To conduct a general educational and informational service on consumer problems.
3. To promote a common understanding of consumer problems among consumer organizations in order to achieve effective protection for the consumer.
4. To establish criteria by which bonafide consumer organizations may be established.

It has published several numbers of the *Consumer*, which analyzed economic issues involved in current legislation, such as price control. In 1938 a committee was set up under the chairmanship of Professor Anton Friedrich, of New York University, to study the Patman proposal for a federal antichain-store tax bill. The report was completed and circulated early in 1939. At the 1938 annual meeting of the National Education Association the federation provided an opportunity for a discussion of consumer education in the schools and colleges and of the materials in use in consumer courses. An exhibit of consumer study materials was held at this meeting. The High Cost of Living Conference in New York City in 1938 was sponsored by the federation. As a result of this conference a delegation of consumer representatives from 25 civic, welfare, consumer and labor organizations in a number of states went to Washington and presented to the President a two-point program asking for an investigation into the reasons for underconsumption in the midst of potential wealth, and pointing out the need for a central consumer agency in the federal government. Early in 1938, in response to a request from the New York State Constitutional Convention Committee, the federation prepared a brief on the subject of an amendment to the New York State constitution to provide for a department of the consumer. One of the leading purposes of the Consumers National Federation as set out in its by-laws is to develop criteria by which bona fide consumer organizations may be identified. It has made a canvass of consumer organizations but the criteria have not yet been set up.

On September 23, 1939, a special committee was appointed to keep consumers informed of price changes resulting from war conditions and to help formulate possible consumer action against profiteering. A price bulletin is issued biweekly to subscribers at the rate of $2 a year, $10 if reproduction rights are wanted. The members of the Special War Prices Committee include: Ruth Ayres, New York City League of Women Voters; Arthur Burns, professor of economics, Columbia University; Wallace Campbell, assistant secretary, Cooperative League of the U.S.A.; Mary Dublin, general secretary, National Consumers League; Anton Friedrich, professor of economics, New York University; Dexter Masters, editor, Consumers Union; George Marshall, labor economist; Colston Warne, professor of economics, Amherst College; Persia Campbell, secretary of the Consumers National Federation. In a memorandum released October 26, 1939, the committee suggested the following steps to prevent a dislocation of prices owing to the new situation:

1. Consumer representation in the membership of all agencies charged with dealing with the effects of war on the American economy.
2. Enlargement of funds and facilities of existing governmental agencies and bureaus giving services to the consumer.
3. The establishment of a new Consumer Protective Commission by the government with adequate staff and publicity facilities to supplement the work now being done and to provide interpretive material enabling consumers to measure the extent of price increases, the deterioration of products, or reductions in the quantity sold at a given price. But it must go further and help consumers to decide how far these increases in price or reduction in quality or quantity are justified.

The federation is supported by individual donations and membership dues and has received one grant of $500 from the Keith Foundation. Its budget for 1938 amounted to $2,000. Membership is based on the following by-laws:

Any organized body, group or association of persons, whether local, state or national, which has as its aim, or which includes in its program the protection of the consumer in the purchase of goods and services and the conditions under which such goods and services are made, performed, and distributed, and which is not operated for profit, nor in the interest of nor connected with profit-making organizations, may become a member of the Federation.

No membership list of affiliated organizations has yet been released by the federation, and it appears that the numerical strength that has been gathered behind it is less than was hoped for. Its leadership in the field is valuable and with the increasing need for this kind of coordination its importance may be expected to grow.

CONSUMERS' COUNCIL AND CONSUMERS' FEDERATION OF ST. LOUIS

When the NRA went out of existence, with it went support for the plan of building up consumer county councils to act as two-way channels of information on consumer interests and the recovery program. Not all the councils went out of existence, however. The Wayne County Consumers' Council, for example, was active in obtaining the establishment of a Consumer Division (now defunct) in the Department of Agriculture in the state of Michigan in 1938. In January, 1939, the office of the Consumers' Counsel of the AAA counted 22 councils still active.

A particularly active consumer group in St. Louis traces its origin back to NRA days. At that time it became widely known for its work in checking up on the effect on coal prices of the NRA codes. It was instrumental in getting public hearings called before the code authority. As a result, price fixing in the retail coal industry was abandoned.

The activity which has been the rallying point of the St. Louis Consumers' Council since the government withdrew its support in 1936 has been milk. Some members from the council served for a while as consumer representatives on the local Dairy Commission, a distributor-producer agency which administered funds for the city milk ordinance. When this ordinance was violated and failed to give St. Louis a pure milk supply—the city health commissioner called the milk "bacteria soup"—the council showed the vitality of a consumer pressure group when organized around a specific community problem. With only a volunteer staff, 110 organizations representing approximately 180,000 individuals were lined up by letter, telephone, and direct contact. Men and women from trade-unions and Junior Leagues, American Legions and social service agencies, service and women's clubs, religious and neighborhood groups added their words of support in an impressive public hearing before the Board of Aldermen. Although the dairy interests and farmers were opposed, their money and legal talent could not prevail against such a genuine expression of public opinion. In the end, the city fathers presented the people of St. Louis with the U.S. Public Health Standard Milk Ordinance—they called it a "Christmas present." Certain members of the Consumers' Council became the only consumer representatives on the local Dairy Council, an affiliate of the National Dairy Council. They have made it their business to check up on the compliance with and financing of the Standard Milk Ordinance.

The Consumers' Council worked to educate local groups as to the need for the new food, drugs, and cosmetics legislation. It supports U.S. grade labelling and endorses the new Wheeler-Lee law regulating advertising. Representatives of the St. Louis consumer groups attended the conferences of the Institute for Consumer Education in 1939 and 1940. After the second conference they arranged a panel discussion for their own members in St. Louis. Esther Cole Franklin, of the American Association of University Women, Donald Montgomery, consumers' counsel of the AAA, Colston Warne, of Consumers Union, and Paul Sifton, consumers' counsel for the National Bituminous Coal Commission participated. The discussion topic, "Consumer Information, Please!" evoked a lively response.

In January, 1940, a beginning was made further to coordinate consumer work in St. Louis. Several consumer, labor, civic, and neighborhood groups formed a federation for the immediate purpose of protecting the consumer against profiteering arising from abnormal prices due to war, substitution of inferior quality in consumers' goods, and the resulting deterioration in living standards. This purpose was later enlarged to enable the federation to exchange information and coordinate activities. The objectives were stated as follows:

To make consumers intelligent buyers. Neither the label nor the advertising nor the price is necessarily assurance of the sound material and competent workmanship at fair wages that, to the informed consumer, mean full value.

To protest effectively in the event of unwarranted rises in price or cuts in values based on war conditions.

The chairman of the Consumers' Council, Mrs. W. V. Weir, is president of the new federation. Miss Alice Rex, of Grace Hill Settlement House, is secretary, and Mrs. Willard Parker, of the League of Women Shoppers, is treasurer.

CONSUMERS' INSTITUTES OF MASSACHUSETTS

Of organizations tracing their origin back to the NRA probably the best known existing ones are the Consumers' Institutes of Massachusetts. At the time of the original project there were three councils in Middlesex, Suffolk, and Hampden. Since then two others in Hampshire and Worcester counties have been added. These "institutes" are coordinated through the office of a state director, Mrs. Elizabeth Cox. Each institute has an unpaid chairman and at least one paid full-time worker. At the present time they function as the Consumers' Institutes of Massachusetts' WPA Education Program, sponsored by the Massachusetts Department of Education.

The institutes work closely with the Boston Better Business Bureau. Total membership is nearly 3,000, but through public meetings, newsletters, radio broadcasts, and publications a much wider group is reached. The Springfield *Shopping News*, for example, with a circulation of 108,000 carries each week a two-column article written by the Hampden County Consumers' Institute. The Worcester *Consumer Shopping News* gives space to the Worcester County Institute. Seven broadcasts are held weekly on food and marketing information especially intended to guide housewives of low-income groups and to assist in economical food buying. The response to these broadcasts has been extremely enthusiastic. The institutes have helped to have courses in consumer education put in the schools.

The Consumers' Institutes cooperated with Labor's Non-Partisan League in sponsoring a Milk Consumers' Committee and have at times represented the consumer in hearings before the Massachusetts Milk Control Board. Mrs. Cox favors a Department of the Consumer in the federal government. Since the outbreak of the European war commodity price fluctuations are being watched.

The Massachusetts Consumers' Institutes have broad interests in consumer education, protection and action in such fields as food and drug legislation, cooperatives, credit unions, instalment buying, life insurance, consumer credit, weights and measures, price fixing, fabric identification, informative labeling, advertising, medical care, housing, milk control, money management, legislation, consumer-retailer relations, etc.

CONSUMER CONFERENCE OF CINCINNATI

This was organized in the fall of 1934 as a result of a class in the Department of Household Administration under Miss Rosamond Cook at the University of Cincinnati to which clubwomen were invited. In 1940 it included 41 organizations such as the American Association of University Women, Business Women's Club, Literary and History Clubs, the League of Women Voters, Women of the Moose, Woman's Auxiliary of Trade Unions, the Cooperative League, and the Better Business Bureau. Seventeen local business firms contributed $5 or $10 during the year. It is an outstanding example of the "city-wide" type of organization, pooling the strength of various local groups in support of consumer programs.

Mrs. Dennis Jackson is president of the conference and has contributed much to its development. Meetings are held once a month during the school year at different places, with a different organization acting as "hostess" for each meeting. The program for 1939-1940 included such topics as protection for coal consumers, modern methods of marketing, government and consumers, quality labels and union labor, chain stores and independent stores. Radio broadcasts are sponsored and a household efficiency class meets under joint sponsorship with the Adult Education Council. Monthly visits to industrial plants are arranged.

Three committees have been set up by the conference: a legislative committee, which investigates and reports to the group on legislation affecting consumers; a speakers' committee, which makes contacts with other groups and provides speakers; a consumer-retailer problems committee, which studies the common problems of consumers and retailers. Delegates from the conference participate in many national conferences. It is a member of the Consumers National Federation.

The conference has been responsible for the adoption of informative labeling and advertising programs by several Cincinnati stores. At present it is particularly anxious to have United States standards and grades for meat adopted and to help abate the smoke nuisance by requiring the volatile content of coal to be given.

HIGH COST OF LIVING CONFERENCES

One of the most spectacular consumer protests in recent years was the Detroit meat strike, led by Mrs. Mary Zuk, of Hamtramck, in the summer of 1935. Little groups of women went from house to house urging other housewives to join in a strike against meat. Other groups called on butchers asking them to close their shops until the packers agreed to lower wholesale prices. Still others acted as pickets. Their demands were a 20 per cent reduction in the price of meat. The news value was so great that papers gave national publicity to their activities. Women's action committees against the high cost of living sprang up all over Detroit. By the end of the third week over 500 women were serving on these committees, backed by thousands of housewives. A permanent organization was formed, called the Women's League against the High Cost of Living. The strike lasted six weeks and the fight was carried to Washington and to the Chicago offices of the meat packers. Although the immediate objective of a 20 per cent reduction was not achieved, credit was taken for halting the rapid rise in meat prices throughout the nation. Actually the supply situation was such that meat prices had probably reached their peak and were due for a gradual reduction. This made the action of these consumer groups particularly timely. The Women's League adopted the following program:

1. To reduce the prices of meat, bread, and other necessities of life.
2. To reduce the rates of gas and electricity.
3. To reduce rents; to improve housing conditions; to lower taxes on small homes.
4. To abolish the sales tax.
5. To cooperate with trade unions, working people's organizations, and farmers to maintain and raise the standard of living.

The idea spread to other cities. In Chicago a United Conference against the High Cost of Living was organized to protest the high price of meat in 1935. It has grown steadily since that time. Its emblem is a market basket enclosed by a triangle whose three sides represent organization, education, and action. Fundamental to its program is the existence of neighborhood consumer clubs which occupy themselves with the buying problems of their members. *Consumers' Guide* and the abridged edition of Consumers Union *Reports* are used for study material. The conference also issues guides for promoting consumer protective leagues and committees to function on a wider community basis.

The conference receives much of its support from labor groups. But at the third annual conference in March, 1937, delegates representing such diverse interests as the following were elected to various offices: Women High School Teachers; Fur Workers Local #45; Mont Clare Boosters' Club; American Lithuanian Literary Society; Postal Clerks Union #1. Delegates from the Parent-Teachers Association also take part in the conference.

All together its program is stated to be endorsed by nearly 200 organizations. At the present time interest is active in a campaign for compulsory meat grading, in lowering public utility rates, in repeal of the sales tax, and in a study of the milk situation. In the spring of 1940 it took part in a conference of rural and urban homemakers, and sent a delegate to the conference of the Institute for Consumer Education in Columbia, Mo.

Behind this organized activity is a definite philosophy of

action much more clearly crystallized than the spontaneous protest against the high price of meat.

We, the people who work for a living, are the consumers as well as the producers. It has been quite natural for us to organize into trade unions and associations as producers. We have been mainly concerned with how much money we can get. But, will high money wages alone purchase any abundant living if as individual consumers we lose as poor buyers across the counter the gains made by our collective bargaining with industry?

We should be concerned with how much we can buy for our money. How often have we as individual consumers complained when dissatisfied with purchases or services. We should know what we are investing our money in.

As organized consumers we are becoming critical. We want a grade labeling system by which we can be informed of quality under standardized grades. We want facts about goods and services; under what conditions the products we buy are produced and distributed; and whether excessive prices arise from monopolistic practices or from inefficiencies that increase costs. We have a right to know these facts.

One of the guiding lights behind the activity is Mrs. Alice Belester, wife of a carpenter with a yearly income of $1,100. Mrs. Belester recently gave testimony on behalf of the consumer before the Temporary National Economic Committee in Washington. She stated that probably around two-thirds of the membership of her organization have incomes of $700 to $800.

High cost of living conferences have been held in other cities such as Baltimore (1937), Washington, D.C. (1938), and New York City (1938). Out of these have sometimes grown more permanent organizations. In New York City a Consumers' Council was formed which meets once a month, acting as a "light brigade" to carry out an action program—such as building support for compulsory meat grading and calling attention to proposals for a state department of the consumer.

MILK CONSUMERS PROTECTIVE COMMITTEE OF NEW YORK

Two examples of local organization with a specific commodity interest are the Milk Consumers Protective Committee in New

York and the Greater Boston Consumer Committee on Milk. The Milk Consumers Protective Committee was organized in August, 1936, under the chairmanship of the late Dr. Caroline Whitney. It was organized after hearings held by the price-fixing state control board to avoid a threatened milk strike of farmers. The fear of higher prices to the consumer brought together a group interested in New York's milk supply under the leadership of Consumers Union. There were 19 people present at this first meeting. In 1938 the committee claimed 72 affiliated organizations. These organizations consist of consumer and civic groups, settlement houses, trade-unions, women's clubs, welfare organizations, teachers' unions, and so on. The organizations affiliated with the committee elect delegates and contribute dues to carry on the committee's work. The delegates meet regularly, discuss policies, and recommend action on particular issues dealing with milk. The object of the committee is "To unite consumers and non-profit organizations of consumers and others interested in milk behind a program." The current program is as follows:

1. Consumers' education on the milk industry.
2. One grade of pasteurized milk, safely sealed.
3. Genuine consumer representation on all public bodies dealing with milk.
4. Establishment of a Department of the Consumer—State and Federal.
5. Opposition to minimum retail price fixing.
6. Adequate provision for supplying milk to those in need.
7. Municipal ownership and operation of a milk distribution system.
8. Support of joint non-profit enterprises of consumers and farmers such as the Consumer-Farmer Milk Cooperative, Inc.
9. Revision of laws affecting consumer and producer cooperatives.
10. Support of dairy farmers in their demands for adequate returns.
11. Support of organized labor in the milk industry.
12. Enforcement and extension of Federal and local legislation to curb monopolistic practices in the milk industry.
13. Cooperation with other groups, national and local, in carrying out this program.

The second major point in the program, "the establishment of one grade of pasteurized milk, safely sealed," has been achieved. The Board of Health in New York City has ruled that after September, 1940, only one grade of "Approved Milk" may be sold. The opposition to this ruling was strong and took place amid a flood of advertisements, public hearings, and propaganda. The New York City Federation of Women's Clubs opposed the measure. The basis for the demand for a single grade of milk was research done by Consumers Union showing that Grade A and Grade B milk commonly were of nearly the same quality. Consumers, they thought, were consequently led by the Grade A label to pay a premium for nonexistent quality. Special milks are not eliminated by the ruling, but consumers will be protected from thinking that by not buying Grade A they are sacrificing safety and nutritive value. More important is the long-run benefit to the consumer which is expected to come through improved market practices and increased efficiency of distribution. The work of the committee in eliminating milk grading is sometimes pointed to as an example of the inconsistency of consumers—first clamoring for grading and then clamoring not to have it. It illustrates rather the need for a continuing consideration of the consumer point of view, once grades are adopted. In problems of the milk supply the factors are particularly complex.

Other accomplishments of the committee include support of the extension of cheap milk depots in New York City, where needy people can come and get their milk at reduced rates. It provides lists and locations of such stations for its members. The committee takes particular credit for eliminating price-fixing provisions from the Milk Control Law in 1937, and has vigorously followed all legislative activity with respect to milk.

Increasing support has been given to a Consumer-Farmer Milk Cooperative, under the leadership of Meyer Parodneck, long active in the consumer cooperative movement. It began delivering milk in paper containers in June, 1938. Membership in the cooperative is by payment of 25 cents membership fee in cash or by deduction from dividends. Dividends are divided in thirds, one-third going to farmers and two-thirds to consumers, according to quantities of milk delivered and bought. The farmer is paid at prevailing milk prices, and the milk is sold at current retail prices. When a federal marketing order went into effect in the fall of 1938, the cooperative went into the distribution of cream and dairy products, believing that greatest profits were to be made in the field of surplus products. It issues its own paper, the *Organized Consumer*, with the slogan "Be an organized consumer. Make your pennies fight." At its second annual meeting in 1940 earnings of $6,000 were declared.

GREATER BOSTON CONSUMER COMMITTEE ON MILK

In January, 1939, a similar committee was launched in Boston. A meeting was called on January 13—the day on which a Greater Boston milk price increase went into effect—jointly by Labor's Non-Partisan League and the Consumers' Institutes of Massachusetts. It was attended by about thirty persons. The executive committee included representatives from the Cooperative Council of the Community Church, the Dorchester Cooperative Society, and the Union Cooperative Buying Club of Cambridge. Subsequently other organizations have joined closely in the work of the committee.

Since its formation the committee has been developing four main types of action: opposition to resale price fixing; analysis of state legislation pertaining to milk; cooperative distribution of milk; marketing efficiency in the milk industry. Plans for further improving the milk situation are based on the formation of neighborhood buying clubs, which will work locally to secure the necessary volume for efficient cooperative distribution. One such group began to purchase milk on May 15, 1940.

In January, 1940, the committee again opposed a price increase which the Massachusetts Milk Control Board proposed. Prior to the hearing the committee raised a question as to legality of further state board resale price fixing, in view of the U.S. Supreme Court decision of June 5, 1939, validating the New York and Boston federal milk marketing orders. The committee claimed that this decision precluded any further necessity or power to fix resale prices by the state board, since producer prices were being maintained by the federal government. At three successive hearings, representatives of consumer and labor organizations went on record before the board. Several score individual consumers, including women with children in arms, appeared. The State House auditorium was packed. Many mothers, pointing to healthy children, stated that they had been brought up on evaporated milk and that thousands of other housewives would do likewise as long as the price of fresh milk remained so far out of line with the prices of milk substitutes.

Consumer groups are also trying to get introduced into Boston many new methods of milk distribution in operation elsewhere, but handicapped under the board's price-fixing regulations. These methods include the paper quart container which now has an extra one-cent charge; two-quart paper and glass containers at a lower price per quart; the gallon container, at a lower price per quart; the Elwell system of pricing for deliveries of more than one quart; every other day delivery of milk, in conjunction with the Elwell system of milk pricing; and reductions in price when a system of payment collection is used different from and cheaper than that now used for home delivery systems.

The Consumer Committee on Milk has worked closely with the Cost of Living Committee of Labor's Non-Partisan League of Massachusetts, which helped to sponsor it. In October, 1939, a Consumer Committee on War Prices was formed by the league. The secretary of the Greater Boston Milk Committee, Eugene Belisle, is secretary of this committee. In addition to working on war prices it is interested in the stamp plan for food distribution, gas rates, and sources of information regarding consumer problems.

NATIONAL CONSUMERS LEAGUE

The National Consumers League was founded in 1899 to awaken consumer responsibility for conditions under which goods are made and distributed, and through investigation, education, and legislation, to promote fair labor standards. The first league was organized in New York under the auspices of the Working Women's Society and some liberal clergymen. They believed that the sympathy and interest of women patrons of retail stores was necessary to ameliorate working conditions.

The idea spread quickly and many leagues were formed in other cities.

The National League was organized to serve as a clearinghouse in the field and to help organize the work on a larger scale. The leagues had their most popular period in the first two decades of the twentieth century; at that time they worked chiefly through the publishing of "white lists" of factories having approved labor conditions. These attracted much attention and served as a forerunner of the union label. With the growing strength of organized labor, the league has confined its activities in recent years mainly to the field of labor legislation. As a lobby group its methods are respected and effective. The league has a membership of about 15,000 through its national and affiliated state leagues.

It was responsible for instituting the "Do Your Christmas Shopping Early" campaign, to eliminate some of the seasonal burden on retail clerks. It has worked from the beginning of its organization for adequate protection to the consumer of food and drugs. At the present time it has added support for compulsory health insurance legislation in the states to its program. Mary Dublin, executive secretary, reports that both the national and state leagues have in recent years been actively concerned in securing the enactment of measures establishing consumer departments or bureaus in the state and federal governments.

The New York league with a membership of 2,500 has been particularly active in the field of consumer interests and was one of the leading groups pressing for a department of the consumer, along with other groups concerned with raising the standard of living of the workers. Fundamentally, however, the concern of its members is with "interpreting industrial problems to the buyer of goods . . . What elements go into the making of a legitimate price to the consumer? To what degree must the buying public take into account desirable social standards, desirable business standards?"

The National Consumers League is interested in the promotion of the Consumers' Protection Label sponsored by the National Coat and Suit Industry Recovery Board and by the Millinery Stabilization Commission. This is based also on the assumption that the consumer is interested in the labor conditions under which the goods they buy are made. It gives a guarantee of sanitary conditions of production. The use of the labels is promoted through a National Garment Label Council with headquarters in New York.

THE LEAGUE OF WOMEN SHOPPERS, INC.

The first League of Women Shoppers was organized in New York in 1935 as a result of a strike at Ohrbach's department store in New York City. A group of store customers noticed the picket line and interviewed the workers. They found that employees had been working excessive hours for mere pittances. They decided to interview the management and felt that the workers' story could be substantiated. The strike was settled almost immediately as a result of the customers' concern. These customers then formed a nucleus for a permanent organization. In Philadelphia a league was organized on an appeal from striking truck drivers at Wanamaker's who had heard of the work of the New York league. In Chicago a league was formed through an interest in the Newspaper Guild.

Nine leagues were operating under a national constitution adopted at the first annual convention at the Hotel Wellington in May, 1938. Other leagues have since become members and the total membership has been estimated as high as 24,000. About 5,000 women belong to the New York league.

The League of Women Shoppers believes in the unionization of labor as a means of improving the workers' condition. Most of their activity is related to the settlement of labor disputes. It uses militant methods to get publicity for the support of labor. It pickets and boycotts stores which its members feel are dealing unfairly with labor and has adopted the slogan "Use Your Buying Power for Justice." Many of its members belong to middle- and upper-income groups, and have high social standing. Whenever it is necessary to bring facts in a particular labor situation to the attention of the buying public the New York league members are prepared to engage in spectacular picketing. In a recent department store strike, for example, the league members gave a fashion show on the picket line. At another time, as former customers of a popular night club whose work-ers were on strike, they picketed in evening dress carrying signs "We Won't be Wined and Dined Until a Union Contract is Signed." The New York league during the five year period 1935-1940 was called upon to investigate labor strikes 174 times and took action in 155.

The most recent pamphlet of the League of Women Shoppers is a study of New York Woolworth workers, written by Therese Mitchell. Another pamphlet which was published sev-eral years ago by the league has had a wide sale. It is *L is for Labor*, a glossary of labor terms written for the consumer lay-man.

SOCIAL UNION, INC.

A different type of organization from any of those already discussed is Social Union, Inc. It grew from a realization of the need for improving *techniques* of organization if obvious human needs were to be met in a democratic way. Not consciously stemming from a "consumer point of view" when it first started in the early twenties, its revival in the thirties soon brought it into close relation with the consumer movement in general.

The origins of the plan go back to experiments made during and after the first World War. The germ of the idea developed out of the need for community education and participation in connection with the establishment of clean milk depots and health centers in New York, Milwaukee, and Cincinnati. Based on experience in these cities, the idea was worked out more com-pletely and plans made to develop it further. National backing was obtained and $90,000 raised. Cincinnati outbid sixteen other cities and raised an additional $45,000 to help carry out the plan. Mohawk-Brighton was chosen as the district. The or-ganization called for a geographic chamber of representatives of the citizens, and an occupational chamber representing the people in their working capacities. These two groups were to meet to work out the problems of the community together. As might be expected, once the plan got under way it quickly came into conflict with the established political machine. The scheme had to be abandoned.

In 1929 plans were projected for a Consumers' and Producers' Foundation of America which received national financial backing and was ready to be launched when the depression came. It collapsed because financial support was then withdrawn. The same plan of community organization worked out earlier was to have been used to make possible the distribution of foods on a scientific basis, with the cooperation of manufacturers, distributors, and consumers. Milk was the commodity chosen to begin the experiment. As a start the zoning of distribution was planned to eliminate inefficiencies due to overlapping deliveries.

In 1939 the plan was launched again as the Social Unit Plan, later changing its name to Social Union, Inc. Mr. Wilbur Phillips, author of *Adventuring for Democracy*, who with his wife Elsie La Grange Cole had put unstinting effort behind the plan in Cincinnati and through all its later stages, is executive secretary. The proposal as outlined at a dinner meeting was given the endorsement of William Fellowes Morgan, commissioner of markets of New York City; Wesley Mitchell, professor of economics at Columbia University; C. E. A. Winslow, professor of public health at Yale University; John Dewey, professor emeritus of Columbia University; Horace Taylor, professor of economics at Columbia University.

The plan as now outlined calls for a geographic council representing consumers. Each block of 100 families is to elect a council. Each block council will choose a working executive, in all cases a woman. These block workers will establish complete, continuous, and friendly contact with the families living in their blocks. Each will study the needs of these families as consumers and carry on education among them. The central council, made up of these block workers, will in this way be representative of all the consumers who live in the district.

An occupational council is also to be elected. Occupational groups in the neighborhood will come together and elect an executive committee. This committee will choose a director to sit on the occupational council of all the directors. The council will consequently coordinate the experience, judg-

ment, and skill of physicians, clergymen, social workers, retailers, businessmen, wage earners, etc.

The two councils will unite for joint study, planning, and
action. The central council is to publish a bulletin going out
regularly to every home in the neighborhood. The program of
work is to be developed gradually. Since women will be chosen
to study the needs of consumers, the initial steps will deal with
consumer problems of immediate practical importance to them
and their children. Milk in its relation to an adequate diet has
been chosen as a product with which to begin operations, and
Manhattan has been chosen to start the experiment. The plan
now is to depend on the purchasing power of consumers rather
than on outside financial backing for making the work effective.

Professor Wesley Mitchell in his foreword to Mr. Phillips'
book points out the significance of the plan as an important type
of social invention. "Recognizing that consumption is basic to
production," he says, "Mr. Phillips has worked out the implications of that fact in a new way. . . . The resulting social or-
ganism supplies a means not only for gathering complete, accurate data on consumer needs and for enabling consumers to
obtain the best scientific advice on how to meet their requirements but also for conveying this information continuously to
producers and manufacturers. On the basis of such information,
the people residing in a Social Unit should be able to get much
more satisfaction now from whatever incomes they have to
spend, while producers should be able to supply goods and
services to them with less waste and risk."[1]

OTHER ORGANIZATIONS

There are many other organizations which on a national or
local scale pursue specific consumer interests. The National
Public Housing Conference established in 1932 seeks to promote
interest in programs of public housing. The Motion Picture Research Council is a citizens' committee organized to abolish the
compulsory block booking and blind selling of motion pictures.
It supports the Neely bill, which deals with this problem. Work

[1] *Adventuring for Democracy* (1940), p. xv.

also is being done by organized groups to promote higher standards in radio programs, particularly for children. Health organizations of various kinds are seeking to advance consumer interests along these lines.

It is sufficient to point out here the existence of these types of organizations. Their growing number is part of the generally increasing consumer consciousness.

CONSUMER ORGANIZATIONS AND THE DIES COMMITTEE

On December 3, 1939, J. B. Matthews—formerly vice-president of Consumers' Research—presented a report to the Dies Committee. Many a clubwoman housewife was startled to read in her newspaper a few days later that the consumer movement was "red." Mr. Matthews claimed that Communist party activities among consumer groups had been "so extensive" and the evidence of it "so vast" that only a mere sketch of it could be made. Specifically he mentioned several organizations and their officers included in the present chapter: the League of Women Shoppers; the Milk Consumers Protective Committee; the Consumer-Farmer Cooperative; the New York Consumers' Council; the United Conference against the High Cost of Living in Chicago, and several other high cost of living groups; and the Consumers National Federation. Consumers Union also was given special attention.

The report attracted wide attention journalistically and aroused much discussion in business and consumer circles. President Roosevelt, according to the St. Louis *Post Dispatch* (December 13), made it clear that he did not approve of the procedure used by the Dies Committee in issuing this report linking consumer groups with communism. Chairman Dies, the President had been given to understand, appointed himself a subcommittee, received the report from Matthews at a special Sunday evening meeting, and then directed that the report be received by the full committee and published. Representative Voorhis, a member of the Dies Committee, publicly accused the committee of undemocratic procedures in preparing and making the report public without informing the full committee. He said that it was "purely and simply the opinion of J. B. Matthews." (New York *Times*, December 12).[2]

The analysis of communistic activities which Matthews made was based on the connections of certain individuals with the organizations in question. Part or all of the evidence against five organizations, for example, was the fact that Miss Susan Jenkins had at one time or other worked in them. The basis for calling Miss Jenkins a Communist was that she had admitted being an employee of the *Daily Worker*, official Communist publication. "It can hardly be alleged," said the report, "that any employee of the *Daily Worker* would be other than a Communist." According to a bulletin of the Institute for Propaganda Analysis issued January 15, Miss Jenkins denied she was ever in the Communist party. She stated that she worked two weeks for the *Daily Worker* at one time while she was on strike against Macaulay Publishers. The *Daily Worker* asked the union to send an operator to help during a pre-election rush and Miss Jenkins was picked because she had dependents. This was the extent of her activity with it. In the New York *Times* of December 11, Miss Jenkins stated

If the rest of Mr. J. B. Matthews' statement on the consumer movement is as inaccurate as his references to my activities, then it is indeed a remarkably inaccurate statement. For instance, I had nothing to do with the organizing of the League of Women Shoppers. That organization had been in existence for many months before I had any contact with it. . . . I am not and have not been a communist or fellow traveler.

Arthur Kallet, director of Consumers Union, was attacked on the basis of isolated and ambiguous extracts from a few of his writings. His answer was reported in the *Times*:

Consumers Union would welcome and fully cooperate in any responsible investigation of the consumer movement and itself. . . .
I want to state emphatically that neither Consumers Union, as an organization, nor myself as an individual, nor to the best of my knowledge any one else connected with Consumers Union has ever

[2] For a survey of press statements see special edition of *Consumer Education*, Vol. 2, No. 4, January, 1940.

had any connection with the Communist party or is even aware of any such broad destructive movement as Mr. Matthews seems to find in operation.

Meyer Parodneck, the report charged, "wrote a glowing account of the position and progress of consumer cooperatives in the Soviet Union" in the *New Republic*, March 20, 1935. He is active in the Milk Consumers' Protective Committee and Consumer-Farmer Milk Cooperative. The Matthews report did not point out that he had also praised in the same article the consumer cooperative movement in Scotland, Denmark, Sweden, and Finland. Mr. Matthews said that "In his article, Mr. Parodneck made it clear that his own ultimate objective was to achieve the abolition of the system of free enterprise and to substitute for it some form of economic collectivism, indicating his special bias in favor of the Soviet Union." The Institute for Propaganda Analysis points out that what Mr. Parodneck really said was, "The uniform success of consumer cooperation in the countries discussed, during the years that profit business has suffered its worst setback, would seem to indicate the power of consumer cooperation as a means of fighting the depression." According to Matthews's report, the chairman of the Milk Consumers Protective Committee was stated to be Susan Jenkins, "who took an active part in its organization." Actually she was acting chairman for only a very brief period after Dr. Caroline Whitney's death. The organization of the committee was definitely the work of Dr. Whitney, who received no mention in the report.

Five individuals were mentioned as being "among those most active" in the formation of the Consumers National Federation. For two of these not even any indirect evidence of communism was suggested. The federation actually has an active executive committee of seventeen and an advisory council of ten. It was also stated against the federation that "one of its early conferences" included sponsorship by six communist "transmission belts." No further analysis of its activities was made, except for reference to an earlier statement by Earl Browder, secretary of the Communist party, mentioning the federation as a transmission belt. In transmission belts, according to Matthews's own testimony, the majority of the members are not Communists or even Communist sympathizers. They are simply organizations where attempts may be made to release communistic propaganda—and so might be almost any kind of organization. Helen Hall, chairman of the Consumers National Federation, president of the National Federation of Settlements, and head of Henry Street Settlement House, along with Robert Lynd, vice-chairman of the federation and professor of sociology at Columbia University, stated (New York *Times*, December 11):

The Consumers National Federation is not a Communist organization nor a "transmission belt" nor do its policies in any way reflect Communist nor any other political control . . . The pity of it is that the resources of the organized consumer movement are inadequate for the tremendous job to be done.

Donald Montgomery, consumers' counsel in the AAA, who was also mentioned in the report as "active from the beginning in the work of the Consumers National Federation" and whose department publication *Consumers' Guide* was stated to have given frequent and favorable publicity to that and other organizations included in the report said (*Editor and Publisher*, December 23, 1939):

I don't know of any consumer organization which is dominated by communists, or any consumer program that is controlled by communists. It is a preposterous canard.

These accusations and answers indicate the general nature of the report. An analysis of the "angles" in the report was made by *Business Week* and sums up general opinion on the matter.[3] For one thing, the timeliness of the report in relation to the Federal Trade Commission case against Hearst's *Good Housekeeping* and the specific defense made of advertising was too obvious to pass unnoticed. Concluding paragraphs of the report, for example, stated:

Communists understand that advertising performs an indispensable function in a mass production economy, and that advertising as an

[3] December 16, 1938, pp. 17-18.

economic process, wholly apart from questions which have to do with good or bad copy, is as essential a part of distributive mechanism as are railroads and outlets. Therefore, communists believe that to sabotage and destroy advertising and through its destruction to undermine and help destroy the capitalist system of free enterprise is a revolutionary tactic worthy of a great deal of attention. . . . This agitation has been going on for years and is now being reflected in government circles as well as in large sections of the population which are wholly unconscious of any influence of communist propaganda.

"Best of all to the ears of Hearst executives was this section of the report," said *Business Week:*

A great part of the current popular and official attack upon advertising is the direct result of communistic propaganda in the field of consumer organizations. This is borne out by the recent action of a government official in the Department of Agriculture who undertook an investigation of national advertising in Good Housekeeping Magazine. This investigation was carried out by WPA employees and paid for out of WPA funds. While there is no record of the findings being used as a basis for action against the magazine it may be assumed that such was the intention.

Good Housekeeping reprinted the Matthews report in the November-December issue of its *Consumers' Information Service* distributed free to club groups and individuals. "If and when reliable information in opposition to the findings of the Dies Committee is at hand, Good Housekeeping Magazine will immediately make it available to you," the issue stated. No further information has been released, however.

"The advertising trade is talking about the Hearst angles in the Dies report," said *Business Week*, "but there are others. The Committee's investigator and author of the report, J. B. Matthews, formerly was an executive of Consumers' Research. In 1935, 70 CR employees went on strike and later under the leadership of Arthur Kallet, set up the rival Consumers Union. Matthews and Kallet are not chums. Consumers Union is No. 1 on the list of organizations which Matthews finds infested with communists."

One final comment was made by *Business Week:* "The Dies
Committee is running out of money. It is due to end with the
new session of Congress, unless new money is appropriated.
Chairman Dies may very well be counting on business interest
in the consumer movement to act as a lever to get the money."

Chapter Six

CONSUMER COOPERATIVES GROW

ONE of the most obvious ways for the consumer to try to get what he wants is by going into business himself through association with other consumers who are similarly interested in economic enterprise undertaken primarily for the benefit of the consumer. The consumer cooperative movement represents the oldest and most important single element in the consumer movement as a whole. Its growing strength is of major importance.

The underlying factors which have produced the general widespread interest in the consumer have reinforced and given impetus to the consumer cooperative movement. Individual consumers have turned to cooperative organization as a direct means of protecting their interests. Many of the organizations previously discussed have given sympathetic or active support to consumer cooperatives. Recent books on consumer cooperation give explicit recognition to its place in the general consumer movement. "Another factor of tremendous importance to cooperative development," writes Orin E. Burley, "is the existence of a strong 'consumer movement' in the United States. This movement originated in the United States and is characteristically American . . . Cooperatives are, however, an active and articulate part of the movement and much of the recent expansion among cooperatives can be traced to the newly aroused interest in economic activity motivated by consumer welfare."[1]

The consumer cooperative movement in America is typically

[1] Orin E. Burley, *The Consumers' Cooperative as a Distributive Agency* (1939), p. 17.

137

American in its origin and genius. Interest in it has been stimulated, however, by examples of its success in foreign countries.
In 1936 President Roosevelt sent a special committee abroad to
study European cooperatives. It published a 321-page report
in 1937. Achievements of Swedish cooperatives such as the cut-
ting of the price of rubber overshoes by one-half and of electric
light bulbs by one-third became well known. The successful
development of consumer cooperation in England, Denmark,
Finland, and other countries was similarly noted.

Closer home, Canadian cooperative experiments at Antigonish in Nova Scotia, and in Newfoundland have done much
to arouse interest in cooperation here. The Nova Scotia movement became important in the late twenties when the ideas of
adult education developed by Father Tompkins and Father
Coady of St. Francis Xavier University were put into practice
through the university's extension program. Basic to the Antigonish cooperative movement is the local study group composed
of fishermen, farmers, or miners who study their problems and
translate what they learn into action. Most rapid growth has
come in the past ten years. Marketing, production, credit, and
housing as well as consumer retail societies have been organized.

The first cooperative store in the new movement opened in
Canso in 1934. Since then over 70 societies have opened for
business in the surrounding area with a membership of nearly
7,000 and an annual turnover of over $2,000,000. The board of
directors of the Sydney Cooperative Society is especially noted
for the efficiency and zeal with which it performs its duties.
The president is a blacksmith, and other board members come
from such callings as machinist, accountant, patternmaker, elec-
trician, boilermaker, furnaceman, millwright, mailman, carpenter, wiredrawer.[2] An older cooperative organization, the British
Canadian Cooperative Society at Sydney Mines, has been in
existence since 1909 and operates four stores. It does a retail
business of over a million dollars a year. Relations between this

---

[2] See Father Martin Schirber, *The Antigonish Movement, Its Method and
Meaning,* Doctoral Dissertation, Harvard University, 1939.

society and the newer Antigonish experiments are increasingly cordial.

Annual tours have been arranged for cooperators from the United States to visit the Antigonish cooperatives and this has done much to stimulate enthusiasm for its potentialities. In particular it has strengthened the interest in the small study group as the basis of cooperative expansion. Adaptations of the study club method have been worked out in American cooperative societies. In Ohio, for example, "advisory councils" have done much to make the work of consumer cooperation effective in that state. There are now over 800 in Ohio, 300 in the Central Co-op wholesale area, 155 in Midland Co-op territory, about 100 organized by the Consumers' Cooperative Association and another 100 by the Eastern Cooperative League. The study circle method is regarded by cooperative leaders as one of the most important factors in the entire educational program.

Cooperatives in America have had spectacular successes too. The most striking development in recent years has been in the sale of oil and gas. The opposition of the big, established oil companies has made cooperatives push farther and farther back into wholesale business and production. In May, 1940, the first complete cooperative oil refinery in the world was dedicated in Phillipsburg, Kansas. The *Cooperative League News Service* reports the ceremonies as being attended by a crowd of between twenty and twenty-five thousand, many of whom were part owners of the $850,000 refinery. They came from eleven states and Canada. A mile-long parade including 15 high school bands and more than 100 oil transports, cars, and floats, was held. Thirty-six hundred pounds of beef were barbecued, and 200 men cut buns for eighteen lines of visitors. Co-op members came from as far as 800 miles away, but the most arduous journey was made by a woman who pushed a baby buggy and led two children a mile and a half from the heart of town for the occasion. The Chambers of Commerce of Phillipsburg and Kensington cooperated to make the dedication a memorable occasion. The refinery is owned by the Consumer Cooperative

Association, a wholesale with 452 societies and 120,000 members in ten states doing $4,225,000 worth of business annually.[3]

Soon after its dedication the refinery emerged successfully from what was called a "squeeze play," when Stanolind (Standard Oil Company of Indiana) proposed to extend its gathering pipe lines into fields in two counties where the co-op had hoped to have a clear field. Two weeks after the dedication the cooperative oil refinery was obliged to shut down. By June it was again operating at full capacity but with construction begun on a $45,000 pipe-line extension which had not been planned originally. The "squeezing" took place amid injunction suits, accusations of promises broken by government officials, and "hot" oil investigations (oil sold in violation of the federal oil laws). The cooperative was helped by the fact that two of its independent sources of supply, the Globe Refining Company and the Sinclair Refining Company, stood by their customer. What finally turned the scale was a barrage of letters written by members of the local co-ops who own the refinery and by members of co-ops affiliated with the Consumer Cooperative Association living in Kansas. Stanolind is reported to have withdrawn from several pools near the co-op pipe line. Officials of the Consumers' Cooperative Association accepted an offer to buy crude from Stanolind's competitive pipe line until the extension of the co-op line is completed. The fight is ended, said *Business Week* on June 15, 1940, "but the cooperators aren't likely to forget the political lesson they learned and almost certainly they will be heard from when the legislature takes up the oil code again at the next session."

While consumer cooperative associations do only a small part of the nation's business, in some regions they are of great importance. In St. Louis County, Minnesota, a sparsely settled area of some 7,000 square miles with a population in 1930 or 204,596, the consumers' cooperatives alone had a combined membership of about 13,500. This did not include the members of the many cooperative associations marketing or processing farm products, nor the families of members of the consumers' societies. In that area cooperative telephone service, credit, lodgings,

[3] Cooperative League News Service, May 4, 1940.

recreational facilities, electric power, insurance, garage service, automobiles, petroleum products, automobile accessories, food, and practically all articles of household and farm equipment are available through cooperative channels. In some of the towns, nearly every family in the area belongs to the cooperative.[4] Similar developments occur elsewhere, frequently among nationality groups.

A fundamental tenet of consumer cooperation is that production must be responsive to the consumption needs of society and not an instrument for private profit making. Consumer cooperative organization is patterned on the principles developed by the Rochdale weavers in England in 1844. From these "Rochdale principles" there may be occasionally minor variations, but true consumer cooperatives are distinguished by their adherence to them. They are: open membership; one man, one vote; limited interest on capital; sale for cash at market prices; dividends paid on the basis of patronage. A group of facilitating principles is also often added: neutrality in race, religion, and politics; constant cooperative education; constant cooperative expansion.

One of the difficult points in defining consumer cooperation lies in the fact that cooperative association may be undertaken solely for the purpose of advancing producer interests, regardless of the ultimate consumer. This is the point of view which is often predominant in agricultural cooperatives, particularly in their marketing activities. It is difficult, however, to draw a distinct line between "vocational" and "household" purchasing, although attempts to do so are frequently made. Consumer cooperative leaders have recently tended to include in the concept of consumers' cooperation the whole field of cooperative buying regardless of whether goods are bought for production or for consumption. The recent rapid expansion of farm purchasing activity into such products as petroleum, which serves both consumer and producer ends, and into household supplies has tended to make it difficult to maintain any real distinction

[4] Cf. Florence Parker, *Consumers' Cooperation in the U. S., 1936*, Bureau of Labor Statistics, Bulletin No. 659 (1939).

between these two kinds of cooperative activity. In recent years, too, there has been a tendency for the "consumer point of view" to be adopted to a greater extent by farm organizations. Typical of this consumer-minded leadership is Murray Lincoln of the Ohio Farm Bureau Federation, who wrote in *Rural America* in April, 1939:

Farmers are inclined to think of themselves as producers first. When you mention the word consumer they think you are talking about the man in town. My purpose is to show how the farmer is a consumer first and a producer second. How the farmers' interests as a consumer are identical with the consumer interests of industrial and white collar workers and of professional people, but often in conflict with the producer interests of these groups, and why consumer action is more effective than producer action.

RETAIL STORES AND THEIR WHOLESALE ASSOCIATIONS

The consumer-owned retail store is generally described as the heart of practical consumer cooperation. It is estimated by the Bureau of Labor Statistics that for the year 1936 there were 3,600 retail distributive associations with a membership of 677,-750 and a volume of business of $182,685,000.[5] Official government estimates for years later than 1936 are not available. In 1939 the Cooperative League reported a membership of 965,000 in consumer cooperatives. These figures may be regarded as lower limits; 12,000 societies and a volume of business of $500,000,000 has been suggested as a reasonable upper limit.[6] These latter figures would include all cooperative purchasing —the cooperative purchasing of farm supplies as well as of ultimate consumer goods. The Bureau of Labor Statistics estimate includes only farm businesses handling consumer supplies for the household.

These stores are set up to act as buying agents for consumers. Cooperatives have a special duty to provide "really good values"

[5] Florence Parker, *Consumers' Cooperation in the U. S., 1936*, Bureau of Labor Statistics, Bul. No. 659 (1939), p. 6.
[6] Orin E. Burley, *The Consumers Cooperative as a Distributive Agency* (1939), p. 60.

rather than merely to stock lines that sell well. How far they succeed in doing this is questioned by some. However, the co-ops do lead in giving customers information about products. Quality grades, supplemented by informative literature available in the stores, are usually indicated on labels of products for which grades have been established. The CO-OP label, used nationally, now has about 600 grocery items distributed under it. Many of these are grade labels. Meat also is frequently sold by government grade. Quality ratings by Consumers Union of various cooperative products have indicated instances of slack fill, low weight, poor grade, and variable quality. A study made by the Boston Better Business Bureau in 1940 also revealed lack of standardization of CO-OP grades. Its scope, however, was very limited.[7] Cooperatives realize the difficulties of controlling their products and have welcomed the ratings of Consumers Union as a basis for standardizing and improving them. A model testing kitchen has been established by the Eastern Cooperative Wholesale, which is intended to accomplish the following: testing of new items, conformation testing on every shipment of goods, preparation of cooperative food facts for consumer education, and the training of store personnel.

Cooperative Distributors, located in New York City, sells cooperative products nationally by mail. It is organized on Rochdale principles. A special feature is made of its tested products and of buying by specification. Examples of its catalogue listing are as follows:

LIQUID METAL POLISH—For brass, bronze and copper. Made to meet U.S. Army Specification No. 3-157.

COLD CREAM—For cleansing and softening the skin and for removing make-up. Made of beeswax, mineral oil, borax, water and perfume. Opal jar.

The fact that cooperatives are closely tied to their membership through education programs and can therefore be more directly responsive to the needs of their customers is an advantage to them over private enterprises when consumers are

[7] See the *Bulletin* published by the Boston Better Business Bureau, July, 1940.

trying to be more articulate about their needs. Better Buyers'
Clubs, such as exist in many associations, can work closely with
their cooperative store manager in getting the kind of information they want about the quality and use of their products,
without meeting the resistance sometimes encountered with private enterprises. In Greenbelt, Md., where most of the business
is run cooperatively, the only enterprise which has difficulty in
maintaining volume is the movie house. The members of the
community find other meetings more absorbing. Cooperative
Women's Guilds both in America and abroad are educational
forces in the movement, and the spearhead for its better-buying
phases.

When cooperatives cannot get what they want at satisfactory prices from established producers, there is always some
possibility that they can undertake production economically on
their own account. The Kansas oil refinery is one example.
A refinery is also being built by the Indiana Farm Bureau Cooperative Association. The Cooperative Grange League Federation Exchange and the Eastern States Farmers' Exchange are
manufacturers or processors of a major part of their inventory.
The Central Cooperative Wholesale owns a bakery and a modern coffee-roasting plant. Practically all the large wholesale
cooperatives engaged in the distribution of petroleum products
operate compounding plants in which lubricating oil is blended
in accordance with their own specifications.

Since consumers are owners of the cooperatives, there is no
reason to make special inducements for buying through advertisements which emphasize the exciting or glamorous features of
the product. Membership is expanded through personal contacts more than through advertising appeals, while for the maintenance of loyalty and continuing appreciation of their services,
the co-ops depend principally on their social and educational
programs. Cooperators believe that business carried on according to their principles is not only socially more desirable but
is economically more efficient. They advocate it as a "type of
business which will function more equitably, which will tend
to undermine monopoly price structures . . . and which will

buttress our political and social democracy by creating a supporting economic democracy."[8]

In other countries cooperatives have been most successful where they have been able to effect economies in distribution or where their competitors were charging monopoly prices. They came on the scene in the United States somewhat late, after the economies of straight-line mass distribution had already been extensively exploited by the chain stores, mail-order houses, and large department stores. For that reason they have not had here the initial advantage they had abroad. American consumers on the whole have not been particularly responsive up to now to cooperative methods and services. Cooperatives have undoubtedly a real contribution to make to consumer welfare, directly to those who like doing business according to their methods and indirectly to all through their attacks on monopoly prices. It is hardly to be expected, however, that in this country they will quickly solve the problems of any large proportion of the buying public.

The influence of wartime demand and its effect on price may serve to give a stronger impetus to the development of consumer cooperatives. In a special peace edition of *Consumers' Cooperation* in October, 1939, the Central Cooperative Wholesale reported that its business during the previous month was the highest for any month in its history. Mr. Woodcock, manager of the Eastern Cooperative Wholesale, stated that "September business showed an advance which must have come at least in part from the fear of profiteering through ordinary commercial channels." His wholesale did twice the business that it did in September, 1938. Cooperatives generally report that there have been unusually large increases in their business during recent months.

One of the biggest problems of cooperative business is to attract managerial skill comparable to that of private industry. In recent years schools have been established to train managers of cooperatives and develop cooperative leadership. The Roch-

[8] Merlin G. Miller, "How Much Emphasis Should Be Placed on Consumer Education in a Cooperative Study Program?" National Conference of the Institute for Consumer Education, April, 1939, *Proceedings*, p. 115.

dale Institute in New York City, established in 1937, provides a national center for this type of education and has provided training for leaders in cooperative medicine and other forms of cooperation besides the retail store. Several district wholesale cooperatives also have training schools. The Consumer Distribution Corporation, established by the department store merchant, E. A. Filene, helps cooperatives by lending money and providing advice in management to cooperatives starting up.

One of the important developments in the United States has been the growth of wholesale societies with which retail clubs can affiliate for at least part of their business. The greatest volume of business is done by this federated type of retail cooperative. To become a member of a wholesale, a society buys at least one share of stock, generally priced at $50 or some multiple of this amount. Members are not bound to purchase through the wholesale as a rule, but usually they buy as large a part of their inventory as possible from this source. The Central Cooperative Wholesale of Superior, Wis., included the following kinds of affiliated organizations on December 31, 1937:[9]

Store societies engaged in merchandising only	59
Stores with production or service departments	24
Active buying clubs	4
Inactive buying clubs and societies	11
Oil associations (regional)	6
Creameries	1
Boarding houses	2
Savings banks	1
Total	108

A type of retail cooperative comparable to the chain store organization where centralized management and control is exercised over a number of local societies has sometimes been attempted. This has been successful in England where the Cooperative Wholesale Society in 1934 formed a CWS Retail Society Limited which opened retail shops, and plans were made to open variety stores of the Woolworth type. Although never actually put into practice the plan made by E. A. Filene for a series of

[9] Orin E. Burley, *The Consumers' Cooperative as a Distributive Agency* (1939), p. 65.

cooperatively run department stores aroused considerable interest. The Midland Cooperative Wholesale has begun a plan of co-op stores which will operate on a centralized plan.

CONSUMER COOPERATIVE SERVICES AND OTHER TYPES OF
   COOPERATIVES

The expansion of consumer cooperative associations into fields other than the retail store is of great importance to the cooperative movement as a whole. Boardinghouses, medical care, burial, housing, electricity, and miscellaneous associations were estimated as totaling 529 societies with 155,293 members and over $5,000,000 in business in 1936. There are about 5,000 telephone associations with 330,000 members doing a business of over $5,000,000 in the United States; 5,440 credit unions with 1,210,000 members made loans amounting to $112,135,000.[10] In 1940 the number of credit unions had increased to 8,000 with a business of $200,000,000.[11] Cooperative insurance is obtained through 1,800 associations with 6,800,000 policyholders and a gross premium income of $103,375,000.[12] These are chiefly farm fire insurance companies.

Such varied enterprises as printing plants, clubhouses, laundries, parks, and cold-storage plants are operated cooperatively. Cooperative boardinghouses have been important chiefly among national groups, such as the Finns in the North Central states. One of the outstanding examples of cooperative restaurants is the Consumers' Cooperative Services, Inc., of New York City which has been operating a chain of cafeterias since 1920. Cooperative restaurants are in operation in Chicago and sometimes operate in connection with cooperative stores such as the Cooperative Trading Company of Waukegan, Ill., and the Consumers Cooperative Society of Maynard, Mass. There is an employee cooperative restaurant with the J. B. Lyons Company at Albany.

Cooperative medicine has come much to the forefront in the

[10] Florence Parker, *Consumers' Cooperation in the U. S., 1936*, Bureau of Labor Statistics, Bul. No. 659 (1939), p. 162.
[11] Official estimate from the Cooperative League of the U.S.A.
[12] Parker, *op. cit.*

past few years and appears to have increasingly favorable prospects. Particularly outstanding instances are the Farmers' Union Cooperative Hospital at Elk City, Okla.; the Wage Earners Health Association of St. Louis, Mo.; the San Diego Beneficial Society, California; the Cooperative Health Association at Superior, Wis. (where the membership of the Central Cooperative Wholesale forms the basis of the organization); the Group Health Association, Washington, D. C.; the Cooperative Health Association, Greenbelt, Md.; and the recently organized group health cooperative in New York City. A Bureau of Cooperative Medicine was set up in New York in 1936. Cooperative medical associations have been under fire by local and national doctors' organizations and several court cases have been necessary to establish their legality. In some states their legality is still in question, and existing laws need to be revised to make their development possible. They have flourished with increasing vigor during recent years and have been a practical answer to many people seeking inexpensive yet adequate medical protection. Most plans provide hospitalization and medical care for $25 a year or less.

The housing projects sponsored by the Amalgamated Clothing Workers in New York are the largest in the United States. They are known as the Amalgamated Housing Corporation and the Amalgamated Dwellings. The 635 members of these associations operate their own milk delivery, laundry service, grocery, dairy store, and electric power plant, as well as a number of cooperative social ventures. In 1940 nearly $28,000 was remitted in cash dividends to the cooperators. Other housing cooperatives include Our Cooperative House, New York City; Cooperative Homemakers, Inc., Boston; and the Farband Housing Cooperative Association of New York. Crestwood, a cooperative housing development "five miles and ten minutes" from the center of Madison, Wis., has drawn high praise for its architecture. It has 20 houses completed and 20 more planned for 1940. By cooperative purchase of land members paid about half of what would usually be needed for suburban lots. Every lot is backed by wooded parklands which make up 20 per cent of the total area. Many of the houses are in the modern trend, and all harmonize with the rolling Wisconsin landscape.

One of the greatest potential fields of expansion provided by any cooperative service is in the rural electrification field. The Rural Electrification Administration reports that nearly 86 per cent of approved loans to project sponsors were to corporations and associations of cooperative character. The larger cooperatives are usually merchandisers of electrical appliances and this field is consequently being opened in a cooperative way. The Electric Home and Farm Authority extends credit to consumers who may desire to purchase appliances on its approved list. Although it is strictly neutral in its relation to various distributor groups, it anticipates an expansion of financing activity to cooperative societies. Since members of the electric cooperative are permitted to pay their bills at the commodity cooperative, however, the two agencies are brought in direct contact, and this may make possible an expansion of the commodity cooperative. There are about 15,000 farms in Ohio that are receiving electricity through cooperative distributors.[13]

Telephone associations represent one of the older forms of cooperative enterprise, the average for the groups as a whole being more than a quarter of a century. Few new associations are being formed. The Bureau of Labor Statistics reports that a surprisingly high degree of conformity to strictly cooperative principles was found among them, but that few of them have any conception of themselves as part of a general cooperative movement. They have been satisfied with furnishing telephone service in territories that would otherwise be without such services. This they are doing through democratic channels at extremely low cost. The yearly average rate per month for a residential subscriber was found to be 92 cents for 415 reporting associations.

The credit union movement in the United States was originally financed through help from the late Edward A. Filene, through the Credit Union National Extension Bureau. In 1934 this was reorganized as the Credit Union National Association.

[13] See Orin E. Burley, *The Consumers' Cooperative as a Distributive Agency* (1939), p. 118.

It consists of 44 affiliated state leagues of credit unions. It operates through a national board of directors composed of 81 members. The national association also maintains various affiliates including the Cuna Supply Cooperative which produces and distributes credit-union accounting forms and supplies to over 6,000 credit unions. It is affiliated with the Cuna Mutual Society. A large percentage of credit union loans are "character" loans without any security except the personal note of the borrower. Formation of new associations was facilitated by the passage of the Federal Credit Union Act in 1934. In 1936 alone over 1,295 associations were formed.

The organized cooperative movement during the past decade has become increasingly aware of the value of cooperative insurance. In 1926 the subject of insurance was given a place on the agenda of the congress of the Cooperative League and since that time has been given special study. The 1934 program of the league called for national associations specializing in various fields, but this has not yet been realized. Many of the insurance agencies are closely related to consumer cooperative distributive organizations.

CENTRALIZATION AND COORDINATION AGENCIES

Up to 1938 the business and education aspects of the consumer cooperative movement were carried on through two separate cooperative structures, the Cooperative League of the United States and National Cooperatives, Inc. The Cooperative League was established in 1915 and its development has been closely linked with the name of Dr. J. P. Warbasse, president of the league. Its primary work is to promote the development of consumer cooperation generally; to give advice to established or new cooperatives; to aid in the organization of cooperatives; to provide protection and assistance, of either a legal or a public relations nature. It accomplishes a great deal of its work through operating wholesales. Its own annual budget is about $20,000.

National Cooperatives, Inc., was formed by eight cooperative wholesale organizations in 1933. It now has a membership of 15, including two in Canada. It was organized because it was found that the eight wholesales by combining their volume could make a better deal with a manufacturer than any one of them could make individually. One of the services it considers most valuable has been the popularizing of the CO-OP trade-mark. Several infringements of the use of this trade-mark by other distributors or manufacturers have been protested or warned against by National Cooperatives. The National office has worked closely with agencies of the federal government dealing with consumer problems and has brought into membership with the Cooperative League cooperatives that normally might not have become affiliated because of their relationship to farm organizations. National Cooperatives has a board of directors of almost 30 which may be increased up to 48. There is fairly equal division in the membership of the board as between consumers' cooperative wholesale societies and the agricultural commodity purchasing cooperatives.

At the biennial congress in 1938 an important move was made to bring the two cooperative structures into closer relation. Joint executive offices of the Cooperative League and National Cooperatives have been established in Chicago and the two groups have an interlocking directorate. The objective appears to be to make cooperative organization adaptable to particular situations and needs as much as possible without losing the sense of a coordinated and unified movement.

It is of interest here only to indicate the growing importance of coordinating and centralizing agencies in the cooperative movement. While this greatly expands its effectiveness, it also creates many of the problems of "bureaucracy" and of democracy of organization within the movement. More and more attention is, in fact, being given to educational measures of a specific type concerned with the cooperative business. Only those matters which cannot be handled locally are delegated to the federation management. The rapid spread of the study club or "advisory council" mentioned earlier in the chapter is an indication of the way in which cooperatives are making local activity the basis of their growth.

CONSUMER COOPERATIVES AND LEGISLATION

Like other consumer groups, consumer cooperators are finding closer attention to problems of legislation desirable. Recent legislative measures tending to discriminate against particular kinds of distribution have made such action more urgent. The board of directors of the Cooperative League on March 23, 1939, authorized the executive committee to open a research and information office in Washington, D. C. In taking this action it was stated that it was regarded as particularly important "because many legislative proposals affecting fields of business and education in which the cooperatives are active are constantly being considered by Congress. Although cooperatives purchase one-sixth of all farm supplies bought in the United States and handle large quantities of petroleum products, groceries, and other commodities and services, they are not regularly consulted on legislative matters directly affecting them. Since approximately two million consumers are buying goods and services through cooperatives, cooperative leaders feel that they have both the right and the obligation to represent cooperative interests on specific proposals. Leaders of the American cooperatives hasten to point out that this action will in no way affect their traditional political neutrality."[14] John Carson, formerly Consumers' Counsel of the National Bituminous Coal Commission, is in charge of the office.

The Cooperative League worked with the Consumers' Advisory Board during the NRA, and has since been interested in the idea of consumer representation in the government. At the eleventh annual convention of the Consumers' Cooperative Association of North Kansas City, Mo., a resolution was passed to request President Roosevelt to set up a consumer board having at least one representative from consumer cooperatives.

Friendly relations are maintained between consumer cooperatives and other consumer groups. They often join forces in working on local issues of interest to consumers. There has been much interest in the place of education about consumer cooperation as part of the school curriculum and of the place of the consumer movement in cooperative education. At the first and second annual conferences held by the Institute for Consumer Education, round tables were held on consumer cooperative education. At the second conference the round table

[14] *Cooperative League News Service*, March 28, 1940.

reported that "The cooperative movement does and must continue to participate with the rest of the consumer movement in advocating research in consumer problems, scientific mass purchasing, standards, grades, labeling and legislation favorable to the consumer."

Chapter Seven

BUSINESS USES AND ABUSES THE CONSUMER MOVEMENT

THE main outlines of the consumer movement have now been drawn. Consumer groups have established certain definite objectives rather clearly: more factual selling, based on standards, grades, and labels; freedom to educate themselves for the independent determination and expression of their wants; representation of the consumer viewpoint in the formulation of public policy.

Business interests are vitally affected by these new developments. Their responses to a movement manifested in so many ways and coming from so many different quarters have shown wide variations. In this connection a few specific considerations affecting their attitudes to the consumer movement deserve special recognition.

One factor of importance is the changing character of the distribution process. Two clear-cut patterns in the marketing of consumers' goods have emerged in the past two decades. A struggle between what is sometimes referred to as "manufacturer-dominated marketing" and "retailer-dominated marketing" is going on. Firms such as Sears, Roebuck and Co., J. C. Penney's, R. H. Macy's, and the A & P, led the way in showing the economies and profits possible by doing their own sales promotion and depending on manufacturers only for the supervision of the actual physical production of the goods. The consumer demand for information and standards has fitted in with this tendency toward greater control by retailers. The promotion of private retail brands is made easier if there is available positive information which permits comparison with nationally advertised "famous name" brands. Retailers who stand to benefit have welcomed and encouraged the consumers' demand for facts. On the other hand, some manufacturers of nationally advertised brands and the advertising media which they largely support have fought against the new trend, and against those aspects of the consumer movement which fit in with it. To some business interests the consumer movement appears to be part of an attempt to undermine the loyalty of their customers and weaken confidence in advertising. They have resented consumers' demand for information almost in the way a hostess would resent it if her guests insisted on knowing what she put into a cake before they would taste it. Advertisers have been particularly vocal. They have attempted to counteract the demand for information by insisting that consumers don't really want it and that there is no need for it. They have tried to promote this idea in all sorts of ways.

Another element in this situation is the fact that chain stores have been under fire from those independent retailers who have not been able to meet the new forms of competition. Through legislation in some states the independents have succeeded in putting tax penalties on chain stores. Representative Wright Patman tried to get a federal "death sentence" law on chains through Congress in 1939. All this brought aggressive retaliation from the chains. Openly, secretly, and semi-secretly, they poured money into a campaign to stimulate consumer organizations to support them. They developed "captive" consumer organizations for their own purposes. The objectives of these organizations often were expanded and support obtained from other interests. They introduced a confusing element into the whole consumer picture.

A second factor of importance is the relation of the consumer movement to the new "public relations" movement developed by business since the New Deal. The first reaction of business leaders to the new spirit bred out of the economic collapse of 1929 was fear and anger. They cried "Radical," "Communist," and "Red" to leaders with new ideas. But the futility of this was demonstrated to some by the sweeping victory of Roosevelt in the election of 1936. Certain business leaders had already developed the idea that it was necessary to work out a different kind of approach. In 1934 Samuel Crowther, a popular writer for business, said:

> Business is highly skilled in informing the public as to its products. The great—and often clever—trade or profession of advertising does a good job. But when it comes to making plain the relation of business to the public, of the public to business, the efforts are mostly feeble and in no wise match the vigor and intelligence, to say nothing of the plausibility, of those who would bring in some other economic system in which private enterprise would not have a part.[1]

Bruce Barton, of the advertising agency of Batten, Barton, Durstine, and Osborn, repeated this idea before the National Association of Manufacturers in 1935. "Research, mass production, and low prices," he said, "are the offspring of business bigness and its only justification. The story should be told, with all the imagination and art of which modern advertising is capable. It should be told just as continuously as the people are told that Ivory Soap floats or that children cry for Castoria."[2] And a little later in the same speech he said:

> If any manufacturer says, "I do not care what the common mass of people think about my business whether it be popular or unpopular with them," that man is a liability to all industry. No major industry has any moral right to allow itself to be unexplained, misunderstood, or publicly distrusted; for by its unpopularity it poisons the pond in which we all must fish.

A campaign to put over business-as-a-whole was begun by management. It was made through the ordinary channels of advertising and became a part of employee, customer, and community relations. Management began to take more interest in what the schools, local clubs, and civic organizations were doing. Consumer organizations naturally played an important part in this new approach. It is true that sometimes management became conscious of the need for reforms within its own enterprise; and closer examination of public attitudes sometimes

[1] See S. H. Walker and Paul Sklar, *Business Finds Its Voice* (1938), p. 6.
[2] *Ibid.*, pp. 6-8.

stimulated a greater sense of social responsibility. But it also brought attempts to prevent any critical thinking at all on the part of the public. There were systematic attempts to weaken the force of consumer organization or to divert its aims.

Another influence which should be mentioned as a contributing element to these other factors was the new opportunity opened for writers and public relations experts by the consumer movement. Good incomes could be made by giving warnings about the consumer movement, and advice as to what should be done. From the point of view of those engaged in this kind of work it was sometimes best to make the movement look wild and dangerous enough to justify the services of their pens, or the need for an aggressive public relations campaign.

Underlying factors such as these need to be kept in mind. New elements—such as the war—are constantly being introduced, which may alter the picture. It is not possible to classify businessmen into hard and fast groups according to their motives in taking action in order to guide the consumer movement into "safe" channels. Most of them, like other human beings, are probably influenced by a combination of factors. Like most human beings, they change their mind as the situation or their understanding of the situation changes. Examples included in the present chapter are simply illustrations of methods of action in which the objective has been primarily to crush, weaken, or guide the consumer movement. By some consumer leaders such attempts have been regarded as a serious threat to the effectiveness of the whole movement; but as consumer groups have realized the character of these attempts they have been drawn more closely together in their common resentment at this kind of action. Relations with business which have been more satisfactory from the consumer point of view are described in Chapter Eight.

DIRECT PROPAGANDA

The most immediate reaction to consumer criticisms and demands was an attempt to discredit the groups felt to be most responsible for the new consumer consciousness—the consumer testing agencies and the writers of the "guinea pig" literature. One of the first leaders in the campaign against them was Anna Steese Richardson, director of the Consumer Division of the Crowell Publishing Company. Speaking about the consumer movement to the Kansas City Advertising Club on May 9, 1938, she said:

> It is a movement . . . organized by men, who posing as protectors of the consumer, attack American businessmen, their methods, and their products. In sensational books, pamphlets, and bulletins, they have built up a very profitable business for themselves, many of us call it a racket . . . Why do you believe this propaganda handed to you by men who have never been in business, as your husbands are, who have never made a payroll or lain awake nights wondering how they could keep their factories or stores going?

More frankly at the Third Annual Editorial Conference at Cleveland in 1939 she pointed out the payrolls most in danger: "Without advertising there can be no magazines, and the downfall of the popular magazine means that a lot of editors will be looking for jobs in the WPA." Mr. Thomas A. Beck, vice-president of the Crowell Publishing Company, has referred to the testing agencies as "burrowing shrimps."[3]

Edward Davenport, a merchandising expert, at a meeting of the Pacific Advertising Clubs in 1938 said, "In a nation whose foundations are being attacked by radical forces such as Consumers' Research and other termites of destruction, it is not only the duty but a matter of wisdom for every merchant, every manufacturer, every advertising agent, to protect the only one free voice of power we have left in America, namely, the newspaper."[4] He suggested a program of "rabble-rousing on the right." The Associated Grocery Manufacturers of America in the fall of 1939, according to *Advertising Age* (November 6, 1939), decided that action should be taken to counteract the "adverse and destructive forces which disseminate false or misleading information about the products manufactured by members of the industry."

[3] Speech before the Associated Grocery Manufacturers of America, New York City, November 28, 1938.
[4] Reported in *Editor and Publisher*, August 6, 1938.

Consumer cooperatives have also been called antagonistic to the "American way" and condemned as undermining the whole structure of the American economy. An attack, for instance, has been launched against cooperative insurance by the Association of Casualty and Surety Executives, through a widely circulated pamphlet, *The Road to Ruin*, by Ray Murphy, which accuses the cooperative movement of "bearing the seal 'made in the U.S.S.R.' "[5]

On March 26, 1940, Miss Katharine Clayberger, representing the *Woman's Home Companion*, spoke to the Advertising Club in Lincoln, Nebr., and was reported to have said, "The consumer cooperative movement is part of a carefully planned drive against our American form of government." She chose a bad place to say it. Local cooperators protested to her and to the newspaper, and in her speech the next day Miss Clayberger was careful to explain to the Woman's Division of the Chamber of Commerce, "Such consumer cooperatives as the ones which exist here in Lincoln are a definitely beneficial thing."[6]

Hostility has been aroused against consumer education, and a systematic and well-planned campaign directed toward the schools. Roy Dickinson, president of Printers' Ink Publications, speaking before the Lithoprinters National Association Convention in 1939, was reported by the *Retail Executive* to have said that students in the universities are being given bigoted, warped, and preconceived judgments about economics and advertising. At the annual convention in 1939 of the Advertising Federation of America, Alfred T. Falk, director of their Bureau of Research and Education, charged that many textbooks treat advertising in an unfair manner.[7]

A high school textbook by Professor Harold Rugg, of Columbia University, *An Introduction to Problems of American Culture*, published in 1931, was specially singled out for attack by Mr. Falk. Speaking before the annual convention of the Advertising Federation in 1939, he said:

[5] *Cooperative League News Service*, December 14, 1939.
[6] *Ibid.*, April 18, 1940.
[7] Reported in the issue of June 28, 1939.

I urge that every advertising club represented here immediately appoint a committee to investigate the textbooks used in the schools of your own city. If the Rugg book is being used, the members of your local school board should be asked whether they approve the teaching of this kind of stuff. If this book is not used then see what books there are.

Your committee should examine every textbook that is used in courses in social science, civics, problems of democracy, citizenship and other modern names given to studies in this field. Whenever you find anything that gives an untrue picture of advertising and business, or contains the type of propaganda found in the sample I have exposed to you, please report the information to Federation headquarters . . . We intend to expose the subtle propagandists and to make a determined effort to cleanse our school rooms of the teaching of subversive doctrines.[8]

In view of this accusation, it is of some interest to examine the sample from Professor Rugg's book which Mr. Falk "exposed." He quoted the following passage (p. 455):

And who do you suppose really pays for the advertising? It is you and your neighbor and every other consumer. The manufacturer adds his advertising costs to the price he charges to retailer; the retailer adds his advertising costs to the price each of his customers pays as the ultimate consumer. Hence it cannot be denied that advertising has increased the cost both of selling and of buying goods. Perhaps you may ask then "Is advertising necessary?"

Professor Rugg has made the essential point in this paragraph that advertising is a cost and that ordinarily the selling price includes all the costs involved. Mr. Falk, however, chose to misinterpret and misrepresent the whole chapter. Commenting on the passage, he said:

So here we have a textbook categorically telling students that advertising raises prices and increases the cost of doing business. Having made this point, the author asks the student to consider whether it is necessary to have advertising at all. His own mind is evidently made up. It seems he wants the student to conclude that advertising is an economic waste and perhaps ought to be abolished.

Actually Professor Rugg concluded, after several pages of

[8] See *Retail Executive*, June 28, 1939.

discussion "summing up the advantages of modern salesman-ship through advertising" (p. 462):

We see, then, that in an industrial civilization such as ours some way of knowing who makes and sells needed products is absolutely necessary. Without such a medium the consumer has a limited means of knowing what goods are for sale. *It is true, therefore, that it is impossible to carry on our economic life today without advertising.* But we must ask ourselves if all the advertising today is wise and necessary.

Again in summing up the whole chapter on page 476, he said:

We see, then, the difficult problems of buying which confront the consumer in our modern civilization. We note the very important role played by advertising in our lives. *That we cannot do without it is clear.* That we must use it wisely so as not to mislead the consumer is equally clear. That there are dangers there can be no doubt. . . . Is it not a very important part of one's education to be taught how to buy?[9]

It is difficult to see how Mr. Falk concludes that Professor Rugg's mind is made up that "advertising ought to be abolished."

Unfortunately such methods as Mr. Falk uses to influence what is taught about advertising do meet with a measure of success. Spokesmen for advertising clubs in New York, St. Louis, Boston, Atlanta, St. Paul, and Minneapolis expressed the opinion that they will take action in line with Mr. Falk's accusations.[10] The Tenth District of the Advertising Federation at Houston, Tex., in November, 1939, passed a resolution urging the Dies Committee to "investigate the subtle destructive forces at work in our public schools."[11] By spring the Dies Committee had voted to undertake an investigation into textbooks.

The New York State Economic Council, an agency supported by business interests, has a special plank in its platform for the investigation of public education and the teaching of "subversive doctrines." In December, 1939, its president, Merton K. Hart, made a speech in Binghamton, N.Y., on "Subversive

[9] Italics in both paragraphs are mine. H. S.
[10] *Consumer Education*, October, 1939.
[11] *Advertising Age*, November 13, 1939, p. 38.

Activities in the Schools." On April 17, 1940, the Board of Education voted to withdraw from circulation the 180 copies of Professor Rugg's books which had been used as supplementary reading in the junior high schools. So great was the feeling aroused that two of the board members actually proposed a public bonfire of the book. Mr. Hart has announced the formation of an American Parents' Council on Education which has the object of "rooting out the subversive teachings which are taking place in many schools." Some of the other towns which have barred Professor Rugg's books are Cedar Rapids, Iowa; Englewood, N.J.; Glen Ridge, N.J.; and Colorado Springs, Colo.

The Inland Daily Press Association has declared war on hostile textbooks, according to *Advertising Age* (May 27, 1940). It was reported also that the Wisconsin Daily Newspaper Association has succeeded in having a textbook, *Modern Economics*, published by The Macmillan Company, removed from Milwaukee schools.

The attempt of one type of industry—and a relatively small one at that—to muzzle teachers and deaden the critical faculty of students for the sake of maintaining its own profits is certainly a good start toward undermining the "American way" which it so vigorously claims to defend. Democracy is founded on the honesty and integrity of its educational institutions and distinguished educators in all fields have risen to defend Rugg's and other textbooks from the kind of attack described. They insist that what should be taught in schools should be decided according to educational standards and not according to the interests of particular groups.

Business spokesmen, too, have recognized the dangers inherent in the type of approach made by Falk, Dickinson, and Hart. Earl Elhart, in an editorial in the *Retail Executive* of July 28, 1939, wrote:

It would be very easy for the whole advertising profession, retail as well as national, to become inflamed over these charges and to start a new kind of witch hunt to reach a climax with the burning of books at the stake. It should be realized, however, that this issue is a particularly explosive one. It must be approached with the greatest coolness and a careful consideration of the social as well as the economic issues involved. . . . The nub of the question is what kind of a picture shall be given to the students in our secondary schools and colleges of this our business civilization. Shall it be a wholly flattering portrait with abuses and evils carefully painted out or shall it show the business world as it is in everyday transactions?

Along with these attempts to discredit the so-called "radical elements" in the consumer movement there has been a type of action aimed at eliminating any recognition of conflict between producer and consumer. It takes its keynote from the new business philosophy of public relations mentioned earlier. Appeal is made through extolling the virtues and essential functions of business enterprise in American life, sometimes giving partial recognition to consumer demands, sometimes ignoring them altogether.

The NRA set an example as well as providing a stimulus to this idea. At the very time when the advice of the Consumers' Advisory Board—advice which would have saved the NRA from some of its major errors—was being impatiently brushed aside, NRA undertook to create a national psychology to aid in putting its program over. "Now is the Time to Buy" appeared on various red, white and blue posters, showing such scenes as the dome of the Capitol, Paul Revere on his steed with the title "Wake Up, Americans," or Uncle Sam in various striking poses. A typical suggestion in one of the letters NRA broadcast to manufacturers called attention to the idea of a national cigar manufacturer in distributing a display card to his retailers bearing the blue eagle and the caption:

When you buy cigars you help provide living incomes for farmers, labor, salesmen, dealers and yourself. Buy now.[12]

This, of course, represents a complete reversal of the theory that production is undertaken to benefit the consumer.

This theme of the mutuality of interests of business and the consumer has been the basis of extensive advertising campaigns

[12] See Walker M. Duvall, *N.R.A. Insignia*, NRA work Materials, No. 22, p. 39.

of the "institutional" type. The Chamber of Commerce advertised widely the slogan "What Helps Business Helps You." Hearst magazines ran a series of advertisements under the heading "Who's a Guinea Pig?" indicating the real guinea pigs to be those who used unadvertised brands. The *Ladies' Home Journal* ran advertisements explaining that this magazine is itself a consumer movement; Crowell Publishing Company ran a series "What Has Advertising Ever Done for Me?" reporting to consumers interviews with leading manufacturers which revealed advertising to have done practically everything. *Liberty* ran a series of articles in 1938-1939 by George Sokolsky on "The American Way of Life" telling the story about how advertising has been responsible for the American standard of living.

Such efforts have attempted to combat the effect of consumer organization by direct appeal to the individual consumer. A further step in promoting better relations with consumers, however, is by contact with organized groups. The Association of Manufacturers' Representatives of New York City under the leadership of Fred C. Wurtz of the Welch Grape Juice Company, according to *Food Field Reporter* (November 13, 1939), started a drive for the betterment of consumer relations in the grocery trade. Mr. Wurtz's plan called for an intensive cultivation of consumer groups by local manufacturers' representatives. It was in line with plans already under way by the Associated Grocery Manufacturers of America. These plans contemplated speaking engagements before hundreds of women's clubs in the metropolitan area, with manufacturers giving "their side of the story" to the public. They were to be interspersed with speaking engagements before headquarters of local chain organizations, wholesale grocers' associations, and before meetings of retail grocers' associations throughout the whole area. Speaking engagements, in addition, featured showings of the talking picture *I'll Tell the World* based upon "The American Way of Life" by George Sokolsky. The New York *Herald Tribune's* Bureau for Clubwomen aided in making arrangements with club groups for such meetings.

The general strategy of this whole approach is perhaps best summed up by the statement of the Associated Grocery Manufacturers of America in outlining the plan they proposed to follow with respect to the consumer movement:

It is generally felt in AGMA circles that the time is coming when a program of cooperation with legitimate consumer groups, armed neutrality with borderline groups and active hostility to radical consumer groups will come as inevitably as did a program for better trade relations after the historic mistakes made in that direction during the twenties.[13]

Consumer leaders feel that for business to evaluate the legitimacy of consumer groups is equivalent to the corresponding effort with respect to labor groups; and that consumer groups should be left alone to iron out or clarify their own differences. They also feel the overwhelming financial advantage of business groups in developing this kind of program. Generally speaking, however, they have been more concerned about attempts made to gain control over the consumer movement in which the commercial or business sponsoring interests have attempted to disguise their plans so that consumers accept their propaganda or advice without being fully aware of the special interests involved. In 1937 Professor Robert Lynd, of Columbia University, in an article in the New York *Times* drew attention to the "captive" consumer movement. No study of the consumer movement would be complete without the inclusion of examples of these organizations, or attempts at such organizations. Few of them have been of long duration.

THE AMERICAN CONSUMER

The consumer program developed around the magazine *American Consumer* furnishes one of the best examples of what might be called a "company union" in the consumer field. It was started in November, 1934, and was issued continuously until January, 1940. It was sympathetic to consumer organization and to many demands of the organized consumer movement, such as informative labeling and grading. The editor, Crump Smith, was formerly in the advertising business and started the magazine because he felt the need of more of the consumer approach in business enterprise. He first established a

[13] *Food Field Reporter*, October 16, 1939, editorial, p. 18.

biweekly organ, the *National Consumer News*. Its policy in 1934 was stated as follows:

National Consumer News is designed for and devoted to the interests of consumers—those who buy at retail for personal consumption. It is thoroughly independent, and knows neither bias nor prejudice. It is dedicated to a career of unswerving loyalty to the welfare of consumers, individually and as a group, and stands free, and always will stand free, of any commercial or other selfish influences.

National Consumer News believes that the interests of consumers can be served best through conciliation and cooperation and that this method will bring government and business to recognize the rights and importance of the retail buying public.

It struggled on without too much success until November, 1937, when it appeared with an almost completely revised setup, an expensive new format, and a rededication to its purpose:

To supply truthful, useful and practical information on consumption problems of American homes.

At the same time it distributed advertising literature describing itself as the "Golden Cord between Business and the New Consumer Consciousness" and sold advertising. In June, 1938, when the name was changed to the *American Consumer*, the position was reaffirmed:

The American Consumer is an independent publication. It is designed for and devoted to the interests of consumers . . . it is unbiased, unprejudiced and points the sane approach to the solution of consumer problems. . . .

In January, 1939, a statement was made to the effect that financial support to the extent of $12,000 had been accepted from the Direct Distributors Group, the Great Atlantic and Pacific Tea Company, Household Finance Corporation, and Sears, Roebuck and Co. This support was stated to be given because of the fundamental belief of these corporations in the policies of the *American Consumer*. The notice was somewhat inconspicuously reprinted in occasional issues afterward.

Editorial policy became increasingly opposed to the independence of the consumer movement. In June, 1939, Crump Smith wrote: "Those who believe in the American system of free enterprise which has made this country the envy of the world subscribe to the fundamental principle of the mutuality of interest between consumers and business." In July the place of business in the consumer movement was more specifically indicated. "It is urgent for progressive business leadership to assert itself," he wrote. "It has an obligation to assume at once the task of providing the consumer movement with the kind of educational information and guidance that will make it a genuinely constructive force. . . . It will save both business and consumers from the wreckage planned by power-hungry saboteurs of the American system."

In January, 1940, the *American Consumer* folded, and Mr. Smith began a "Confidential Interpretive and Advisory Service to Business" called *Consumer Movement Trends* issued weekly, in which the general view of the consumer movement was continued. Originally a printed leaflet selling at $100 a year, it was later made a mimeographed letter with a subscription rate of $25.

Both the original *National Consumer News* and the *American Consumer* particularly championed the case against hidden taxes, chain store taxation, and price-fixing laws. It offered $100 in cash prizes and a free trip to Washington for the best letter "outlining the consumer viewpoint on the new Patman bill," the winner to visit his congressman and present his ideas in person.

The circulation has been estimated as high as 82,000 of which 25,000 was newsstand. In addition to regular consumer or housewife circulation, the magazine went to home economists, home demonstration agents, women's clubs, education groups, and schools and colleges. Single copies were 10 cents; annual subscriptions, $1. Aid was given to the formation of local consumer groups and consumer education in schools. A 9-part study plan for consumer organizations and a mimeographed "Training Course in Consumer Education for Use in Secondary Schools" were prepared. An important part of the study programs for adult groups was a scheme for testing samples of advertised products by housewives. Manufacturers provided free samples and were furnished with the resulting indications of consumer preferences.

CONSUMERS FOUNDATION, INC.

A more short-lived but well-publicized organization was Consumers Foundation, incorporated in January, 1938. Its aims as stated in an organization bulletin issued at that time were as follows:

To promote the consumer interests of the people of the United States.

To encourage, assist and engage in research and education devoted to that end.

To ascertain those matters, measures or positions favorable to, or opposed to, the consumer interest, and to state in clear and objective terms where the consumer interest lies.

To obtain, correlate, interpret and make available to the public by publishing, broadcasting, or by any other means, information and results of research concerning the production, distribution and consumption of goods and services; prices and forces which influence them; monopolies and free competition; trade practices, codes and agreements; taxation; governmental and trade regulation of industry; the operation of the national economy and proposed changes affecting it; the establishment of standards, informative labeling, uniform terminology and truthful advertising, with respect to consumers goods; and any other matters of value to consumers or affecting the consumer interest.

To aid consumers in judging the value and quality of goods and services.

To foster cooperation of consumer and producer interests in the public welfare.

To assist by grant, or otherwise, other organizations which promote these purposes.

The prospectus in this bulletin was stated to be the final draft as prepared by Mrs. Bert Hendrickson, Mr. Stacy May, and Mr. Donald Montgomery of the Committee on Organization and approved by the entire board. An advisory council of one hundred civic and other leaders was also appointed. Financing was to be from individuals, private foundations, commercial and other sources, with the understanding that the foundation would have complete and unconditional freedom of action. A preliminary gift of $25,000 was made by the Institute of Distribution for necessary research.

Press comment indicated skepticism concerning the foundation's program: *Business Week* said that "it sounds like an A-1 opportunity for business to win the consumer over to its side." Actually Stacy May, Donald Montgomery, and Mrs. Hendrickson had resigned before the organization bulletin went to press. Their reasons are indicated in the following letter:

Bulletin Number One of Consumers Foundation, marked for release January 8, states that the prospectus included in the bulletin is the final draft as prepared by Mrs. Bert W. Hendrickson, Mr. Stacy May and Mr. Donald E. Montgomery, and as approved by the entire committee. This statement is misleading. The prospectus was not originally drafted by us, although it now incorporates suggestions which we made and omits many things to which we objected in the draft originally submitted to the Organization Committee.

The statement is further misleading in that it fails to disclose that we had resigned from the Organization Committee before the bulletin went to press. We resigned because we were not convinced that the procedure followed was such as to insure an organization that would operate effectively and honestly in the consumer interest.[14]

Testimony by Persia Campbell of the Consumers National Federation before the Temporary National Economic Committee made still more evident the purposes behind the formation of the foundation.[15] Quoting from a confidential report distributed in 1937 by Wheeler Sammons, managing director for the Institute of Distribution entitled "An Outline of Direct Distribution Public Relations—With the Consumer Speaking," she said:

This outline proposed a three-point program of organization: (1) a national consumer organization, (2) Consumers Foundation, Inc., (3) a national consumer mouthpiece or voice—National Consumer News or similar publication.

According to this testimony, plans for developing such a

[14] See CU *Reports*, January, 1938, p. 2.
[15] Verbatim record, Vol. 3, pp. 298-299.

program of public relations had been in process since 1935. The
Wheeler Sammons report described experiments which had
been undertaken to organize housewives with $2,500 a year or
less. This was done to determine whether enough of such low-
income housewives could be brought together to "make effective the appearance of selected housewives . . . before legislative committees and meetings of state legislators." The experiment was reported as successful.

Dr. William Trufant Foster, director of the Pollak Foundation, was director of the Consumers Foundation. Since the issuing of the first bulletin and the resignations connected with it,
the foundation has been inactive although not defunct.

NATIONAL FOUNDATION FOR CONSUMER EDUCATION

In 1936, Don Francisco, president of the Lord and Thomas
advertising agency, organized a successful campaign for the
chain stores in the fight on the Pacific Coast over the proposed
tax there. In it the help of prominent clubwomen was found
useful. After the fight was over it was decided to continue the
work according to a long-run plan, based on the principles
evolved out of the twelve-month California experience. In
June, 1937, a Foundation for Consumer Education was incorporated, with the Board of Directors of prominent educators
and citizens including Dr. George C. Mann, chief of the Division of Adult Education, Mr. Armistead B. Carter, a member
of the State Board of Education, Mrs. Doris Haney Jones, personnel director of the city of Santa Monica and legislative
chairman of the California League of Women Voters, and Mrs.
Gertrude P. Millikan, formerly connected with the State Board
of Education. The directors were stated to feel "that the consumer movement will become a great and constructive force if
it has sound leadership and sound materials with which to work.
Unfortunately the movement here, as elsewhere, has been handicapped, and at times diverted into unproductive channels,
because the sound leadership and materials have been lacking."
The object of the foundation was to act as a clearinghouse of
information available in the field, to obtain the facts and to make
them available to the public, to study groups, and to all interested

consumers, in convenient and understandable form. The lack of consumer confidence in advertised brands owing to "widespread attacks" was felt to be an obstacle in gaining chain store support and this partly explains the undertaking of such a broad program. Release of educational material through women's clubs was a major objective.

The Home-Owned Business of California, Inc., representing organized independent retailers, also waged a campaign for support among women's clubs, and in their organ, *Home-Owned News*, brought to light some interesting side lights on the Foundation for Consumer Education, as well as on how economic issues may be worked out between unwary clubwomen and high-powered publicity experts. One of the employees of the foundation resigned and took with her personal correspondence relating to the foundation activities. These were printed in the *Home-Owned News* and their authenticity has not been denied. An extract from one of the letters dated May 7, 1937, in the nature of a progress report by a foundation officer is as follows:

Just a memorandum of this week's activities.

At the meeting of the California Housewives' League in the Oakland City Hall, April 28th, I steered a resolution through commending the President on his stand against the Tydings-Miller Bill. Last Monday, I went over to Berkeley and advised Mrs. Cleverdon upon the content of the letter to the President.

On Tuesday I went over and had a very agreeable chat with Mrs. M. Ward Campbell, following up the advance work done by Mrs. Bevil. She agreed to come in on our Board of Directors on the same conditions Mrs. Clark agreed to. I feel that this is somewhat of an achievement in view of the fact that Mrs. Campbell is extremely suspicious of chain stores.

On Wednesday Mrs. Cleverdon's letter came through and we publicized it all over the State. . . . On Thursday, upon instructions from Jean Spear, I went over to Berkeley and got Mrs. Cleverdon to write a very militant telegram to the State Senators and Assemblymen against Assembly Bill 409 which is the California Robinson-Patman Act. . . .

Charlie Jacobs has been doing everything in his power to find out what our set-up is all about—without any success. Apparently he is gathering about him the same old cats and dogs he had during the campaign. If we can set up our Board of Directors as planned, we will have him licked insofar as the club women are concerned. Politics are a different matter, but I am hopeful that this will straighten itself out within the next year.[16]

As a result of the bitter opposition from the *Home-Owned News*, the foundation was forced to acknowledge the source of its funds, which it had previously felt wiser to keep undisclosed.

In the fall of 1938 a reorganization was effected partly in order to extend its scope to a national scale and partly because of the withdrawal of some of the chain store financing. A campaign for broader financial support was launched and a tentative budget set up of $60,000. Contributions came chiefly from the drug, insurance and refrigerator fields. Dr. Mann, Armistead Carter, and Mrs. Millikan were included again in the Board of Directors and E. J. Murphy, West Coast manager for the Dictaphone Sales Corporation and past president of the Pacific Advertising Clubs, added. The plan in this case was to attempt to work through the schools and teachers rather than through women's clubs and adult groups. Within a short time, however, this project also collapsed. The present status is uncertain.

NATIONAL CONSUMERS' TAX COMMISSION, INC.

In 1937 the Atlantic and Pacific Tea Company, in view of the mounting wave of antichain-store legislation, announced its intention of embarking on a thoroughgoing public relations program to make known the contributions of chain stores to general welfare. Carl Byoir and Associates were hired as public relations counsel. This agency spent a considerable amount of time gathering figures on taxes, particularly hidden taxes, and then launched a drive to build up an effective consumer pressure group of a general antitax nature. According to the trade journal *Tide*, Byoir assisted Mrs. Dick Sporburg, chairman of the Consumers' Tax Committee of the Women's National Exposition of Arts and Industries, with the results of this research.[17] Aid was given also to the organization of the New Jersey Emergency Tax Councils which were developed under the leadership

[16] *Home-Owned News*, October, 1937.
[17] September 1, 1938.

of Mrs. Ada Sackett in 1938. Byoir's organization lent six men to help organize other councils. Despite the rapid growth of these efforts, taxes were passed in five townships. Similar proposals were, however, defeated in ten other towns. Besides the A & P, contributors to the council's support were other chains, a furniture manufacturer, a shoe manufacturer, a milk distributor, a couple of farm groups, and one or two department stores. These preferred to remain anonymous.

The New Jersey Councils later affiliated with a bigger organization, the National Consumers' Tax Commission which was incorporated in June, 1938, by four businessmen. It was described in its promotional literature as a women's movement. The program and study material are planned and prepared at the Chicago headquarters.

As outlined in the official publication, the *NCTC News*, the plan is by means of study units and publicity to make a "coast-to-coast crusade against taxes that penalize the consumer and increase the cost of life's necessities." Men are permitted to join the study units as well as women, but not to become leaders. The movement spread rapidly and in March, 1939, claimed over 4,000 groups in action.

A monthly news sheet and periodical study bulletins are issued. Mrs. Kenneth Frazier, of Dallas, Tex., was the first president, and Mrs. Sackett was secretary. The women who organize units and the officers of the units are allowed travel expenses and other privileges. The *NCTC News* carries six to ten pictures of the clubwomen leaders of the units in each issue. Generally speaking, the women do not seem to be aware that the movement is not a spontaneous consumer organization.

There are no membership dues and no fees. In the first issue of the *NCTC News*, John A. Hartford, of the A & P, pledged his organization "to go along as far as it is necessary for us to go to see that your work is not hampered by lack of funds."[18]

OTHER EXAMPLES

Organizations which have been supported by groups opposing antichain-store taxes and price-fixing legislation have furnished the outstanding examples of consumer organizations deliberately

[18] November, 1938.

set up for special purposes. Examples in other fields are numerous also, though on a smaller scale.

During the fight to obtain new food and drug legislation representatives of a Joint Committee for Sound and Democratic Consumer Legislation testified at the hearings and supported legislation along the same lines as many industry groups. At later hearings witnesses appeared on behalf of the National Advisory Council of Producers and Consumers. This council was stated to be:

A cooperative council sponsored by representative consumers in consultation with manufacturers, dedicated to a better understanding between producer and consumers; the fostering of adequate and democratic laws governing consumer goods and the encouraging of an intelligent and sympathetic approach to a study of advertising regulation and other economic problems.

It was proposed to sponsor similar councils of a local nature on a nation-wide basis. Walter Pitkin, the well-known writer, Mrs. W. D. Sporburg, an officer of the General Federation of Women's Clubs, and Lee Bristol, of the Bristol-Meyer Company, appeared on the promotional literature as executive directors. Mr. Pitkin claims that the use of his name was entirely unauthorized. A survey of the opinion of 10,000 homemakers was distributed among consumer groups. According to the results of this survey:

With regard to food, drug, and cosmetic products, this cross-section of public opinion would indicate only a very small percentage of dissatisfaction in them and that largely a matter of personal preference . . . Advertising stands, in the opinion of the family purchasing agent, as an economic servant of real worth. A small percentage indicate their dissatisfaction with it. Manufacturers approached on this particular point assure us that steps are being taken within the industries and more will be taken when it is shown how advertising can be made more effective.

Another group which came to light during legislative hearings was the Consumers' League for Honest Wool Labeling. This organization prepared and distributed pamphlets and other material supporting Schwartz Senate Bill 162 and Martin House Bill

944, which provided for the labeling of virgin and reworked wool. Mr. J. B. Wilson, who represented the National Wool Growers' Association at the hearings, acted as secretary for the organization. During the course of the hearings the existence of the league was uncovered. When Senator Austin asked Mr. Wilson if there was any such thing as the Consumers' League for Honest Wool Labeling, he replied:

> The Consumers' League for Honest Wool Labeling, Senator, is the outgrowth of organizations we have had in Wyoming for some 19 years that we have been attempting to secure truth-in-fabrics legislation. The organization you speak of is an organization of which I suppose if there be a head, I am the directing head, but there are no salaries connected with it, and it is just an organization to disseminate information regarding this particular bill that is now under consideration before your committee.
>
> SENATOR AUSTIN: What kind of organization is it?
>
> MR. WILSON: Well, it is just a loose organization of friends of mine from Wyoming, with no dues.[19]

Senator Lyle H. Boren, also on the committee, questioned Mr. Wilson still more closely concerning his association with the Consumers' League and brought out rather clearly that it was simply a propaganda organization of woolgrowers whose printing and mailing costs were partly borne by Mr. Forstmann of the Forstmann Woolen Company.[20]

So great was the confusion introduced at these hearings that a representative of the National Consumers League felt it necessary to appear to testify that their organization was not related to the Consumers' League for Honest Wool Labeling; and a representative of the General Federation of Women's Clubs appeared to testify that they had not endorsed the bill, as stated in the literature issued by the league.

An organization which, under the guise of a women's group,

[19] Wool Products Labelling Act of 1939. Hearings before a subcommittee of the Committee on Interstate Commerce, U. S. Senate, 76th Congress, 1st session, on S.162, Feb. 20, 21, 22, and March 2, 1939, pp. 209-210.

[20] Wool Fabrics Labelling Act. Hearings before a subcommittee of the Committee on Interstate and Foreign Commerce, House of Representatives, 76th Congress, 1st session, on H.R.944, March, 1939, pp. 430-435.

sponsors particular commodities is the Women's National Institute. It functions as a division of the Women's National Exposition of Arts and Industries, an organization which sponsors yearly expositions featuring items of interest to housewives. The institute was founded in 1933 and conducts educational forums and exhibits. It has a National Advisory Committee with nearly sixty members, mostly prominent clubwomen. The institute prepares reports on its forums which are distributed among women's clubs and educational groups throughout the country. In 1938 it prepared a report endorsing Crown Quality rayons. In 1939 a lengthy report heavily weighted with scientific data was issued. The chief purpose seemed to be the endorsement of Vicks VapoRub and Vicks Va-tro-nol. In the same year it issued a report advocating the patronage of dry cleaners using the seal of the institute for Maintaining Dry Cleaning Standards.

The report on the common cold recommending the Vicks products has been specially condemned. In the *Journal of the American Medical Association* for February 4, 1939, it was stated:

Much of the material contained in the summary and the recommendations is satisfactory, but the obvious purpose of the whole performance was the ultimate recommendation for use of these proprietary medicines. Having secured by this circuitous technic what appears to be scientific sponsorship for the products concerned, the next step was the circulation of this leaflet. For this purpose a double barreled shotgun was employed. The first barrel was released "To the Women of America" particularly leaders of women's organizations, urging "that they present it to their organizations at an early date." The second was released "To the Educators of American Youth." In one instance the latter was distributed without first obtaining the opinion or advice of the school medical department.

The programs of the institute are concerned with health, housing, food, textiles, and finance. Its theme is "The Interdependence of Industry, Labor and the Purchasing Public." Besides its activities in promoting forums and issuing reports, it has issued a questionnaire to consumer leaders designed to sound out the extent of consumer activity and consumer attitudes toward business. It asks these leaders if they would be willing to organize study groups "to obtain information regarding the activities of consumer organizations in your community, and forward this information to our committee each month." In return for this information the institute sends the groups its reports, bulletins, and other material.

An example of consumer indignation at attempts to use consumer leaders to promote commercial ends arose in connection with the New York World's Fair. The fair included a special Consumer Interests Building. A Consumers' Advisory Committee was appointed to take charge of the building. Twenty-one of the members resigned in February, 1939. In their letter of resignation to Grover Whalen they stated:

We accepted membership on the committee with your assurance that it would be empowered to develop plans in good faith to enhance the value of Fair exhibits to consumers. We are forced to the conclusion that the purpose of the committee, as you see it, is solely to advertise the Fair to consumers and to others and to promote the commercial interest of persons enjoying the confidence of the corporation . . . the use of our names may lead consumers to the false conclusion that representation has been accorded to their interests in the planning and execution of exhibits.[21]

CONSUMER TESTING RACKETS

Flagrant attempts have been made to capture consumer trade, or to operate profitable "rackets" against distributors and manufacturers by the establishment of pseudo-testing agencies. The Consumers' Bureau of Standards was one of the outstanding examples of this type. The director, Albert Lane, operated by obtaining samples from distributors and manufacturers (in suitable sizes for personal use). Then he issued bulletins rating them. If a business man appeared unwilling to cooperate he was threatened with unfavorable ratings. The Consumers' Bureau of Standards *Reports* represented their ratings as impartial and independent, although they were only gleaned from various secondhand sources. They implied an affiliation with the Mellon Institute and the National Bureau of Standards which was actually nonexistent. On the complaint of Consumers Union, Albert Lane was ordered by New York courts to change the name of his publication. The Federal Trade Commission also brought action

[21] New York *Times*, February 28, 1939.

against him. He has since attempted to start up again and to issue a Consumers' Bureau *Guide*.

The FTC has also issued a cease and desist order against the Ross Roy Service, Inc., which tested "impartially" various makes of refrigerators showing the superiority of Kelvinator models. It was found that it had actually been set up as a selling device by the Kelvinator Corporation and the FTC found that the handbook issued and the comparisons made were not "accurate, authoritative, or unbiased," as claimed.

Another short-lived service was the Consumers' Informer of California, which also undertook to rate various products. While the directors had no apparent connection with commercial interests, no attempt was made to ensure the scientific accuracy of the information. In one issue, for example, aluminum cooking utensils were said to contaminate food, a statement with no foundation in fact. Examples could be multiplied to show the variety and extent of possibilities in misusing the testing idea.

USING THE CONSUMER AGAINST LABOR

In recent years several organizations have sprung up which have been hostile to organized labor on the basis of the consumer interest. An organization called the Women of the Pacific offers its support to firms which have strikes in progress. It makes contacts through a fortnightly newspaper, the *American Worker-Consumer*, which is dedicated to the consumer and the open shop. A similar organization, the Neutral Thousands, was started on the West Coast for the same purposes. No elections of officers are held, but these organizations have been stated to be "spontaneous rebellions of women against labor tyranny." Although contributions are accepted from anyone interested, there are no dues or assessments on members and the names of contributors are not published. Hearings before the Senate Civil Liberties Committee and before the National Labor Relations Board have indicated that they were organized and backed by employer interests. Other organizations hostile to labor have traded on the names of consumer organizations favorable to labor: for example, the Consumers' League of America, in Akron, Ohio, and the American Consumers' Union in St. Paul.

Chapter Eight

BUSINESS AND CONSUMERS MEET HALFWAY

THE consumer movement was at first regarded by businessmen as a passing fad of idle clubwomen who had temporarily taken to protesting about their purchases as a diversion from their bridge. Now they recognize it as one of the most important features of the world in which they operate, not to be lightly dismissed, not a thing to be easily discredited or controlled. The trade journal *Advertising Age*, in January, 1940, stated that "the record of discussion, action and comment on this subject in business and marketing circles during 1939 indicates that it has now indubitably moved into the position of No. 1 problem of American business and industry."

The serious interest business now has in the consumer movement is indicated by the large number of surveys made during the past two years. One of the first of these appeared in June, 1937, in *Sales Management*. Next came an important special study by the Crowell Publishing Company, which was issued in bulletin form of that same year. It filled 25 pages and was extensively used in the bitter campaign referred to in the previous chapter which Crowell's carried on against the consumer movement. In 1938 the *Retail Executive* began a weekly column friendly to the movement under the caption "The Consumer Wants to Know." In May, 1938, this paper issued the first of its special annual supplements covering the year's developments in the consumer field. In April, 1939, a significant 14-page survey of the consumer movement was published by *Business Week* as a special report to executives. At about the same time an article describing the growth and importance of the consumer movement appeared in the *Harvard Business Review*. The most notable of all these publications appeared in 1939 when the American Retail Federation issued a 58-page study (with a 45-page appendix) dealing with the rise of the consumer movement and the character of its present composition. Within three months the first printing of 1,500 copies of the pamphlet was exhausted. Not long after this the Association of National Advertisers issued a 171-page confidential study of the consumer movement, containing analyses of the programs of most of the component organizations together with short statements of the affiliations and activities of consumer leaders. This was sold to members at $7.50 a copy. Although it was in some ways the most comprehensive of the surveys, the picture it gave of consumer activities was considerably distorted by the bias with which it was written. At the annual meetings of the Association of National Advertisers in October, 1939, the results of a survey on "The Scope and Penetration of the Consumer Movement" were reported by Dr. George Gallup. The poll was financed by the Advertising Research Foundation. Although not actually a project of the Institute of Public Opinion, it was carried out according to its methods. It was one of the most important documents contributing to an appreciation of the importance of the consumer movement. *Advertising Age* in a special issue in January, 1940, gave six full pages to the history and background of the consumer movement. In March it offered $500 in prizes for the best essay on the subject of improving consumer-advertising relations. Crump Smith's weekly "Confidential Advisory and Interpretative Service," *Consumer Movement Trends*, referred to in the previous chapter, was started in January, 1940. Trade journals such as *Printers' Ink, Advertising and Selling, Tide, Food and Drug Trade, Food Field Reporter, Women's Wear Daily,* and many similar publications have given a good deal of attention to the consumer movement.

By the prominence given to consumer activities of all kinds, consciousness of the consumer movement has been developed among the rank and file of subscribers to these various trade publications. Whether or not they themselves have felt any direct impact from the consumer movement in their own business experiences, the effect of reading such captions as "Consumer Problems Monopolize Attention at Ad Men's Meetings," "Advertising and Business Put on Grill at Consumer Meet," "Emergency Seen as Stimulus to Consumer Action," has made them keenly aware now of the growing force of the movement. The passage of the new Food, Drug, and Cosmetic Act and of the Wheeler-Lea amendment to the Federal Trade Commission Act, both specifically concerned with greater consumer protection, further served to give a feeling of reality to this new awareness.

On numerous occasions business leaders have stated their recognition of the right of consumers to organize and their acceptance of the movement as a natural economic phenomenon. Edgar Kaufmann, president of the Kaufmann Department Stores, Inc., of Pittsburgh, in the spring of 1939 declared that he believed consumer organizations are now strong enough to be able to force retailing to deal with them as it does with other groups such as manufacturers and laborers. "It is the duty of the retailer," he said, "to make an effort to understand the fundamental problems and needs of the consumer. This may require patience and tact, which do not always seem advantageous at the moment, but which are bound, in the long run, to keep this country the worthwhile place to live and to work, which we all want to see it remain."[1]

The right of consumers to establish consumer cooperatives and to form testing agencies of their own has also been recognized by many of the more progressive business groups. In discussing the interest of the retail industry, Louis Kirstein, chairman of the Board of Trustees of the American Retail Federation, indicated the position he thought the retailer should take with respect to consumer cooperatives. "The retail industry should recognize the growth of consumer cooperatives as a legitimate form of retail distribution," he stated.[2] Public statements in support of the work of the testing agencies are not so

[1] First Retailers' National Forum, May 22-23, 1939, *Proceedings*, p. 36.
[2] *Ibid.*, p. 127.

common, but in private discussions recognition of the value of their contributions is frequently given.

It is, of course, the idea of the consumer as a buyer that is uppermost in the minds of businessmen. When they think of consumer demands, they naturally have in mind the people who come and buy their particular goods and services at their own counters. And since the general plea of the consumer-buyer at the present time is for more information, this is the central theme of current consumer-business relations. While the demand for commodity information by no means represents the entire scope of the consumer movement, it has significance as a concrete illustration of the way in which organized consumers may take part in direct relations with other economic groups. The satisfactory working out of such relations gives consumers a recognized place in the economic affairs of the market through their organizations, as well as through their activities as individual buyers.

Many sellers have welcomed the opportunity to work with consumer groups. The seller, in fact, finds many advantages in considering favorably some of the demands of consumers. To give more information voluntarily about goods may forestall stricter government regulation. The more honest and efficient sellers have much to gain from an orderly market in which customers are both discriminating and informed. Lack of information creates problems for the commercial buyers in individual stores just as it does for household purchasers. The commercial buyers would like the manufacturers to give them more information too, and can use the demands of consumers for more information to reinforce their own requests. More knowledge regarding what the consumer wants would eliminate some of the expense involved in carrying on an unnecessarily wide range of goods and would lessen the need for the drastic markdowns that now have to be made periodically. Many retailers feel that if customers were better informed as to what performance could reasonably be expected from their purchases the mounting costs caused by returned goods would be diminished.

Retailers who are promoting their private brands have reason to welcome information and standards which enable consumers to compare their products objectively with those that are nationally advertised. The outstanding examples of this are found in the drug field. Montgomery Ward's mail-order house advertises Bayer's aspirin at 59 cents per 100 tablets side by side with their own brand at 16 cents per 100. Information about standards of purity and the quickness with which the aspirin dissolves leaves no doubt that the private brand tablets are as good as or better than the expensive advertised product.

For one reason or another, then, consumers and businessmen have come together to consider their mutual interests or to try to iron out their differences. The actual kinds of machinery which have been developed to promote closer business-consumer relations are considered in the present chapter.

THE NATIONAL CONSUMER-RETAILER COUNCIL AND THE ADVISORY COMMITTEE ON ULTIMATE CONSUMER GOODS OF THE AMERICAN STANDARDS ASSOCIATION

Retailers have the closest contacts with consumers. They have taken the lead in recognizing the consumer movement and setting up machinery to discuss the mutual problems of the retail seller and the household buyer. In 1937 the National Consumer-Retailer Council was organized for this purpose.

The council was developed out of the work of the Advisory Committee on Ultimate Consumer Goods of the American Standards Association. The American Standards Association had since 1928 included the American Home Economics Association in its membership and had taken part in various standards projects of interest to the ultimate consumer. The growing strength of the consumer movement led to the establishment in 1936 of an Advisory Committee on Ultimate Consumer Goods to promote further the work on consumer standards. Household consumers are represented on this committee by the American Home Economics Association, the American Association of University Women, the General Federation of Women's Clubs, the National League of Women Voters, and Consumers Union; and institutional, commercial, and government buyers through the National Association of Purchasing Agents. Retailers are represented through the National Retail Dry Goods Association, and by merchandising executives and technical advisers from larger stores. The federal government participates through five agencies: the Bureau of Home Economics; the Bureau of Foreign and Domestic Commerce; the National Bureau of Standards; the Retail Price Division of the Bureau of Labor Statistics; and the Consumers' Project of the Agricultural Adjustment Administration. In addition to the above groups, the American Association of Textile Chemists and Colorists and the American Society for Testing Materials have recently accepted invitations to membership in this committee. Manufacturers are not represented on the Advisory Committee, for manufacturing groups in the consumer field are so numerous and so diverse that it would be difficult to get adequate representation in a committee small enough to work effectively. Manufacturers are, however, represented on committees that do the actual work of drafting standards.

Work in the field of consumers' goods represents only a small and comparatively recent part of the activities of the American Standards Association. This organization is a federation of 72 trade associations, technical societies, and government departments. For the past twenty years it has been serving as the national clearinghouse for private standardization work. During that time, the present methods for developing national standards have been built up and also policies for dealing with intergroup problems. These ASA methods are based on the fundamental principle that all groups affected by a standard have an inherent right to participate in its development. The underlying philosophy of all their standardization work is well summed up in the association's motto: "Standardization is dynamic, not static. It means not to stand still, but to move forward together."

The Advisory Committee on Ultimate Consumer Goods advises the association in all consumer goods work. The committee has advisory supervision over the selection of new projects for standardization. It checks on the personnel of technical committees engaged in developing standards. It follows up the work in progress. It makes recommendations as to the advisability of approving standards, but does not itself develop standards.

In carrying out its functions, the Advisory Committee exercises supervision and conducts investigations in a variety of ways. Supervision to assure maintenance of the consumers' and retailers' point of view is obtained through continuing contact with technical committees. These are now engaged in the development of standards for domestic refrigerators (both electrical and those cooled with ice); standards for bedding and upholstery; sizes of children's garments and patterns; sheets; photography, gasoline, sun glasses; devices for the hard of hearing; household ladders; and valid certification.

The work on the development of standards for sizes of children's garments has aroused much popular interest. The standards are to be based on the results of a nation-wide survey of 36 body measurements made on 147,000 children between the ages of four and seventeen. This was carried out by the Bureau of Home Economics and completed early in 1940. One of the most confusing and inconvenient situations in the retail market should be greatly improved if these standards are put into practice. Children's garments will be sold according to such things as height, weight and arm length, rather than the customary method of adding anywhere from one to four years to the child's actual age.

Through subcommittees, the Advisory Committee is investigating the possibilities of developing standards for shoes, silver-plated tableware, coordination of testing methods for consumers' goods, and laundering and dry cleaning. Activities of the subcommittee on shoes have already led to a publication by one government agency (Circ. National Bureau of Standards C149 —Shoe Constructions) and to the appointment of an interdepartmental committee by agencies of the federal government, which has led to the initiation of comprehensive studies of the foot and the effect of footwear on health.

The difficulties in the way of developing standards for consumer goods are so frequently stressed that it is of interest to point out the fact that examples of their successful application do exist. One of the most noteworthy cases is found with the standards for gas ranges. These are in four parts: The first lays down requirements for sound, rigid, durable construction necessary for the safe and convenient operation of all types of gas ranges. The second part lays down performance requirements for domestic ranges for use with natural and manufactured gas. It covers gas consumption, leakage, completeness of combustion to prevent contamination of the air by carbon monoxide, operation of safety devices, surface temperature of ovens and broilers in insulated stoves, efficiency of thermostats, no-rusting oven interiors, etc. An elaborate baking test is provided to ensure that "the heat distribution in the oven shall be so uniform that cookies distributed in the oven, heated to 375 degrees F., will be evenly browned in not more than 11 minutes." Parts three and four contain similar performance requirements for ranges which burn bottled gases. The work has been done under the leadership of the American Gas Association and it has been an important factor in the radical improvement in gas-burning appliances in the past few years. For example, when a study of gas-fired water heaters was undertaken, it was found that all such heaters then on the market permitted the escape of an amount of carbon monoxide which was dangerous to health. This discovery led to redesigning of all water heaters on the market at that time. Ninety per cent of the gas appliances made in this country now comply with these standards.[3]

A number of attempts to formulate American standards for consumer goods have failed, however, even though they were undertaken by unanimous agreement of all the groups concerned. Plans for a dictionary of terms used in the retail trade were stymied by the failure of a retail group to follow through. Similarly, one on bed blankets, and one providing for the labeling of shrinkage of cotton textiles failed because of a change of heart on the part of the manufacturers. In the latter case, the proposed standard on shrinkage was later embodied in a mandatory standard by the Federal Trade Commission to prevent unfair trade practices.[4]

The use of specifications in merchandising goods involves the problem of how the customer can be assured that goods comply with the standard. An individual consumer, unlike a corporation,

[3] P. G. Agnew, "Standards on the Way," *Industrial Standardization,* February, 1940.
[4] *Ibid.*

has neither the knowledge nor the facilities to test his purchases. When standards are used in merchandising, manufacturers and retailers state on the labels and in their advertising and other sales representations that the goods comply with the standard. Then comes the question of verifying such statements. To meet this question, many forms of "certifying" compliance by independent laboratories, by other testing agencies, and by manufacturers and stores have been used. The consumer finds himself confronted with literally hundreds of such seals of approval, verifications, and so on with no way of judging their actual merits.

One now often hears, "Who is to certify the certifier?" The American Standards Association is studying the subject actively. A representative committee, appointed to lay down principles that ought to underlie a valid public certification has been at work for some time, and the association has adopted the following policy:

1. Any program of certification, labeling or grade marking, in order to be adequate should be based upon specifications which are publicly available and nationally recognized.

2. It is for the group or groups substantially concerned with the specifications to decide whether there is to be certification or labeling; and the ASA itself cannot directly take any primary responsibility in respect to such activities.

3. Any certification or labeling program should be effectively supervised by a properly qualified body; e.g. a trade association, or a testing laboratory, operating under proper administrative management.[5]

The consumers' goods program of the ASA does not touch the style element, nor is it in any sense the purpose of the work to force any product off the market or to control in any way the lines of the products offered for sale. The objective is, in a word, to bring about standards that will make words mean the same to both buyer and seller, and will in this way give consumers more intelligent and effective control over their purchases.

The work of the Advisory Committee on Ultimate Consumer Goods is limited to the question of determining what acceptable

[5] *Ibid.*

standards are. Out of the experience of the groups working together on this problem grew the idea of a broader forum where consumers and retailers might discuss other mutual problems and engage in more active promotional work for increasing the use of standards. In the fall of 1937 a Consumer-Retailer Relations Council was set up. The name was later changed to the National Consumer-Retailer Council. The basic purposes of this council are educational. Its objectives as revised in June, 1940, are as follows:

(a) To educate consumers, distributors, manufacturers, and the general public with respect to the value and use of adequate standards for consumer goods and the value and use of uniform terminology in describing consumer goods.

(b) To promote the general use of informative labelling and to educate consumers, distributors, manufacturers, and the general public with respect to the use thereof.

(c) To promote the use of truthful and factual information in advertising and to educate distributors and manufacturers with respect to the use thereof.

(d) To promote informative salesmanship and to educate distributors and manufacturers with respect thereto.

(e) To develop and promote the use of suggested codes of ethics for both retailers and consumers.

(f) To encourage practices which will tend to reduce abuses of such privileges as customer accounts, returning goods and deliveries, and to educate consumers, distributors, and the general public with respect to the benefits to be derived from such cooperation.

The establishment of the council was largely due to the enthusiasm of some of the members of the Advisory Committee on Ultimate Consumer Goods. The original organization members of the council were: the American Association of University Women, the American Home Economics Association, and the General Federation of Women's Clubs, representing consumers; the National Retail Dry Goods Association and the American Retail Federation, representing retailers. Since then the National Association of Food Chains and the National Shoe Retailers' Association have joined the council. Consumer groups have the power to veto plans. The council engages in no legislative activities and in no commercial activities.

Harold W. Brightman, vice-president of Bamberger's Department store in New Jersey, is chairman of the council. The board of trustees in 1939-1940 included: Sadie Orr Dunbar, president of the General Federation of Women's Clubs; Harriet Howe, in charge of Consumer Education, American Home Economics Association; P. G. Agnew, executive secretary of the American Standards Association; D. M. Nelson, vice-president of Sears, Roebuck and Co.; and Faith Williams, of the American Association of University Women. The executive secretary of the council is Roger Wolcott, whose advertising agency in Boston was a pioneer in advocating informative selling. The 1939 budget amounted to approximately $15,000. The membership fee is $100 for each organization. This is supplemented by retailers.

Committees have been set up including representatives from both consumer and retail organizations. Where manufacturing interests are involved, representatives are invited to participate, and recently some advertising groups have become interested in taking part in the work of the council. Each committee in itself serves as a forum for a specific phase of the council's work. The standing committees functioning at present are: Informative Labeling, Promotion of Standards, Store Program, Customer Program, Advertising, Customer Abuses of Stores Services, and miscellaneous committees such as those on library research and other phases of the council program.

Evidence of concrete achievement is expected to appear first from the work of the Labeling Committee. Its first publication was a tentative guide on informative labeling. This included a discussion of the general aspects of informative labeling, grades, and standards and their advantages to each economic group. A proposed outline for informative labels covers the following points: composition, construction, performance, care, uses, and sponsor of the product. Specific check lists have been prepared for labels for blankets, mattresses, cotton sheets, terry towels, kitchen knives, window shades, men's hosiery, men's shirts, woven piece goods, women's hosiery, slips and petticoats, and women's wash dresses. These check lists have been submitted to thousands of consumers, retailers, and manufacturers in order to secure a consensus of their opinion as to what information should appear on labels. Similar check lists are being prepared for other products. The committee tries to get the best advice possible from experts in government bureaus, from manufacturers, technicians, and other qualified people.

The success of this committee is central to the whole program of the council. Concrete achievements are already in evidence. In mail-order catalogues and in some department stores, labels modeled on the informative methods advocated by the council can be found. The National Association of Food Chains, to which all the major chains except the A & P belong, is considering the adoption of informative grade labels on foods, a practice which the A & P has already used for several years. An impetus to the use of grade labels may come from their adoption in 1940 by two California canners, N. Schuckl Co. and U.S. Products Co.[6]

A separate committee works for the promotion of standards by educating consumers, distributors, and manufacturers to understand the value and use of existing standards for consumers' goods; and by obtaining financial assistance to provide technicians necessary to further the work of the Advisory Committee on Ultimate Consumer Goods of the American Standards Association.

Many retailers have appeared skeptical as to the need for giving more information to consumers and the program of the council has even been regarded with hostility in a few quarters. A program of informative labeling would naturally have some tendency to alter consumer choices both among products and among items of the budget. Less money, for example, might be spent on sheets by a program of informative labeling which would enable the buyer to get sheets suitable for her purpose at lower prices than she usually pays. Money saved by better buying might be spent outside the retail store for recreation or medical care. Conversely, of course, as many retailers argue, the consumer might buy higher quality goods if she had assurances that the higher price really represented worth-while extra quality.

[6] Cf. *Tide*, July 15, 1940, p. 16.

How an individual store would be affected by a program of informative labeling would depend on the nature of the demand for the product and how keen price competition would be if the customer were fully able to compare qualities.

Considerations such as these make the reluctance of some sellers to participate in the scheme understandable. To many the hazards and discomforts of change seem great, perhaps disastrous. The real strength of the consumer movement has not been proved to them. It appears likely, therefore, that the effectiveness with which the program can be carried on will partly depend on how insistent consumer groups are on obtaining results, either through machinery such as the council or through legislative means.

It will also depend on how effectively merchants can be educated to newer forms of merchandising, to the general conditions of the market, and to the problems of consumer demand. Only in this way will they become less anxious about the effects of yielding to consumer demands for information and more aware of the immediate and long-run advantages they may gain through improved store practices. In line with this, the Store Program Committee of the council works out procedures which may be followed when adopting a policy of informative merchandising. It is based on the experience of stores already carrying out such a program.

A pioneer project in developing a program of informative labeling was that started by Gimbel Brothers in Philadelphia. This large department store appeals mostly to middle and lower-middle income customers. The company had been using the services of a commercial testing laboratory for five years on a fee basis. The laboratories were housed in the store building. They were used chiefly to help the store buyer in making purchases, as an aid to promotion, and to analyze customers' complaints on returned goods. In December, 1936, a research department was established to work out a consumer relations program. This was adopted by the management in February. For seven months the research department and a testing committee worked on the plans before actually launching the program.

The entire project was based on giving informative labeling

and complete testing reports to the public. The testing reports were used to supplement the labels and were made accessible to customers who wished to find out more than could be put on the label. When the program was actually started in September, 1937, the store had over 200 items which had informative labels and complete testing reports. These 200 items were sold in approximately 35 departments. Between September, 1937, and March, 1938, the number of tested items was more than doubled.

Before launching the program, complete backing by top management was obtained, cooperation sought from the store buyers, and the sales force educated regarding the program. When the store was ready to put the scheme into operation, a luncheon meeting of consumer representatives was arranged. About 150 women from clubs, colleges, and consumer groups were told about the new program. Their criticisms and suggestions were invited and their cooperation asked in explaining it to the members of their organizations. A director of customer relations was appointed to take over the function of supplying speakers and information of all kinds. The store took an active part in the formation of a local consumer relations group in collaboration with the local Chamber of Commerce. It also collaborated with the National Consumer Retailer Council. Advertising publicity was kept as conservative as possible. The program is of special interest because it is an example of how a particular store placed its entire organization and its merchandising policy in line with a new appreciation of the importance of the consumer movement.

Another store which has adopted a program of consumer-retailer relations is the William F. Gable Company of Altoona, Pa. It is particularly interesting because of its cooperative relations with the local high schools and colleges. The store's facilities are offered to students for instruction in store selling, buying, and management through a "College and High School Cooperative Service." The store itself has adopted a program of informative selling.

One of the most outstanding examples of a long-time successful consumer relations program is that of Sears, Roebuck and Co. In recent years, its work has been tied in more closely with the program of the National Consumer-Retailer Council. As part of its general public relations program, Sears has a consumer education division which since 1930 has been developing educational exhibits and sending them to farm women's groups, home economics classes, and women's clubs. In 1939 exhibits were used 6,638 times, a 400 per cent increase over 1936. Testing of products and factual information is basic to its mail-order method of selling. In 1940 a new series of merchandise labels was introduced—"Infotags." The tag tries to give all the information about materials and workmanship which the consumer might want to know—such as thread count, breaking strength, weight, facts about selvages, sizing and hemstitching, for sheets. In addition, the tags indicate the reasons for price differences among different qualities of the same product. The labels are used to train salespeople as well as to inform customers. Sears has special advantages in that its large-scale operations permit the use of its own specifications in buying and manufacturing. Its 29-year-old testing laboratories have contributed greatly to the development of the consumer program.

R. H. Macy's department store in New York has used a consumer testing laboratory for a specification buying and selling for some of its stock. It features a "Red Star" label on goods which it claims have met the "rigid specification requirements" of its testing bureau. The qualities for which the product has been tested are indicated on the label. A successful radio program, "Consumer Quiz Club of the Air," was started in 1938 and is broadcast daily. From the studio audience of ordinary housewives three or four are chosen by lot to answer questions about the performance and uses of different products. Whether the answers given by the housewives are right or wrong, the facts in each case are stated, as based on information from Macy's Bureau of Standards. No specific reference is made to Macy products. Typical questions answered are: Is a mouthwash a deodorant? What can you do to overcome a shine on your nose? What is taffeta? What is the advantage of a bias-cut slip? When should a baby first wear shoes? What is the difference between single and double damask? Should a dog wear a coat when he goes out in cold weather? How can you get the maximum amount of efficiency from a vacuum cleaner? Why does it appear to be practically impossible to get sheets with two-inch hems on both ends? How can you tell a good quality mirror? What type of roller skates should you buy for a child under five years of age?

Similar plans have been developed in other cities and in other stores. Successful ventures such as these are largely dependent on a store's being big enough to have testing facilities of its own. One of the hopes of the National Consumer-Retailer Council is that smaller stores will be able to share in the advantages of specification buying through the acceptance of common standards for consumers' goods. The Store Program Committee has sent out questionnaires to the operating, merchandising, advertising, laboratory, and training divisions of a selected group of stores known to be carrying on a consumer relations program. A manual of recommended procedures for stores based on the returns was published in 1940. The object is to approach the problem from the point of view of store management rather than from the merchandising, training, or promotion department standpoints. The essence of the program for stores interested in adopting the policies of the council, according to the manual, lies in knowing more about the quality characteristics of the merchandise sold, in making this knowledge available to customers, and in developing facilities for a closer and more friendly contact with customers on an organized and continuing basis. At the Chicago meetings of the American Retail Federation in 1940, the council's executive secretary, Roger Wolcott, said to merchants, "It is not a publicity stunt or device for quick sales. It is a long-term program which affects every function of your store."

A Committee on Customer Program is developing techniques for local consumer groups to enable them to attain a better meeting of minds between their members and local merchants on mutual problems regarding the buying and selling of merchandise. These activities are coordinated closely with those of the Store Program. Test campaigns are being conducted in two cities to determine the effectiveness of the suggested program.

At the suggestion of consumer representatives, a study of customer practices which add unnecessarily to the cost of distribution has been undertaken. Its function is to encourage practices that will tend to reduce abuses of such privileges as charge accounts, returns, deliveries, and similar services. The first job it proposes to do is the preparation of a manual of suggestions of how returns can be reduced.

Although the council was originally formed by retailers and consumers, it has brought in the points of view of manufacturers and advertisers. Manufacturing representatives are sometimes included when commodities in which they are directly concerned are under discussion. A standing committee on advertising was formed in 1940 in which representatives from the Association of National Advertising Agencies, the Advertising Federation of America, and the Advertising Bureau of American Newspaper Publishers Associations are included. It discusses methods of bringing the attention of manufacturers and retailers to the value and use of more truthful and factual information in advertising by inaugurating test campaigns—both retail and national—which will incorporate the kind of information asked for by customers.

Particular attention has been given to the work of the Council because it is believed that as an example of a joint attack on the mutual problems of buyers and sellers it illustrates a new type of collective bargaining between organized consumers and organized sellers. Its major function so far has been educational for both groups.

As far as the growth of the consumer movement itself is concerned, it has given added significance to the work of the women's clubs. They have been the main source of consumer support in these efforts, although all consumer groups have regarded the experiment favorably. It has helped to give the women a clearer understanding of business problems and philosophy. It has also been a strong coordinating force in their consumer work. They do not ordinarily work so closely together, especially on controversial questions. Not since the demand for suffrage have women been drawn so closely together on a common issue. They now have much more experience both in the legislative field and in the public relations field. Business and government have become more aware of the quality of their leadership. In spite of individual differences, they have been able to put forward a basic platform of consumer relations with business. The platform is such an important formulation of policy that it may be quoted in some detail. It opens with a careful statement of the general point of view:

We believe that:

1. American democracy is based upon a recognition of the dignity and worth of the individual, and upon the willingness of the individual to accept a limitation of personal liberty in order to make possible a maximum of freedom and equality for all. We recognize that the self-interests of individuals as well as of economic groups are frequently in conflict and that the maintenance of our democracy depends upon establishing and maintaining a balance in our economic life which insures an equal recognition to the interests of each group.

2. Consumers have two major interests: to secure enough income to buy goods and services which will satisfy their needs and provide them with the greatest possible satisfaction; to be able to identify those products and services which are best suited to their special needs at prices they can afford to pay.

3. In order to protect these interests, consumers need to understand the basic economic principles which affect our standards of living; to take an intelligent part in the formulation of policies and legislation that promote or hamper the general welfare; to promote the development and general use of simple methods of identifying quality and performance in consumer goods that make intelligent buying possible.

4. Consumers must have the opportunity to make those free and intelligent choices among the goods and services available which are possible only when consumers are given adequate and accurate statements of fact about the relative quality and performance of the goods and services offered to satisfy their needs.

5. Many traditional practices of manufacturers and retailers leave consumers without an opportunity to exercise real freedom of choice based upon their own judgment and experience. This lack of opportunity creates a sense of helplessness and frustration in the individual which in turn has brought about an extensive and unfortunate re-

sentment against business which, while often vague and indiscriminate, tends to be vindictive.

6. It is possible for the consumer and business to work together in good faith to their mutual advantage and without jeopardizing the legitimate self-interest of either group.

7. Constructive work of this kind will contribute more to the welfare of consumers, distributors, and producers than restrictive legislation and punitive measures.

8. The goal of cooperative work between consumers and business should be: an intelligent and sympathetic understanding of the problems of business by consumers, and the problems of consumers by business; active work on the development of useful and accurate definitions, standards, and performance specifications for consumer goods and services which will make intelligent buying and selling possible; active promotion of the use of sound factual information now available in the distribution, promotion, and sale of consumer goods.

Other points in the platform include a statement of their belief in the necessity for making definitions of goods and services by standards and specifications and by simple grade labeling systems where possible, through machinery such as that of the American Standards Association. Methods of informing the consumer through labels, advertisements, and other selling devices are developed in detail. The value of using the machinery of the National Consumer-Retailer Council and the importance of consumer education are stressed. Worthy of special note is the specific mention made of the need for independence in the education of the consumer:

The education of the consumer, like all other education, must be kept comprehensive, objective, and without bias. To this end, special care must be taken to safeguard the consumer point of view: (a) in the use of speakers or materials from commercial sources; (b) in organizations formed to protect or further consumer interest, or when cooperating with other groups promoting a common interest.

Whenever consumers participate in cooperative activities they must name their own representatives.

No funds should be accepted for the promotion of consumers interests or activities without full publicity as to their source and full control over their use.

No other group should be delegated to speak for them.

No cooperative program should be undertaken in which business interests are in a position to dominate or outvote the consumer interest.

The platform has been frequently presented to business groups and is becoming recognized as the basis for consumer-business relations.

The American Retail Federation has become one of the most active promoters and supporters of the council. This federation includes the National Retail Dry Goods Association and several other national retail trade associations as well as 24 state organizations. It is devoted to promoting the welfare of the retailing occupation and a recognition of its importance in national life. At its first annual forum in Washington in 1939, particular attention was given to a consideration of the interests of consumers. John M. Cassels, director of the Institute for Consumer Education, was invited to present the consumer case at that meeting. In 1940, at the Chicago forum, a special luncheon session on consumer relations was scheduled, at which Mrs. Sadie Orr Dunbar, president of the General Federation of Women's Clubs, was a featured speaker. The pamphlet prepared by Werner Gabler, distribution consultant for the federation, "Labeling the Consumer Movement," has already been referred to at the beginning of this chapter. Dr. Gabler analyzed the background which makes the consumer movement an inevitable part of economic life today and stressed its importance as a constructive factor in social and economic adjustments.

BETTER BUSINESS BUREAUS AND THE CONSUMER MOVEMENT

Another example of the effect of the growing interest of business in the consumer movement may be found in the extension of the activities of Better Business Bureaus. While they have contributed to the work of the National Consumer-Retailer Council, new emphasis has also been given to their own efforts in the consumer field.

These bureaus grew out of a "Truth-in-Advertising" movement which began about 1911. In 1940 there were Better Business Bureaus in over 70 cities representing an aggregate population of more than 60,000,000. There is a National Association of Better Business Bureaus which affiliates all the local independent bureaus and a National Better Business Bureau which is concerned with national advertising. About 25,000 business concerns and professional men support these organizations and contribute approximately $950,000 a year to their activities.

The Better Business Bureaus have tried to educate gullible consumers in the interests of fair trade. Businessmen through the bureaus have attempted to establish fair competition and to eliminate fraudulent advertising. Speaking before the second annual conference of the Institute for Consumer Education in 1940, Mr. Kenneth Backman, of the Boston Better Business Bureau, pointed out that in addition to this selfish desire there is a "community interest, a desire to make the business world a better world. Actually the support and expansion of Better Business Bureaus is a recognition, on the part of business, of increased social responsibilities."[7]

Stores joining a Better Business Bureau pledge themselves to maintain fair trade practices, and pressure is brought by the manager of the bureau on members who fail to conform to them. A *Guide to Retail Selling* describes proper use of names for fur, linens, etc., and enumerates acceptable trade practices. It is based on legal decisions, Federal Trade Commission rulings, government standards, and similar sources of information. A series of Fact Booklets, such as *Facts about Furs, Facts about Jewelry, Facts about Cosmetics,* has been prepared to explain to the consumer the nature of products and what claims can be made for them accurately. These are carefully prepared and have been generally accepted as unbiased and useful material of value to the consumer. A *Guide to National Advertising* has been issued to help national advertisers. Particular emphasis is given to the terms and meaning of the Food, Drug, and Cosmetics Act of 1938.

These guides have tended to promote more informative advertising and selling by prohibiting the use of terms and phrases which are misleading or confusing to consumers; by promoting

[7] *Proceedings,* p. 14.

the use of uniform terminology, standardizing the definitions or meanings of various terms; and by requiring, in many instances, the disclosure of material facts. In developing these definitions of terms the bureaus have made surveys of consumer opinion and knowledge which have yielded interesting results. On one question concerned with the meaning attached to terms describing woods, 50 per cent of the consumers surveyed understood that the term "combination mahogany" referred to an article composed of mahogany and some other wood, while 8 per cent thought it meant furniture composed of wood other than mahogany; 5 per cent thought it meant mahogany and mahogany veneer; 15 per cent thought the term meant mahogany veneer and some other wood, while the balance said they didn't know what the term did mean. This indicates the confusion which exists in the understanding of selling terminology, and the need for standardization and education in the use of terms.

Another investigation, as to the meaning of the word "mothproof," indicated that it meant something entirely different to the industry than it did to the public. Consumers thought that an article so designated was immune from attack for the life of the article with no reservations. With few exceptions manufacturers of textiles and insurance companies appeared to have a more qualified meaning in mind.[8]

The work of the bureaus was summarized by Mr. Backman as following a four-point program:

1. Fraud prosecution
2. Fraud prevention
3. Promotion of fair advertising and selling practices
4. Consumer education in money management, in buying and taking care of merchandise, in everyday relations with business

Most bureaus operate several divisions, including a financial division, merchandise division, and publicity division. Many maintain separate consumer service divisions. Others have special divisions for certain industries, such as coal, schools, lumber.

Approximately 138,000 complaints on fraud are handled annually through the bureaus. Where the facts warrant such

[8] Cf. Kenneth Backman, *loc. cit.*, p. 15.

action, they are, with the additional evidence uncovered in the investigations, referred to the appropriate government agency, whether federal, state, or municipal. Approximately 12,000 complaints are referred to government agencies annually. Thousands of inquiries also are received from these sources. The bureaus sometimes assist in the enactment of laws that act as fraud preventives, such as jewelry auction laws and state advertising laws. Normally, however, they stay out of legislation.

In 1939, 106 radio stations gave 1,400 hours (over 58 days) of time to the bureaus. Over 6,000,000 lines were devoted to bureau advertisements in more than 371 newspapers, with a total circulation of 12,000,000. These advertisements generally appeared weekly. Over 5,430 news items were published. Nearly 2,000,000 bureau bulletins were printed and distributed, while over 700,000 pamphlets and posters prepared specifically for consumers were distributed. Over 120,000 posters were displayed on employee bulletin boards, in libraries and other places, illustrating and warning against various fraudulent schemes and unfair practices. Over 350,000 of the *Fact* booklets were distributed in 1939.[9]

Two important events in the growth of the consumer movement have been the annual Business-Consumer Relations Conferences sponsored by the National Association of Better Business Bureaus in 1939 and 1940. At each of these conferences leading representatives from business, government, education, and consumer organizations took active parts in comprehensive two-day programs. At the Buffalo conference in 1939 Harry Riehl, of the St. Louis Better Business Bureau, outlined a plan for the establishment of a Better Business Bureau Research Institute. It was approved by the Board of Governors and is now under consideration by members. The general purposes of the institute would be to conduct research and make surveys in advertising and selling practices affecting the public interest; to conduct, assist, and encourage educational research in, and studies of, commodities, investments, and services, and of related advertising and selling practices; and to gather and dis-

[9] *Loc. cit.*, pp. 18-19.

seminate impartial, factual information so developed in order
to foster more informative selling and more intelligent buying.
The management and control of the corporation would be
vested in a Board of Directors made up of the persons consti-
tuting the Board of Governors of the National Association of
Better Business Bureaus. The board would appoint committees,
including an Advisory Committee and representatives of the
consumer, educational, business, professional, and technological interests needed to assist in accomplishing the purposes of
the institute. The institute would be financed by contributions
from bureau members and other sources which subscribe to
the purpose and nature of the institute's activities and approved
by the board. The proposed draft of the institute activities includes the possibility of establishing their own research laboratory facilities if needed in obtaining facts. The distribution and
collection of facts through an agency such as this would add
greatly to the strength of the bureaus. It would, also, make
available material of great value to all workers interested in
consumer problems. If accepted by the bureaus, it should do
much to promote harmonious consumer-business relations by
clarifying on a factual basis the issues involved.

It is interesting to observe that developments among retailers
in this country have been paralleled elsewhere. In 1935, a Retail
Trading Standards Association was established in Great Britain.
This was organized largely through the leadership of the Amer-
ican-born London merchant, H. Gordon Selfridge. It grew
out of the work of the Retail Distributors' Association and has
included some manufacturers and wholesalers. It was designed
to form a basis for a long-time campaign to improve public
relations between retailers and the public, the manufacturer,
and the legislature. One of its chief aims is to eliminate misleading advertising.

The association has issued a handbook, *Standards of Retail
Practice* for use by retailers to define terms and practices in
common use. To give the consumer corresponding information
less technically, it issued an *Intelligent Woman's Guide to Shopping*. It publishes a bulletin which gives publicity to firms vio-

lating their rules, and its members are entitled to display an insignia indicating their support of the objectives and policy of the association.

The machinery for dealing with the infringement of its standards consists of a Tribunal, composed of five people: an experienced arbitrator, a commercial lawyer, a women's club leader, an editor of a woman's magazine and testing institute service, and an economist. Legal action under the Merchandise Marks Act of 1887 is taken by the association against members of the trade who are found misrepresenting their products.

In 1938 it established a Testing House which tests and certifies merchandise in the textile field. The association works closely with the British Standards Institution and an agreement has been made which precludes the Retail Trading Standards Association from setting up standards of quality without the approval of the British Standards Institution. Membership dues and gifts for the Testing House support its work.

According to the Fifth Annual Report the education of the consumer and of its own staff is considered of special importance. "The mere compilation of descriptions and practices," it says, "is of little value if the results repose on library shelves and are not brought forcibly to the attention of every manager, sales person, and purchaser in the country . . . consumer education has made rapid strides in the United States and an even greater problem had to be faced there."

When the war broke out, the association was faced with the problem of whether its work should be continued. Its members unanimously decided to do so. Although finances had to be somewhat curtailed, they felt that "Now that the adequate and orderly distribution of merchandise to the ordinary consumer is a matter of national policy, it is imperative that distributors should think in terms of quality, adequacy of description, and the elimination of misleading practices." The work of the Testing House was found useful too. When the British Standards Institution, for example, introduced specifications for the obscuration value of curtain and blind materials for black-out purposes, applications were received for tests on fabrics to be carried out against the new specification. Special apparatus was installed for dealing with this type of work.

CONSUMER-RETAILER RELATIONS AND NATIONAL DEFENSE

On August 29, 1940, merchants from more than fifty different retail trade groups sent representatives to a conference called by Miss Harriet Elliott, consumer adviser on the National Defense Advisory Commission. The purpose was to discuss cooperation between her office and retail merchants. With this new and major problem of national defense in the foreground, consumers and retailers have found further opportunities to work together on questions of mutual concern. The outstanding characteristic of their previous discussions had been their concern with methods of obtaining and presenting information about product characteristics and performance. Now the matter of prices in relation to quality is becoming more prominent. To distinguish between justified and unjustified price increases, to recognize changes in quality, are matters of growing importance to household consumers now that they must compete with the new demands made on national resources for defense.

In opening the conference Miss Elliott said to the retail representatives: "You as retailers and all of us as consumers have a common concern at the present moment. We all know the danger we face in a time like this of prices going into an upward spiral that would seriously upset the functioning of the whole economy. . . . It is my hope that out of the present conference will come machinery for continuing cooperation between the retailers of the country and the Defense Commission for dealing with this type of problem and all the other economic problems in which we have such a real and urgent interest in common."

The afternoon session of the conference was devoted to a discussion of "A Practical Program for Retailers' Participation in National Defense." Mr. Fred Lazarus, vice-president of the F. R. Lazarus and Co., Columbus, Ohio, stressed the urgent need for retailing to take an active part in developing an effective and efficient program if government controls were to be avoided. Discussion on "Checking Unwarranted Increases at the Pre-Retail Level" was introduced by Mr. Oswald Knauth, president of the Associated Dry Goods Corporation of New York; on the "Problems of Speculative Buying," by Mr. Lewis Cole, chairman of the Executive Committee, National Association of Food Chains; on "Quality Changes, Standards, and Substitution," by Mr. H. W. Brightman, chairman of the National Consumer-Retailer Council; on the "Retailer Interest in the Free Flow of Goods," by Mr. Hector Lazo, executive vice-president, Cooperative Food Distributors of America.

At the close of the conference an advisory committee of nine members was appointed to formulate methods for continuing cooperation between retailers and the Consumer Adviser's Office. It is studying methods for putting into effect the unanimously adopted resolution:

The representatives of retail merchants here assembled announce that it is their intention to devote their efforts to prevent so far as possible any unjustifiable rise in retail prices, by urging upon the general retail trade vigorous opposition to all price increases which appear to be unwarranted and which might cause difficulty to the Government and the consuming public.

We agree to cooperate wholeheartedly with the National Defense Advisory Commission in determining the justification of any price rise that might take place; in exchanging information; and in advising with the National Defense Advisory Commission as to the wisest plan to pursue.

We announce that, providing the cost to us of the merchandise that we sell does not vary substantially, and providing also, that our cost of doing business does not increase substantially, we will not alter past methods and practices in arriving at our selling prices.

Mr. Ben Lewis, chief economist in the Consumer Adviser's Office, pointed out that "The prime characteristic of a free, open, effective market is the ready availability of information which will permit interested buyers and sellers to make intelligent decisions concerning quality, price, and timing. This means abundant information—complete, accurate, pointed, and available to all. The free market as an instrument of defense will fail, and our democratic program of total defense will be impaired to the extent that consumers must make their purchases on the basis of fragmentary, inaccurate information and rumors concerning qualities, available and potential supplies, and prices." He warned that "We shall not ignore the appearance of out-of-line prices, nor shall we accept them as inevitable features of a production and marketing system busy with defense. To the best of our ability, we shall undertake a realistic analysis of threatened or actual increase in prices, and shall seek an explanation from parties participating in the increase in those cases where our study discloses no sound economic cause or purpose. If the explanation does not explain, and if the increase is not abated, we shall be prepared to resort, through the Commission, to publicity. In extreme cases, where the facts warrant and will sustain such action, we shall not hesitate to call upon the assistance of the appropriate government agencies in breaking log jams which clog the channels of consumer goods and threaten the program of civilian defense."

OTHER EXAMPLES OF CONSUMER-BUSINESS RELATIONS

An attempt to promote the use of standards for consumer goods was proposed in the spring of 1940 as the Institute of Standards, Inc. The project was first conceived several years ago by A. A. Mezerik, of *McCall's Magazine*, as the Scientific Research Institute. Although it has not yet been put into operation, the procedure outlined in the original plan is of interest, because it embodied special features to win consumer support. A system of certification based on voluntary standards set up by recognized standardizing bodies was the essence of the scheme. The plan was to license manufacturers to use a seal indicating conformity to "American Standard No. . . . Grade . . . (obtainable on request and verified by the Institute of Standards)."

Procedure was outlined as follows: A manufacturer or any other member could ask for adoption by the institute of a standard for, perhaps, an electric refrigerator. The institute staff would then assemble all standards available or under discussion in recognized standardizing bodies such as the American Standards Association. The staff would discuss these standards with member manufacturers. When their willingness to produce and advertise according to the standard would be evident the standard would be submitted to a Consumer Board of Review for acceptance or rejection. This board, composed of representatives of consumer organizations, would be provided with facilities for the study and consideration of the standard. The board could call in outside technical assistance if it desired. When a standard was considered acceptable by the Consumer Board of Review manufacturers could request selected testing laboratories to confirm their adherence to it and receive the certifying seal.

The manufacturer member then would send his refrigerator to any of the member testing laboratories equipped for this type of testing. The laboratory report would be confidential and the private property of the manufacturer who paid for the test. If the refrigerator met the standard, the manufacturer would be automatically entitled, upon application to the institute, to use the official institute symbol, subject to the conditions of the licensing agreement which he would execute with the institute. The symbol would be intended as impartial proof of conformance to a published, recognized standard. The manufacturer could use the symbol in all his advertising if statements made about the technical character of the product were consistent with the standard and if he agreed to submit the product to periodic tests. Provision would be made for taking into consideration changes in standards.

A manufacturer would become a member of the institute by payment of a $200 fee. He would pay the cost of the test and a 10 per cent fee assessed by the laboratory for institute maintenance. This would pay for the laboratory membership. Consumer organizations would pay a fee of $50 a year.

Publisher members would pay a fee of $200 a year plus a pro rata assessment to make up the institute budget. They would elect the Board of Trustees and give the institute editorial support. Eligibility for membership was stated as follows:

1. Any manufacturer who is in sympathy with the objectives of the plan, even though standards may not be available at the time for the product which he manufactures.

2. Any laboratory possessing the facilities, test procedures and integrity to perform testing adequately.

3. Any publisher whose editorial policies are in accord with the objectives of the Institute.

4. Any consumer organization, unless it was founded to further an economic interest other than consumption, or unless its consumer program embraces objectives which are in conflict with those of the charter organizations.

The primary purpose in establishing the institute was to increase confidence in advertised products. Otto L. Wiese, editor of *McCall's*, in launching publicity on the plan in the fall of 1940, wrote to manufacturers:

—I am writing to you in the hope that we, as publishers, and you, as manufacturers, can collaborate—with consumers and testing laboratories—to bring order and direction to the consumer movement in America. This movement has grown out of discord into a position of prime importance to manufacturers and publishers alike. . . . In considering membership in the Institute of Standards, I hope you will recognize the wisdom implicit in a united approach of leading manufacturers to the consumers—an opportunity that is offered by the Institute. I am sure you will also grant that a consumer movement co-operating in this program with you may be a valuable force in your merchandising efforts. In effect, the Institute of Standards, established under the leadership of Business—and not Government —provides a sound basis for the stabilization of confidence in advertising.

Consumer groups which were invited to become charter members of the Consumer Board of Review were the same as those supporting the National Consumer-Retailer Council: the General Federation of Women's Clubs, the American Association of University Women, and the American Home Economics Association. Participation in a proposal of this sort would, of course, require sanction by the organizations involved, through their boards of directors, council meetings, or other machinery. The publicity released by the Institute of Standards in the summer of 1940 indicated that the women had already given support to the plan, although this official action had not been taken. In November 1940, the executive committee of the American Home Economics Association voted against participation in the Institute of Standards. The following statement was released with the announcement of this decision:

The executive committee of the American Home Economics Association has voted not to participate in the Institute of Standards, Inc., the organization sponsored by McCall's Magazine as a means of increasing consumer confidence in advertising and advertised products through the development and use of standards for consumer goods. The American Home Economics Association, which has worked consistently for more than thirty years to promote standards for consumer goods, is already a member body of the American Standards Association and the National Consumer-Retailer Council, Inc.

This action, which was taken only after extended study of the proposed Institute, was based on the belief that the Association's own work to improve the situation of the consumer buyer, in which the promotion of standards for consumer goods is one phase, could be done most effectively if it was not identified with the Institute.

Last July when the plans of the Institute were discussed in the press, it was erroneously reported that the American Home Economics Association, the General Federation of Women's Clubs, and the American Association of University Women had agreed to participate in the Institute. This action of the American Home Economics Association is believed to be the first official action taken by a consumer group with regard to the Institute.

The details of the original plans for the Institute have been altered, but the project was still being discussed in the winter of 1940-41.

The Institute symbol was not intended to be a seal of approval, but an impartial proof of conformance to a published, recognized standard. In this it differs from the great number of seals and certification symbols now in existence. Best known of commercially backed seals is the long-established Seal of Approval of the Good Housekeeping Institute. The Federal Trade Commission case against it for misrepresentation to the consumer and unfair competition was still pending in the fall of 1940. As a result of this action, changes in the claims for some seals and guarantees have already been made. Just before the Federal Trade Commission issued its complaint, *Good Housekeeping* reworded its statement "every product guaranteed as advertised—see page 6" that had adorned advertising-page margins. For it there was substituted a more cautious direction to "see Good Housekeeping's advertising guarantee" where the limits of its scope are carefully explained. *Parents' Magazine* dropped its two seals, one "Accepted-Parents' Magazine Consumers Service Bureau" and the other "Guaranteed by Parents' Magazine as advertised therein," and substituted one new seal reading "Studied and Commended—Parents' Magazine Consumer Service Bureau." The final outcome of the suit against *Good Housekeeping* is being awaited with interest by both business and consumer groups, since it may have some influence in determining the course of future consumer-business relations.

The preceding examples have been described because they are specific instances where the impact of organized consumer activity on the practices of organized business groups may readily be seen. There are many cases where trade associations and individual business enterprises have worked to improve competitive practices, to promote factual selling or to collect and disseminate general information about commodities or family finance. This has often been done without any particular pressure coming from consumers and the results have been valuable to them. It is, however, a wide field of investigation beyond the scope of the present study.

One example of trade association activity which may be mentioned, however, is the action taken recently by the National Association of Broadcasters. In accordance with the commercial section of the code adopted in 1939, provisions for the acceptance of accounts became effective in October, 1940. These provisions limit the acceptance of accounts to "products and services offered by individuals and firms engaged in legitimate commerce; whose products, services, radio advertising, testimonials and other statements comply with pertinent legal requirements, fair trade practices, and accepted standards of good taste."

Time limitations (with ample provision for exceptions) are

made for the length of commercial copy. These vary from 2½ minutes for nighttime 15-minute programs to 9 minutes for hour daytime programs. The matter of "standards of good taste" is clarified by listing the following types of advertising and products as not acceptable:

1. Any spirituous or "hard" liquor.

2. Any remedy or other product the sale of which or the method of sale of which constitutes a violation of the law.

3. Any fortune-telling, mind-reading, or character-reading, by handwriting, numerology, palm-reading, or astrology, or advertising related thereto.

4. Schools that offer questionable or untrue promises of employment as inducements for enrollment.

5. Matrimonial agencies.

6. Offers of "homework" except by firms of unquestioned responsibility.

7. Any "dopester" tip-sheet or race track publications.

8. All forms of speculative finance. Before member stations may accept any financial advertising, it shall be fully ascertained that such advertising and such advertised services comply with all pertinent federal, state and local laws.

9. Cures and products claiming to cure.

10. Advertising statements or claims member stations know to be false, deceptive or grossly exaggerated.

11. Continuity which describes, repellently, any functions or symptomatic results of disturbances, or relief granted such disturbances through use of any product.

12. Unfair attacks upon competitors, competing products, or upon other industries, professions or institutions.

13. Misleading statements of price or value, or misleading comparisons of price or value.

In releasing the statement of the code, Edgar L. Bill, chairman of the Code Compliance Committee, wrote: "Here is an industry code which has won support of both consumer and business, liberal and conservative, press and government, Catholic and Protestant. It is, in effect, an insurance policy for the American system of privately managed, commercial and competitive broadcasting. It is an insurance policy whose beneficiary is, as well, the American public itself." How effective the code will actually be in raising standards remains to be seen.

Chapter Nine

DO THE PIECES MAKE A PATTERN?

PRECEDING chapters have indicated the variety of interests which go to constitute the consumer movement. On the surface at least, it looks like a confusing and somewhat surprising mixture. There are, however, common underlying threads running through the different kinds of activity. These were summed up in the first chapter under four headings: the general desire for the greatest possible real income; the demand for more information about commodities, about wise choice, and about the economic system; the recognition of the need for integrity in buying and selling; and the insistence on independence in education and action. Some groups put emphasis on one or the other of these, some are concerned with all of them. Clearly the movement taken as a whole does make sense.

The maturity of the consumer movement may be illustrated by contrasting the organization and work of the Consumer Adviser's Office of the Advisory Commission to the Council of National Defense with the earlier efforts of the Consumers' Advisory Board of the NRA, described in the first chapter. With the institution of this office, provision for consumer representation has been made once again in a program calling for major changes in public policy. A woman has again been chosen to head the office. Miss Harriet Elliott, dean at North Carolina College for Women and a specialist in social sciences, is in charge of the program.

The National Defense Advisory Commission was appointed in May, 1940, and has seven members. Their functions are concerned with: production resources and production structure; raw materials necessary for national defense; transportation; labor; agriculture; price stabilization; consumer welfare. In some cases, of course, these functions overlap. Housing, for example, includes problems concerned with materials, prices, transportation, labor, and consumer welfare. In this case a housing coordinator was appointed responsible to the whole commission. The Consumer Adviser's Office is organized into four divisions. These are: economics, welfare and security, civic contacts, and housing. Its functions may be classified under six headings roughly arranged in the order of their immediacy with relation to the current activities of the commission as a whole:[1]

1. *To make sure the commission, in reaching decisions on matters that come before it, gives due consideration to the effects of one course of action or another on the welfare of people as consumers.* This does not mean that Miss Elliott opposes every proposal that involves any sacrifice of consumer welfare. If ordering planes means that there would be minor changes in automobile models next year, for example, the loss to consumers would obviously be slight. If, however, the buying of quinine or any other drug by the army and navy in large quantities might raise the price so high that low-income families could not buy it, thus endangering their health, Miss Elliott would certainly be expected to question the necessity of the order.

In performing the foregoing function, Donald Nelson, coordinator of purchases, who is responsible and reports directly to the President, is also in a position where he can keep consumer welfare in mind in planning defense orders. As vice-president of Sears, Roebuck and Co., Mr. Nelson is well known among consumer leaders for his favorable attitude toward the consumer movement.

2. *To make sure that the specific problems created by particular military measures are dealt with as satisfactorily as possible.* It is Miss Elliott's duty to minimize or offset the ill effects

[1] See John M. Cassels, "The Program of the Consumer Division," in *The Consumer and Defense*, edited by Frances Hall, Institute for Consumer Education, 1940.

of the problems that will naturally follow newly expanded or developed munitions plants and training camps, including housing, sanitation, recreation facilities, milk supply market arrangements, economic relations, welfare and security. She will also be concerned with problems arising out of the draft and the calling of the National Guard, such as the basis of selection, the provision for dependents, and the status of men in service in regard to social security. Some of these will be shared with other members of the commission. The responsibility of seeing that adequate housing is provided is shared with Sidney Hillman, head of the labor division; matters of the food supply, with Chester Davis, head of the agriculture division; and making sure that supplies of drugs or chemicals are adequate, with Edward Stettinius, head of the raw materials division.

3. *To promote economic efficiency by efforts to secure the effective functioning of the price system and advising on matters of monetary and fiscal policy from the consumer point of view.* It is Miss Elliott's duty to help to "preserve economic stability" by preventing unwarranted price increases, restraining speculation or panic in purchasing, and dealing with similar problems. In this she works closely with Leon Henderson, head of the price division, with the Consumers' Counsel of the Department of Agriculture, with the Consumers' Counsel of the Department of the Interior, and with many other government agencies. If after investigation an unwarranted price increase is discovered, the people responsible are called into a conference and warned of the possible ill effects of their actions. If this fails, the division may resort to publicity. If necessary, the Federal Trade Commission, or the antitrust division of the Department of Justice can be called in. To check hidden deterioration in products, Miss Elliott's office is supporting the work of the Consumer Standards Project in the Department of Agriculture and is cooperating with the National Consumer-Retailer Council in promoting the use of standards and informative labeling. Close cooperation is planned with state and local defense commissions, which have been set up in practically all the forty-eight states.

4. *To promote and coordinate positive measures for consumer welfare that are essential to a total defense program.* Under this heading Miss Elliott is concerned with the problems of welfare, education, recreation, housing, and nutrition. One of the main problems to be tackled is to educate consumers to choose the right kinds of food in the right proportions, and to develop distribution arrangements which will make more adequate diets available for those in the lowest income groups, where the most important cause of malnutrition under existing conditions is sheer lack of income. Last month she issued a call for concerted action to "make America strong by making Americans stronger" in a special issue of *Consumers' Guide*. She urged organized groups and individuals to bring this about by: starting a municipal radio market news service and school lunch program; working for low-cost ways of selling milk, fruits, and vegetables for low-income families; establishing diet clinics for food-buying problems; encouraging production of home-grown foods and their preservation, when possible; supporting the Food Stamp Plan; and promoting government grading of food, by urging merchants to sell and consumers to buy by grades. She advised consumers to keep in touch with what their local, state, and national governments are doing toward these ends.

In the field of housing, positive measures are needed to bring standards up to the levels required for health and efficiency. Work toward this end has been carried on for some years by the U.S. Housing Authority through its slum-clearance and public building programs. The Consumer Adviser's Office has a responsibility to see that the normal development and expansion of this work is not dangerously interfered with by the diversion of public attention and public funds to military defense activities.

5. *To consider the possible consequences of an intensification of the present emergency and to prepare, in anticipation of certain situations that might arise, preliminary plans for meeting them.* Since this function is less urgent than the preceding four, nothing of importance has yet been done along these lines. Under this heading would fall the enlisting of the cooper-

ation of consumers in directly promoting military defense objectives. Urging consumers to buy coal in the summer to lessen
the strain on transportation facilities in the autumn would be
an example of this kind of work.

6. *To look still farther ahead to the problems that will arise in
readjusting the nation's activities to a normal peacetime basis
when the emergency is over and to anticipate some of the steps
that must be taken in dealing with them.* General plans with
regard to this have not yet been developed. In the matter of
housing for defense workers, however, the Consumer Adviser's
Office has taken the long-range view that the new projects
should be permanent wherever the community is permanent
and time allows for this type of construction.

Actually this part of the program is of special importance
since the problems with which Miss Elliott's office is concerned
are as vital for peacetime objectives as for national defense.
Many people feel that one reason for the tragic world situation
today lies in the failure of governments to marshal the resources
of their countries toward doing something in more prosperous
times and under more favorable conditions to provide for basic
consumer needs. Frank Graham, president of North Carolina
University, last August struck the keynote of this consumer
position in presenting the report of a round-table discussion on
Social Well-Being at a national conference of civic organizations
called in Washington by the Consumer Adviser's Office:

> As we look at the national situation, we see a peace-loving people
> only recently being totally geared with coordinated military and
> industrial defenses against invasion and attack from without, and
> only a little less recently being equipped with many vital social
> defenses against poverty, unemployment, insecurity, disillusionment
> and despair, those socially poisonous causes and recruiting areas for
> disruptive incursions and attacks from within. . . .
>
> There are democratic defeatists in America, members of the
> Sixth Column, unbelievers in the resources of this land and the
> ability of the people of this democracy; disbelievers in the American
> dream of the freedom and equal opportunity of all the American
> people. They patriotically stand for the military and industrial
> defense of America, but sincerely do not believe we can afford to

provide for total defense of America. . . . We have the economic resources, the industrial plants, the sciences and technology, the human skills, the creative intelligence, and the democratic responsibility . . . to make total defense a defense of, and a step toward the total abundance of freedom and democracy of all the people, who are what the defense is all about, from whom all our defenses come, and without whose spiritual faith and democratic morale all our defenses collapse. . . .

Members of Miss Elliott's staff include Caroline Ware, chairman of Social Studies for the American Association of University Women; John Cassels, director, Institute for Consumer Education; Ben Lewis, professor of economics, Oberlin College; Gay Shepperson, formerly state director of the Works Progress Administration in Georgia; Carleton Sharpe, manager, Green Hills Housing Project near Cincinnati; Mrs. Minnie Fisher Cunningham, General Federation of Women's Clubs; M. L. Wilson, Department of Agriculture; Leland Gordon, professor of economics, Denison University; and Ruth Ayres, chairman, Consumer Division, New York City League of Women Voters.

The Consumer Adviser's Office swung into action quickly. On August 1 and 2 of 1940 a conference of national civic organizations met in Washington. Over 80 leaders participated in the conference and 55 specialists attended as consultants. Round-table sessions were held on: Consumer-Buyer Problems; the Consumer Adviser's Office and Organized Civic Groups; Social Well-Being; Nutrition as a Basis for Physical Fitness; and Public Health and Consumer Aspects of Housing. Mrs. Sadie Orr Dunbar led the discussion on consumer-buyer problems and the group reported their basic positions as follows:

Consumers wish to see the defense program carried on vigorously and effectively. They are prepared to make sacrifices *if* and *when* they are *necessary*, but, we agree that the making of *unnecessary* sacrifices will only undermine population efficiency and add to the maladjustments in the functioning of the economy. . . .

We agreed that, in general, consumers will serve best, not only their own interests, but also those of the whole economy, by insisting that all the unemployed workers, idle plants and unutilized resources be brought into effective use in production as a means of maintaining the best possible standard of living.

The following recommendations were suggested for consideration by the Consumer Adviser's Office:

(a) That accurate, up-to-date information be made available on the prices and quality of consumer goods, and on the general situation with regard to inventories and supplies which may affect prices.

(b) That consumer groups be aided in developing the necessary understanding and interest to get such information used effectively.

(c) That, since information as to the quality of consumer goods is particularly necessary in a period when quality changes and substitutions are likely, existing standards for consumer goods should be compiled and disseminated widely among consumer groups; that the cooperation of business people in the use of standards should be sought. Where standards are not available, informative labeling should be considered and new standards developed.

(d) That the Consumer Adviser's Office consider steps to prevent unwarranted increases in price.

(e) That the Consumer Adviser's Office try to see that the effects on consumers are duly considered in planning rearmament measures, that the problem of taxation be considered as it falls on consumers; that the Commission be urged to be wary of special interests cloaking selfish ends in terms of national defense.

The other round tables similarly emphasized the importance of their special subjects. Particular stress was laid throughout on the obtaining of continuous and accurate information and on the need for working closely with existing local groups in every community. As a result of the discussion on "Nutrition as a Basis for Physical Fitness," for example, the following was recommended for consideration by the Consumer Adviser's Office:

(a) That local groups, recognizing that a well fed people is essential to defense, support school lunch programs and other projects, both to teach the proper use of food and to make such protective foods as fruits and vegetables more available to low income families.

(b) That in these efforts local groups call upon the professional nutritionists in their communities in order to insure the soundness of their efforts.

(c) That the Consumer Adviser's Office consider issuing "kitchen front" pamphlets so that the food people eat and the food which the women of America prepare for them will aid in raising the physical fitness of our people.

The round table on Social Well-Being recommended that the Consumer Adviser's Office work to fill the gaps in social defenses such as low labor standards, low levels of health and nutrition, exclusions and prejudices among different groups, low living standards, and lack of understanding and participation in democratic life. It also recommended that the Consumer Adviser's Office set up means of communication with national and local organizations which could serve as a two-way channel of information between the office and private groups.

Miss Elliott, in addressing the conference, explained the responsibility of the Consumer Adviser's Office as extending in two directions: on the one hand, to the protection of American consumers against the hardships and maladjustments to which they might be subjected in the course of armament construction if attention were not continuously directed to civilian as well as military needs; on the other hand, to a positive responsibility for strengthening the human defenses of the country through achieving and maintaining standards of health, nutrition, physical fitness, and social well-being necessary for adequate defense. "In assuming this responsibility," she said, "we are thinking of consumers in the broad meaning of the word, and are viewing our task in terms of the realities of the American situation today. Someone has said that in the United States we can have guns and butter too. You might say that one of the functions of the Consumer Adviser's Office falls under the word 'butter.' "

The conference held by the Consumer Adviser's Office with representatives of retailing was described in the previous chapter. Similar work has been undertaken with wholesalers and manufacturers.

The rapid organization of the Consumer Adviser's Office and its prompt action are significant witnesses to the rapid strides that the consumer movement has made in the past few years.

Yet the question still is sometimes raised as to whether the movement is really a healthy growth in economic and political life. Does the introduction of specific consideration of the consumer interest weaken public administration by removing a sense of government responsibility for the welfare of consumers? An idealistic view of government functions must recognize some validity in this position. Realistically considered, however, the specific recognition of the consumer interest plays a vital role in our present scheme of things.

How to get effective action taken for the general good of the community as a whole is, of course, the basic problem of government. If it is argued that the representatives in a democratic government should renounce all local or partisan claims upon them, and should each attempt to reach conclusions on the basis of what he thinks would be in the best interests of all; if, in other words, we would like to see more conscious thought given directly to problems of the whole community, then we will still find consumer views congenial. Because we are all consumers the consumer point of view must include a consideration of the interests of society as a whole. Most of us can figure out our own consumer interests—perhaps calling on the aid of specialists in food, clothing, or housing—and can present them with some degree of certainty. That at least should be a responsibility of democratic citizens. We can also recognize directly the consumer needs of other citizens. Only as consumers succeed in making known their needs and wants can we expect to attain a truly democratic solution to the question of what constitutes national economic welfare. A democratic society, therefore, is justified in recognizing and encouraging an articulate consumer movement as an aid to establishing public policy.

Sometimes it is argued that if the representative of every group effectively presents his own point of view a balance will be worked out through discussions and pressure which will promote the general welfare more satisfactorily than would any other practical procedure. If this is so, then the need for consumer organization becomes even more vital. Active and aggressive consumer groups would need to be developed on issues where they have special interests, or these interests would be entirely neglected. We have already seen this neglect on tariff questions. We have seen some beginnings of effective consumer action in the case of milk and of meat. If we accept the view that our national policies are to be developed through the balancing of the claims of all the different special interest groups we can hardly deny that the consumer interest needs to be much more effectively brought into the picture than it has been in the past.

In observing the growth and place of the consumer movement, the presence of conflicts of interests with the interests of other groups cannot be ignored. This is true whether we are thinking of the broad interests of consumers as a whole or of groups with special consumer interests. Consumers themselves may sometimes be shortsighted and by failing to recognize their long-run interests may come into conflict with the public interest. In recognizing the need for a consumer movement these considerations must, therefore, be kept in mind.

It has been emphasized before that the immediate interests of the consumer as a buyer are naturally in conflict to some extent with the interests of sellers. The businessman wants to make as much profit as possible; the consumer to get as much for his money as he can. Businessmen want high prices if they will result in higher profits for them; the consumer-buyer wants the lowest price possible. The same is true of the relation of the immediate interests of consumers and those of farmers and laborers. That does not mean, however, that the consumer necessarily wants the lowest price possible, nor that the consumer-buyer is always entitled to the "best of the bargain." Even though his immediate interest may be to get an article at the cheapest price, he has a long-run interest in the efficient functioning of the economy. This may require a rise in the prices of particular products. Many consumers do not feel that, if the price of wheat is lowered through the wasteful cultivation of plains that are better designed by nature for grazing, that it is in the consumer's interest. If the price of milk is reduced through uncontrolled expansion of production to a level that prevents farmers from adequately maintaining their facilities, that is not in the consumer's long-run interest. If lower prices of industrial products result from a prolonged competitive struggle in which the permanent plant and equipment of a whole group of manufacturers is seriously run down, or if low prices are obtained through employment of sweated labor in the dressmaking industry or the extreme depression of wages in the coal-mining industry, consumers will suffer from the instability of economic conditions that may be expected to result. If the price of apples did not go up in a year when the crop was short, consumers, guiding their purchases by a price inappropriate to the circumstances, would exhaust the available stock early in the season and find themselves without any supply of that commodity for months before the new crop came in. It is clear from some of these cases that low prices today may mean high prices tomorrow. If we use up irreplaceable natural resources too quickly, if we wear down the capital equipment of an entire industry too ruthlessly, or if we undermine the health and efficiency of large sections of the population by squeezing their incomes down to inadequate levels, the higher cost of goods tomorrow may much more than offset the gains that consumers get from cheapness today. In other words, although many individual consumers may be short-sighted in their actions or demands, particularly with respect to price, the true consumer interest must be taken to represent also the consumers who look at questions from the long-run point of view. This long-run point of view is more likely to appear among organized groups than among individuals. As consumers study their problems longer and more carefully they become aware of the many ramifications of their objectives.

HOW STRONG IS THE CONSUMER MOVEMENT?

A fundamental question is raised by those who ask how many people really may be included in the consumer movement as it exists today; how lasting their interest may be expected to be; how much the expressions of consumer interest represent actual informed interest by members of organizations and how much they are the opinions of organization leaders. None of these can be answered conclusively. Further study of the organizations would be needed, and further evidence of their actual effectiveness in action. It is probably safe to say, however, that the ordinary member of a consumer group is as well or better informed and is more intelligent about consumer problems than is the ordinary trade association member about the problems of his industry and social questions generally. No movement in recent years has been more specifically concerned with education at both the school and the adult level. In some form or other it is an integral part of every organization program. This gives special strength to the consumer movement and assures its upward trend.

In the survey made by Dr. George Gallup of the scope and penetration of the movement among the consuming public, it was found that approximately one out of four consumers was familiar with the consumer movement. Persons in the higher income levels were much more familiar with it than those with lower incomes. Most teachers interviewed knew about the consumer movement. It was found that knowledge of the consumer movement had actually influenced buying habits. The conclusion was reached that the consumer movement had reached proportions of significance to American business, and would continue to grow in strength and importance.

In trying to total actual membership in organized groups anywhere from five to twenty millions has been estimated, depending on how many of the groups with minor consumer interests, as well as those with major consumer interests, are included. It may be more definitely said that there are at least 5,000,000 women in national organizations with major consumer interests. Consumer cooperatives have well over 1,000,000 members.

The problems of the consumer movement are not so much those of obtaining membership, important as that is. They are those connected with making consumer influence effective. This was recently pointed out by Thurman Arnold in his book *Bottlenecks of Business*: "I think that the consumer movement is strong enough today; the only question is whether it can be sufficiently informed about available procedures to insist on practical action."

Consumers are awake to their problems; they are studying them intensively. The challenge which they must meet is this urgent need for practical *consumer action*.

Appendix

SELECTED ORGANIZATIONS

Note: These lists do not constitute a comprehensive survey of the consumer movement nor of the business organizations reacting to it. The groups included are representative of important national organizations and typical local groups. Workers interested in more extensive and detailed information about the organized consumer movement should consult the files of the Institute for Consumer Education, Columbia, Missouri, or of the Consumer Standards Project of the AAA, Washington, D. C. Bibliographies on selected or general consumer topics may be obtained from the Institute for Consumer Education.

Data on the membership of organizations were taken chiefly from 1939 and 1940 official sources, in a few cases from 1938 reports.

A. WOMEN'S GROUPS, RELIGIOUS AND WELFARE ORGANIZATIONS

American Association of University Women, 1634 Eye Street, N.W., Washington, D. C. Organized 1882. Membership about 62,000 in 880 branches. An important group in the consumer movement.

American Home Economics Association, 620 Mills Building, Washington, D. C. Organized 1908. Membership over 15,000. Interested in all problems affecting family living. Often acts in an advisory capacity for private and government groups.

Federal Council of Churches of Christ in America, 297 Fourth Avenue, New York City. Organized 1909. Includes 24 religious denominations with approximately twenty million members. Specially interested in the consumer cooperative movement.

General Federation of Women's Clubs, 1734 N Street, N.W., Washington, D. C. Organized 1890. Includes 15,000 clubs with total membership of over two million. An important group in consumer movement.

Girls' Friendly Society, 386 Fourth Avenue, New York City. Organized 1875. Membership about 26,000 in 900 branches. Sponsored by Episcopal church. No specific consumer interests but publishes articles on consumer problems and appeared for consumers at food and drug hearings.

National Board of the Young Women's Christian Association of the United States, 600 Lexington Avenue, New York City. Organized 1906. Membership 120 representing about 1000 local associations. Has given specific recognition to the encouragement of consumer cooperatives and to other organized consumer efforts.

National Congress of Parents and Teachers, 1201 Sixteenth Street, N.W., Washington, D. C.; 600 South Michigan Boulevard, Chicago, Illinois. Organized 1897. Membership nearly two and one-third millions. Has active consumer interests.

National Council of Catholic Women, 1312 Massachusetts Avenue, N.W., Washington, D. C. Organized 1920. Interested in the development of consumer programs. Has a legislative program.

National Council of Jewish Women, 1819 Broadway, New York City. Organized 1893. Membership about 40,000 in United States and Canada. Has a study program on consumer problems. Also has legislative interests in food and drugs, housing, motion pictures.

National Council of Women of the United States, Inc., 501 Madison Avenue, New York City. Organized 1880. Includes women's organizations having a combined membership estimated at seven million. Has held consumer programs and prepared consumer material. Not as important as other women's groups in the consumer movement.

National Council of the Young Men's Christian Associations of the United States, 347 Madison Avenue, New York City. Organized 1924. Membership 325 representatives elected by organizations totalling over one million members. Has some study groups interested in consumer education and consumer cooperatives.

National Federation of Business and Professional Women's Clubs, Inc., 1819 Broadway, New York City. Organized 1919. Membership about 71,000 in 1600 clubs. Includes consumer problems in its program.

National Federation of Settlements, 147 Avenue B, New York City. Organized 1911. Membership of 156 agencies. Has a Committee on Consumer Education and definite consumer interests.

National League of Women Voters, 726 Jackson Place, Washington, D. C. Organized 1920. Membership about 50,000 in state and local leagues. An influential group in the legislative field, with broad consumer interests.

New York City Federation of Women's Clubs, Room 132 Hotel

Astor, New York City. Very active in promoting labeling of textiles and in other consumer problems. Not a member of the General Federation of Women's Clubs.

Women's Joint Congressional Committee, 620 Mills Building, Washington, D. C. Organized 1920. A legislative clearing house for women's organizations totaling about five million members.

B. Groups Primarily Interested in Farm or Labor Welfare

American Federation of Labor, Labor Building, Washington, D. C. Organized 1881. Has endorsed the consumer cooperative movement.

Associated Women of the American Farm Bureau Federation, 58 East Washington Street, Chicago, Illinois. Has indicated interest in consumer protection.

Congress of Industrial Organizations, 1106 Connecticut Avenue, Washington, D. C. Organized 1935. Has indicated interest in consumer protection and endorsed the consumer cooperative movement.

International Ladies' Garment Workers' Union, 3 West 16th Street, New York City. Organized 1900. Has consumer education study groups and prepares consumer material.

Labor's Non-Partisan League of Illinois, 35 South Dearborn, Chicago, Illinois. Cooperates with other groups interested in improving labor's position. Similar labor groups have been active with the consumer movement in other centers, such as Boston and New York.

League of Women Shoppers, 220 Fifth Avenue, New York City. National organization formed in 1938. First local league about 1935. Interested in helping organized labor when it feels claims are justified.

National Consumers League, 114 East 32nd Street, New York City. Organized 1899. Membership of about 15,000 individuals in state leagues and local committees. Main interest is in improving labor legislation, but sometimes includes consumer interests. An important legislative group.

National Garment Label Council, 322 Metropolitan Tower, New York City. Established 1935-6. Membership includes 1600 members of the coat and suit and millinery industries. Sponsors Consumers' Protection Label guaranteeing sanitary conditions and fair working conditions to the consumer.

National Women's Trade Union League, 306 Machinists' Building,

Washington, D. C. Organized 1903. Membership of over one million. Interested in consumer problems and consumer protection. Includes in its platform the objective of a standard of living commensurate with the nation's productive capacity.

Union Label Trades Department, American Federation of Labor, 901 Massachusetts Avenue, N.W., Washington, D. C. Organized 1909. Promotes the use of a union label and educates consumers to buy merchandise made under union standards.

C. Groups Organized Specifically to Promote Consumer Welfare

Consumer Conference of Greater Cincinnati, c/o Mrs. Dennis Jackson, 144 Louis Avenue, Cincinnati, Ohio. Organized 1934. Membership of about forty civic, welfare, religious, labor, business, and other groups. Specially interested in promoting better merchandising practices.

Consumer-Farmer Milk Cooperative, 215 Fourth Avenue, New York City. Organized 1937. Over 7000 members. Works closely with Milk Consumers Protective Committee of New York.

Consumers National Federation, 110 Morningside Drive, New York City. Organized 1937. Acts as a clearing-house for consumer groups. Prepares consumer material of a general economic nature.

County Consumer Councils active in January 1939:
Arizona: Maricopa County Consumers' Council, Phoenix.
Arkansas: Pulaski County Consumers' Council, Little Rock.
Connecticut: Connecticut Consumers' Council, New Haven.
Delaware: New Castle County Consumers' Council, Wilmington.
Georgia: DeKalb County Consumers' Council, Avondale Estates.
Kentucky: Jefferson County Consumers' Council, Louisville.
Maryland: Baltimore Consumers' Council.
Massachusetts: Consumers' Institutes of Massachusetts, Boston.
  Hampden County Consumers' Institute, Springfield.
  Hampshire County Consumers' Institute, Northampton
  Worcester County Consumers' Institute, Worcester.
  Eastern Massachusetts Consumers' Institute, Boston.
Missouri: St. Louis County Consumers' Council.
Montana: Silver Bow County Consumers' Council, Butte
Nebraska: Omaha Consumers' Council, Omaha.
New Jersey: Camden County Consumers' Council, Camden.
New York: Tompkins County Consumers' Council, Ithaca.
  Erie County Consumers' Council, Buffalo.

Ohio: Hamilton County Consumer's Council, Cincinnati.
   Butler County Consumers' Council, Oxford.
Pennsylvania: Allegheny County Consumers' Council, Pittsburgh.
Tennessee: Davidson County Consumers' Council, Nashville.
   Knox County Consumers' Council, Fountain City.
   Shelby County Consumers' Council, Memphis.
Texas: Brazos County Consumers' Council, Bryan.
Washington, D. C.: Washington Consumers' Council.
Wisconsin: Milwaukee County Consumers' Council, Milwaukee.
Greater Boston Consumers' Committee on Milk, 80 Federal Street, Boston, Massachusetts. Organized 1939. Membership of delegates from organizations interested in milk supply of Boston consumers.
Miami Consumer League, c/o Mrs. G. M. Labuzen, 3821 N.W. Sixth Avenue, Miami, Florida. Organized 1939. Developed out of an interest in consumer problems taught in an adult education class. Objective to develop more intelligent consumer-buyers through a careful study of consumer goods.
Milk Consumers' Protective Committee, 215 Fourth Avenue, New York City. Organized 1936. Membership of delegates from nearly 100 organizations. Interested in all questions related to the milk supply of consumers in New York City.
National Public Housing Conference, Inc., 122 East 22nd Street, New York City. Organized 1932. Membership of over 1000 persons and organizations interested in promoting good housing at low cost for low-income groups.
St. Louis Consumers' Federation, c/o Miss Alice Rex, Grace Hill Settlement House. Organized 1940 to coordinate work of Consumer groups in St. Louis.
United Conference Against the High Cost of Living, c/o Mrs. Alice Treleaven, Hull House, 800 Halsted Street, Chicago, Illinois. Organized 1935. Coordinates consumer work of organized groups in Chicago.

D. NATIONAL CONSUMER COOPERATIVE ORGANIZATIONS

Bureau of Cooperative Medicine, 5 East 57th Street, New York City. Organized as a division of the Cooperative League. A research and education organization for studying various methods of collective purchase of medical care on a pre-payment plan.
Consumer Distribution Corporation, 420 Lexington Avenue, New York City. Organized 1936. Helps existing cooperatives with pro-

vision of capital and management. Financed by the Good Will Fund, a foundation set up by E. A. Filene, Boston merchant.

Consumers' Book Cooperative, Inc., formerly Cooperative Book Club, 118 East 28th Street, New York City. Membership about 2000 individual members as well as libraries, cooperative organizations and other associations. Wholesale department has operated since 1939.

Cooperative Distributors, Inc., 116 East 16th Street, New York City. Organized 1932. Membership more than 3600 individuals and 225 clubs. Sells goods chiefly by mail-order. Maintains a testing laboratory, and has a labor committee which is supposed to make sure that concerns selling to CD maintain union standards.

Cooperative League of the United States of America, Inc., Executive Office 608 South Dearborn, Chicago, Illinois; Education offices 167 West 12th Street, New York City. Organized 1916. Total membership includes nearly a million members in affiliated cooperative associations.

Credit Union National Association, Raiffeison House, Madison, Wisconsin. Organized 1935. Membership about 8,500 credit unions with over 2,500,000 members.

National Cooperative Women's Guild, 167 West 12th Street, New York City. In 1932 National Guild Committee elected. In 1940 decided to organize Women's Guild on a permanent basis. Total number of guilds, 122 from 14 states, membership approximately 3000.

National Cooperatives, Inc., 608 South Dearborn, Chicago, Illinois. Organized 1932-33. A federation of regional cooperative wholesales.

Rochdale Institute, 167 West 12th Street, New York City. Organized 1937, under sponsorship of the Cooperative League, to train and educate men and women for service in the cooperative organization of consumers.

E. EDUCATIONAL ORGANIZATIONS AND SERVICES

American Association for Adult Education, Inc., 60 East 42nd Street, New York City. Organized 1926. Membership about 1500. Gathers consumer education material, and assists in organizing consumer groups.

American Association for Economic Education, 141 Milk Street, Boston, Massachusetts. Particularly interested in promoting education in money management and personal economics.

American Committee for Democracy and Intellectual Freedom, 519 West 121st Street, New York City. Organized 1939. Has defended rights of schools against attacks from special interests. Has protested attacks made by some advertising groups on Professor Rugg's Social Science Series.

American Home Economics Association, Inc., 620 Mills Building, Washington, D. C. Organized 1908. Membership over 15,000. Interested in all problems affecting home living.

Consumer Education Association, 45 Sunnyside Avenue, Brooklyn, New York. Organized 1938. Membership of around 500. Coordinates the work of consumer educators in different fields.

Consumer Education Service, American Home Economics Association, 620 Mills Building, Washington, D. C. Established 1936. Subscription nearly 800. Digests news of consumer interest over a wide field.

Council of Business Education, Ohio University, Athens, Ohio. Membership about 15,000. Interested in developing business education from the consumer point of view.

Institute for Consumer Education, Stephens College, Columbia, Missouri. Organized 1937. Holds conferences, collects consumer material, and prepares educational material.

Institute for Propaganda Analysis, 40 East 49th Street, New York City. Organized 1937. About 7000 subscribers to the Institute's Bulletin, which is issued periodically and analyzes current propaganda.

National Education Association of the United States, 1201 16th Street, N.W., Washington, D. C. Organized 1857. Membership about 775,000 teachers. Interested in the development of consumer education.

Progressive Education Association, 310 West 90th Street, New York City. Organized 1919. Membership about 10,000. Holds consumer sections at annual meetings.

Service Bureau for Adult Education, Division of General Education, New York University, 20 Washington Square North, New York City. Issues materials occasionally on consumer education.

F. Professional Organizations

American Association of Scientific Workers, c/o W. T. Martin, 64 Dana Street, Cambridge, Massachusetts. Organized 1938. Branches in Boston-Cambridge, Philadelphia, New York, Chicago, and Berkeley. Membership about 800. Has consumer committees.

American Dental Association, 212 East Superior Street, Chicago,
Illinois. Council on Dental Therapeutics established 1930. Issues
seal of acceptance for dentrifices, mouth washes, etc.

American Medical Association, 535 North Dearborn Street, Chicago,
Illinois. Established Council on Pharmacy and Chemistry 1905,
Bureau of Investigation, 1906, Council on Physical Therapy, 1925,
Committee on Foods, 1929. Council on Pharmacy and Chemistry
and on Physical Therapy help guide the doctor in the purchase of
drugs and appliances. Bureau of Investigation investigates patent
medicines, etc. and exposes frauds and quackery in the medical
field. Committee on Foods awards a seal of acceptance to foods
which are advertised honestly.

American Public Health Association, 50 West 50th Street, New
York City. Organized 1872. Membership about 6700. Interested in
all problems affecting public health.

National Lawyer's Guild, 1653 Pennsylvania Avenue, N.W., Washington, D. C. Has a committee on Consumers and Cooperatives.

G. Consumer Testing and Rating Agencies

Consumers of Canada, Inc., c/o Charles Nix, 14631 Summit Avenue,
Edmonton, Alberta, Canada. Organized 1939. Not active at
present.

Consumers' Research, Inc., Washington, New Jersey. Incorporated
1929. Membership about 60,000. Tests and rates consumer goods
by brand names.

Consumers' Union, 17 Union Square West, New York City. Organized 1936. Membership about 80,000. Tests and rates consumer goods by brand name.

Intermountain Consumers' Service, Inc., 435 Marion Street, Denver,
Colorado. Organized 1932. Membership probably about 3000.
Tests and rates consumer goods.

H. Buying Agents for Consumers

Babson Statistical Organization, Babson Park, Massachusetts. Organized about 1903. In 1938 opened schools for training in purchasing
for families and individuals. Offers a special housewives' course.
On a fee basis will prepare budgets, keep accounts, and do purchasing for clients.

Consumers, Inc., 655 Shatto Place, Los Angeles, California. Organized 1938 as a limited profit corporation. Nearly 1000 members.
Serves as purchasing agents for its membership.

I. Institutional and Commercial Buying Organizations

Hospital Bureau of Standards and Supplies, Inc., 247 Park Avenue, New York City. Established 1910. Membership of over 200 hospitals and similar institutional members for whom it buys by specification and analyzes brands.

National Association of Purchasing Agents, 9 Park Place, New York City. Organized 1915. About 5700 members. Devoted entirely to the development of information and services for its members. Members can in no way be connected with selling.

J. Consumer-Business Groups

Advisory Committee on Ultimate Consumer Goods, American Standards Association, 29 West 39th Street, New York City. Organized 1936. Consumer representatives from the American Home Economics Association, the American Association of University Women, the General Federation of Women's clubs, the National Congress of Parents and Teachers, the National League of Women Voters, and Consumers Union. Provides a forum where business and consumer representatives may cooperate in the development of standards for consumer goods.

American Society for Testing Materials, 260 South Broad Street, Philadelphia, Pennsylvania. Established 1902. Over 4000 members. A standardizing body. Does not undertake certification of consumer goods. Cooperates with other groups in developing standards.

National Consumer Retailer Council, 8 West 40th Street, New York City. Organized 1937. Membership organizations representing business and consumer groups. A forum for the discussion of mutual problems of consumers and retailers.

K. Some Trade and Manufacturing Associations Conscious of the Consumer Movement

Advertising Federation of America, 330 West 42nd Street, New York City. A. F. Falk, Director of Research Division, has been active in attacking treatment of advertising in some widely used text books.

Advertising Women of New York, Inc., 47 West 34th Street. Has held annual consumer forums.

American Association of Advertising Agencies, 420 Lexington Avenue, New York City. Has a Committee on Consumer Relations.

American Retail Federation, 1627 K Street, N.W., Washington, D. C. Organized April 1935. A federation of individuals and state and local associations to protect retail interests and collect facts relating to the retail industry. Recognizes the importance of an independent consumer movement.

Associated Grocery Manufacturers of America, 205 East 42nd Street, New York City. Organized 1908. Membership about 250 manufacturers, with annual sales of four billion dollars. Has a special department dealing with consumer relation activities.

Association of National Advertisers, 330 West 42nd Street, New York City. Prepared a comprehensive confidential survey of consumer organizations in 1939.

Institute of Distribution, Inc., 570 Seventh Avenue, New York City. Interested in developing consumer opposition to chain store taxation.

National Association of Better Business Bureaus, Inc., Chrysler Building, New York City. Better Business Bureau began about 1911. Now over 64 Better Business Bureaus in cities in U. S. and Canada.

National Association of Manufacturers, 14 West 49th Street, New York City. Founded 1895. Created Women's Division in 1939. Home and Industry Committee formed on which representatives of manufacturers and women's organizations serve.

National Association of Retail Grocers of the United States, 360 North Michigan Avenue, Chicago, Illinois. Established 1893. Opposes grade labeling.

National Canners Association, 1739 H. Street, N.W., Washington, D. C. Organized 1907. Favors descriptive rather than grade labeling.

National Retail Dry Goods Association, 101 West 31st Street, New York City. Has gone on record as officially sponsoring a program to advance the movement for consumer goods standards.

Retail Trading Standards, Association, Inc., 207-13, Oxford Street, London, W.1. Organized 1934. Designed to form a basis for a long-time campaign to improve public relations between retailers and the public, the manufacturer and the legislature.

L. PSEUDO CONSUMER GROUPS

The American Consumer, 205 East 42nd Street (defunct). Published 1934-40. The editor, Crump Smith, began a confidential service for businessmen "Consumer Movement Trends" in January, 1940, when the *American Consumer* became defunct.

Consumer Credit Institute of America, Woolworth Building, New York City. Organized 1930. Issues monographs on consumer credit and a periodical for educational use called the *Family Dollar*. Receives major support from one of the personal finance companies, as well as from other commercial sources, although this is not clearly stated. Appears to be trying to expand distribution of the *Family Dollar* because of its public relations value in putting over the business point of view.

Consumers' Foundation, c/o Pollak Foundation, Newton, Massachusetts. Organized 1938. Not active now. Designed primarily as public relations for chain store interests.

Home Maker's Education Service, 31 South Grove Street, Freeport, New York. Organized 1916. Issues Bulletins giving names of products awarded "Symbol of Reliability." No laboratory tests other than those of manufacturer, although this is not explicitly stated. Prepares lesson helps and provides samples of products sponsored.

National Consumers' Tax Commission, 310 South Michigan Avenue, Chicago, Illinois. Organized 1938 by four business men. Had over 500 active units in 1939. Members have no control over the national organization. Financed by business interests. A & P pledged support openly.

The Neutral Thousands, 510 South Spring Street, Los Angeles, California. Organized 1937. Took over activities of the groups sometimes known as Women Consumers or Women of California, or Women of the Pacific. Interested in promoting the company union. Posed as an independent organization but really sponsored by Southern Californians, Inc., a business organization dedicated to the open shop. For details of relationships about the organizations and the publication *American-Worker Consumer* see report of the National Relations Board IR-112, Case No. XXI-C-1007, 1113, 1114, 1116, September 26, 1940.

New York State Economic Council, Inc., 505 Fifth Avenue, New York City, also First National Bank Building, Utica, N. Y. Organized 1931 by business interests. Has led attacks against Professor Rugg's text book. (See *Consumer Education*, November 1940 issue, for details.)

Women's National Institute, 247 Park Avenue, New York City. Organized 1933 as part of the Women's National Exposition of

Arts and Industries which was organized in 1920. Has issued several pamphlets promoting particular products such as Vicks Vapo Rub and Crown Quality Rayon. Holds forums and supplies consumer materials for study groups.

M. MISCELLANEOUS

American Investors Union, Inc., 10 East 40th Street, New York City. Organized 1939. Subscription approximately 3,500. Formed to aid the small investor.

Legal Aid Society of New York, 11 Park Place, New York City. Organized 1876. At present about 100 legal aid organizations in the United States and Canada. Object is to render legal aid to all who appear worthy but who are unable to procure assistance elsewhere, and to promote measures for their protection.

School of Living, Suffern, New York. Organized 1934, Ralph Borsodi, Director. Interested in home production and decentralization of industry.

Social Union, Inc., 118 East 28th Street, New York City. Organized 1939, as Social Unit Plan. Developed out of earlier experiments in the twenties. A technique of organization to get a better adjustment of production and consumption by cooperation of all interests concerned.

INDEX

Aaron, Dr. Harold, 40
Adult education, 63-67, 103, 106, 129-130, 171, 176
cooperatives, 138-139
radio, 117
Adult Education Council, 119
Advertising, 28, 134-135, 160-161, 164, 171, 195
and public relations movement, 156
and testing agencies, 37-38
consumer poll, 174
control, 14
cooperatives, 144
materials used in schools, 68-69
National Parent-Teacher Magazine, 95
"truth in advertising," 11, 198-199
Advertising Bureau of American Newspaper Publishers Associations, 195
Advertising Club, Lincoln, Neb., 159
Advertising Federation of America, 159, 195
Advertising Research Foundation, 180
Advisory Commission to the Council of National Defense, 50, 212-219
Advisory Committee on Ultimate Consumer Goods, 72, 87, 183
Agnew, P. G., 189
Amalgamated Dwellings, 148
Amalgamated Housing Corporation, 148
American Association of Scientific Workers, 36, 41
American Association of Textile Chemists and Colorists, 184
American Association of University Women, 84-89, 100, 118, 183, 188, 208
New York branch, 112
American Consumer, 165-167

American Consumers' Union, St. Paul, 178
American Economics Association, 73
American Federation of Hosiery Workers, 106
American Federation of Teachers, 72
American Gas Association, 186
American Home Economics Association, 6, 13, 58-72, 85, 100, 183, 188, 208-209
legislative program, 70-71
work with other groups, 71-72
American Hospital Association, 109
American Labor Party, 107
American Marketing Association, 34, 73
American Medical Association, 55
American Parents' Council on Education, 162
American Pure Food League, 7
American Retail Federation, 180, 181, 188, 198
American Society for Testing Materials, 184
American Standards Association, 66, 67, 72, 87, 183, 184
American Worker-Consumer, 178
Antigonish cooperative movement, 138-139
Arnold, Thurman, 223
Associated Grocery Manufacturers of America, 158, 164-165
Associated Women of the American Farm Bureau Federation, 108
Association of Casualty and Surety Executives, 159
Association of Manufacturers' Representatives of New York City, 164
Association of National Advertisers, 180

237

A CENTURY OF MARKETING

An Arno Press Collection

Alderson, Wroe. **Marketing Behavior and Executive Action.** 1957

Assael, Henry, editor. **The Collected Works of C. C. Parlin.** 1978

Assael, Henry, editor. **Early Development and Conceptualization of the Field of Marketing.** 1978

Assael, Henry, editor. **A Pioneer in Marketing, L. D. H. Weld.** 1978

Bartels, Robert D. W. **Marketing Literature: Development and Appraisal.** 1978

Blankenship, Albert B. **Consumer and Opinion Research.** 1943

Borden, Neil H. **Advertising in Our Economy.** 1945

Breyer, Ralph F. **The Marketing Institution.** 1934

Breyer, Ralph F. **Quantitative Systemic Analysis and Control.** 1949

Clark, Fred E. **Principles of Marketing.** 1922

Clark, Lincoln H., editor. **Consumer Behavior.** 1958

Coles, Jessie V. **The Consumer-Buyer and the Market.** 1938

Collins, V[irgil] D[ewey]. **World Marketing.** 1935

Converse, Paul D. **The Beginning of Marketing Thought in the U.S.** *and* **Fifty Years of Marketing in Retrospect.** 1959

Copeland, Melvin Thomas. **Principles of Merchandising.** 1924

The Ethical Problems of Modern Advertising. 1931

Frederick, John H. **Industrial Marketing.** 1934

Frederick, J. George. **Modern Salesmanagement.** 1921

Hower, Ralph M. **The History of an Advertising Agency.** 1939

Longman, Donald R. **Distribution Cost Analysis.** 1941

Lyon, Leverett S. **Salesmen in Marketing Strategy.** 1926

The Men Who Advertise. 1870

Nystrom, Paul H. **Economics of Retailing.** 1930

Reilly, William J. **Marketing Investigations.** 1929

Revzan, David A. **Wholesaling in Marketing Organization.** 1961

Rosenberg, Larry J., editor. **The Roots of Marketing Strategy.** 1978

Scott, Walter Dill. **The Psychology of Advertising.** 1913

Sorenson, Helen. **The Consumer Movement.** 1941

Starch, Daniel. **Advertising Principles.** 1927

Terry, Samuel Hough. **The Retailer's Manual.** 1869

Tosdal, Harry R. **Principles of Personal Selling.** 1925

White, Percival. **Advertising Research.** 1927

White, Percival. **Scientific Marketing Management.** 1927